OPERATION BETHLEHEM

OPERATION BETHLEHEM

YARIV INBAR

TRANSLATED BY DALIT SHMUELI

Copyright

Credits

Cover design by Gerzon branding agency
Proofreading by Ally Mitchell

The quote in the author's note is from Yeftah Getz, "Excerpts from the diary of Rabbi Getz on his search for the Ark of the Covenant and the Temple's vessels," 7/10/2013, http://rotter.net/forum/scoops1/53378.shtml

Dedicated to all those who were privileged to serve their country away from the spotlight.

Home is where the heart is.

Pliny the Elder

CONTENTS

Prologue

The freezing, howling wind was deafening. At first, it was like freefalling into an abyss. A few seconds later, he felt the exhilarating sensation of floating spread-eagled, cushioned by air. But it was a fleeting pleasure. After one minute, the alert in Daniel's helmet rang near his ear. He pulled the ripcord handle and the noise stopped. There was no trace of the C-130 Hercules aircraft above, flying without the identifying Star of David, and clusters of orange lights flickered on the ground far below. His eyes didn't have to adjust to the darkness – it had been dark inside the aircraft, too.

Suspended between the earth and sky, Daniel enjoyed these final moments. It was his first operation in enemy territory. If only Grandpa could see me now, Daniel thought, but maybe he can, from somewhere up above. Only Daniel's immediate family was still alive, his sister, father, and mother. He had spoken with his mother the night before and felt a twinge of sadness thinking of her. He hadn't seen her in almost a year. Although video calls bridged the distance, they were no substitute for a hug, a kiss, or her loving, gentle touch. The conversations with his father had always been impersonal and emotionless, but recently something had changed between them. Maybe it was the hundreds of miles that separated them and perhaps the path Daniel had taken – although, officially, his family wasn't supposed to know about it.

He looked up; the canopy blended into the darkness and was barely visible. This wasn't his first time. When he served in Duvdevan, the IDF elite unit that operates undercover among the Palestinian population, he trained with the paratroopers and jumped several times with his fellow soldiers. When he returned to his unit after completing the officer training course, he also jumped with the team he commanded. But this time was different. Combat freefall into enemy territory alone was part of the Mossad training. As he fell, he suddenly recalled reading about the legendary Zionist and paratrooper Hannah Senesh and her friends and felt a surge of pride. Like them, he was doing his part; a European-born Jewish intelligence field agent jumping from a plane into enemy territory. Daniel always searched for meaning and found it in unexpected places. His Israeli-born friends often teased him about it. "Israel is a given for you," he would rant, "You only heard secondhand accounts from your grandparents about what it feels like to be cursed at and called a dirty Jew." But he never said anything beyond that.

Daniel pulled the parachute steering lines to land. The ground was rapidly getting closer. Seconds later, he landed in the arid desert. Quickly releasing the bag strapped to his legs, he gathered the canopy and rolled it into a tight bundle. He stuffed the rest of the gear into a small cloth bag and placed it on the rolled parachute, peeled off the black jumpsuit that added bulk to his lean body, and added it to the pile. Underneath, he wore khaki cargo pants and a gray plaid shirt. His helmet hid an unruly mass of black hair, which would normally be tamed with gel.

Kneeling on the ground, Daniel tuned in to his surroundings. Howls of jackals in the distance broke the peaceful silence. He retrieved a small, old-school video camera from his backpack, powered it up and set it to night vision. The hidden infrared light helped the sensor to capture and display his surroundings better. He surveyed the area. Not a soul in sight. He put the camera back, pulled out a large multi-tool from a side zipper in his backpack, unfolded a narrow spade, and searched for a suitable cluster of rocks. When he found the right spot, he cleared the ground, dug a hole, then buried the parachute, bag, and jumpsuit. He covered them with dirt and put the rocks back as they were. The camouflage wasn't perfect, but it was good enough. The desert wind would cover the area in sand within minutes.

Daniel put the multi-tool back, took out a cellular device tethered with a thin, black paracord, and turned it on. The display, set on low brightness, was covered with a filter coating to block the glare so it wouldn't project into the barren desert. He opened an app that looked like a simple game but was programmed to turn into a GPS navigator by pressing a sequence of buttons. The app showed his navigation route on maps uploaded by the tech team. Daniel identified his position on the map and put the cellular device in a zippered pocket. Every time he entered his exact location, an automatic notification would be sent to command post confirming his progress. Finally, he adjusted his backpack on his shoulders and started quickly walking a route he'd repeatedly reviewed and memorized while preparing for the operation.

Around a mile ahead on the horizon were the slopes he would shortly cross. Besides reflecting on the surprising similarity to the familiar landscape of Israel, Daniel didn't allow random thoughts to enter his mind. Half an hour later, he was sitting on the ground just below the top of the hill. Daniel took a few sips from his water bottle, feeling the heat and throbbing pulse in his temples. He hadn't shaved in a few days, and the stubble was irritating. Checking his position on the navigation app, he set out. Forty-five minutes of strenuous walking, crossing hills and ravines, brought him close to the target area – a twisting dirt road between two stone walls, about fifteen feet high. Although he had never been there before, Daniel felt like he knew every rock, bush, and mound of dirt. The intelligence he'd received, satellite photos, and drills in similar terrain – it was just like any other full dress rehearsal. The feeling surprised him – he had expected to feel more excited.

With sure steps, Daniel navigated to the exact spot where he had to hide the device he carried in his backpack. He took out the large multi-tool and a camera disguised to look like part of the surroundings. "A sensor will turn the camera on every time a convoy of vehicles passes by, and it will send us pictures," the technical operations officer had explained, "that way, we'll be able to intercept a convoy we suspect to be smuggling weapons."

Daniel felt a sense of satisfaction. This had been his dream for so long, to play a critical role in the security of his ancestral homeland. The boy who had felt like an outsider in Paris where he was born flipped an imaginary bird at everything and everyone that had knocked him off balance and caused such insecurity.

After a quick assessment of the camera's location, Daniel worked on the camouflage. Then he took his cell phone, opened one of the apps, and waited. Seconds later, a confirmation message appeared on the screen. The device was ready. "*Superbe*," he whispered, smiling as he got ready to leave.

The night vision camera confirmed that nothing was left in the field. When he bent over to lift his pack, he heard a rock hit the ground as if someone behind him had thrown it. Daniel felt his heart race as he rose slowly, slinging the backpack over his shoulders. He looked around and listened closely, using the camera to carefully survey the area around and above the stone walls, but didn't hear or see a thing. He tried to think of a logical explanation; maybe it was an animal or a loose stone.

Daniel started to walk away slowly and quickened his pace when he felt confident. It was already three am, two and a half hours until the sun was "six degrees" below the horizon, just before dawn banished the absolute dark of night. He covered the distance in an hour and a half and navigated right to the lone tree just a few hundred feet from the meeting point. For the first time that night, he sat down to rest. Leaning against the rough bark, he devoured two sandwiches, drank some water, and stared into the infinite darkness. He put on a fleece jacket and a beanie to protect against the cold wind but kept his ears exposed and alert to any sounds. There was nothing to do but wait patiently and fight the fatigue following the adrenaline rush.

The last few days had been very intense, with final preparations, orders, briefings, memorizing navigation routes, and cover stories to ensure a flawless operation. The accumulated exhaustion and stress demanded relief. Arik, the course commander and the most significant person in his life over the past year, had drummed into their heads during training that the professional life of an intelligence officer entails endless waiting. "It doesn't matter what your role is in the information gathering process; ninety percent of the time, you'll be waiting, whether it's for a meeting with an informant, for an answer, for the person you're speaking with to say what you want to hear. Just waiting. You're in the wrong profession if you don't have patience."

Daniel had innate patience. An introvert by nature, he could spend hours quietly observing. He stared into the night, listening to the sounds of the desert and fighting to keep his eyes open when suddenly, twin beams of light flashed through the darkness. It was too early for the rendezvous; maybe it was just a car. Now he could make out headlights and the shadow of a cargo van driving slowly. Another beam on top scanned the road, swinging from side to side deep into the desert. He crawled behind the tree trunk. For the first time that night, he felt fear. The intelligence briefings did not mention patrols on this road. Questions raced through his mind, and he recalled the falling rock. Maybe someone had seen him? If they didn't notice him now, it really didn't matter what the van was doing there. Daniel saw the light coming toward him and flattened his body against the cold, sharp desert stones. He lay still, breathing in the dry desert dust until the lights drove out of sight.

When the beam of light was far enough away, he got up and watched the van drive off until it suddenly stopped. Daniel froze. The doors opened, and a few soldiers got out. He quickly crawled back into the darkness and lay behind a small ridge. The soldiers circled the vehicle. One of them lit a cigarette and opened the hood. Why here, of all places? He realized that the extraction would likely not happen as planned. Fifteen nerve-wracking minutes later, just before he decided to go to the alternate meeting point, the soldiers got in the van, turned around, and drove back in the direction they came from. Daniel breathed a sigh of relief and walked toward the road.

Dawn was breaking. Daniel climbed down into a dry gorge and walked through it toward the road. Pebbles crunched under his feet. Around fifty feet before the road, he sat by a huge boulder and leaned against it. The sun rose and brought the desert landscape to life, the stones casting long shadows. It was freezing, and Daniel could barely keep his eyes open. Removing the black filter from his cellular device, he pulled out a lighter and burned the plastic film. He released the lanyard loop from the cellphone case, threw it into his backpack, checked that his wallet and passport were in the inner pocket, and reviewed his cover story. A few minutes later, a car drove up and stopped a few feet away from him. Daniel sat still. He heard people speaking in Arabic, then a door opened and slammed shut. He stood up, stretched his limbs, and took a few deep breaths – mentally switching modes from commando operating under the cover of night to daytime field agent with a fake identity. It was a subtle, unnerving shift.

He came out from behind the boulder and climbed up the dirt embankment. A red pickup truck was parked on the side of the road, the license plate matching the one he was given – his extraction.

"*Bonjour*," he said to the young man standing outside the vehicle, pulling a faded canvas bed cover over the back of the truck.

The man nodded awkwardly. Daniel came up to him. "Need help?" he asked in English.

The man shrugged and handed Daniel the rope he was pulling.

"Can I get a ride?" Daniel asked as he'd been instructed.

The man nodded and opened the door. Daniel got into the back seat, keeping hold of his backpack. The sweet smell of hookah tobacco enveloped him. A young woman with a colorful head covering sat in the front seat. "*Bonjour, madame,*" he called out, and she nodded without turning her head.

The man sat behind the wheel, started the truck, and drove. The woman slid a CD into the player, and modern Arabic music filled the cabin. She stole a glance at him in the rearview mirror, and Daniel got a quick look at her almond-shaped, hazel eyes. He tried to imagine the rest of her face, seeing only her creamy complexion. His last relationship had ended shortly after he started the training course. It had been a while, and as time passed, every encounter with an attractive woman stirred a spark of desire. Even now.

"Music okay?" the driver asked.

Daniel gave a thumbs up and smiled. The young woman's almond eyes met his in the mirror again, and she lowered them quickly. It was six thirty in the morning; he had the whole day ahead of him, hours of driving with the local couple. He would cross this enemy country with them, hundreds of miles, until they reached the isolated area where the commando unit would pick him up to take him home. Daniel stared out the dusty window at the desert view, feeling enormous satisfaction in this unreal situation.

"Checkpoint," the driver suddenly announced in Arabic, and slowed down.

Daniel tensed. The intelligence briefings hadn't mentioned checkpoints. He immediately recognized the cargo van as the patrol vehicle he'd seen several hours earlier. It was parked perpendicular to the road and blocked one of the lanes. Images flashed through his mind: the Hercules, the jump, the camera, the thud of the rock, the beacon of light – incriminating thoughts that were better left suppressed. What he felt right now was nothing like in the exercises – that was pure anticipation like before an exam. Now he felt the dread of what might lie ahead: arrest, maybe torture, or even death.

The driver stopped the truck and opened the window for the soldier armed with an AK-47.

"Where are you coming from?" the soldier questioned the driver in Arabic. The driver gave the name of one of the nearby villages. The woman fixed her head covering and avoided eye contact with the soldier. Another soldier circled the truck, and a third sat in the patrol vehicle at the wheel. "Where are you headed?" the soldier asked, and the driver gave the name of another village in the area. Daniel looked outwardly calm even as his heart threatened to explode.

"And who is this?" the soldier asked.

"A tourist. I saw him a few miles back, and he asked for a ride."

The soldier nodded a few times. "Open the window," he ordered Daniel in Arabic and mimed rolling the window down.

"*Bonjour, monsieur,*" Daniel opened the window and greeted the soldier.

"Passport," the soldier demanded.

While Daniel was digging for his passport, the young woman turned to the soldier and asked through the driver's window if everything was all right.

"We will see!" he said to her, taking the passport and flipping through it. After examining all the rubber stamps, he compared the picture to Daniel's face. Then, after a long look at him, he returned to the cargo van and spoke with the soldier sitting inside. After a few minutes that seemed like an eternity, the soldier returned and asked the driver to follow them.

The driver looked worried, "Please don't be angry... can I ask what's wrong?"

Daniel, who understood every word, felt his heart drop and tried to keep smiling.

"Is this your wife?" the soldier asked.

"Yes," the driver affirmed, "my wife."

"Show me your IDs."

The driver handed over the plastic card that his wife took out of a small green purse and his own.

"Follow me," the soldier ordered and turned to the cargo van.

"What's going on, sir? What did we do?" The young woman got out of the truck and followed him, and her husband silently joined her. Daniel stayed in the car and looked at the woman, who was wearing an ankle-length brown dress with long sleeves.

"Ma'am," the soldier said impatiently, "get back in the car and follow us, don't give us any problems. Last night a plane penetrated the border, and we received orders to stop anyone who looked suspicious."

Daniel's heart skipped a beat. They had detected the aircraft, but the soldier hadn't said anything about a parachute. How could they know?

"An aircraft?" the young woman scoffed as she fixed her flowered head covering. "What has that got to do with us? I've never even been to the airport. I don't understand..."

"Move it." The soldier barked at the man. "Take your wife, get back into the car and drive after us, or you're coming in the van with us."

The woman turned to her husband, "What does he want? Are we suspects? Let them take the Frenchman and leave us alone..."

"Okay, okay," the man grabbed his wife's arm and pulled her toward the truck. "Keep your mouth shut! We'll go. Let them check what they need to, and then they'll leave us alone."

"I am not going with them. Are you crazy?" The woman stood there and yelled. "Just let them take him!"

The soldier circling the truck came up to Daniel's door and signaled with his rifle to get out. Daniel took his backpack with him.

"What's the problem?" he asked in French. The soldier responded by motioning toward the cargo van with his rifle.

The other soldier, holding the passport and ID cards in one hand and the AK-47 in the other, motioned the driver and his wife to get into the back of the van. The three of them got in while the woman continued her shrill complaints. The door slammed shut and locked automatically. They backed up, turned toward the road, and drove off quickly.

The back of the van was pitch black. The windows were painted over, and very little light could get through.

21

"It's all your fault," the woman wailed and pointed at Daniel.

"Are you crazy? Shut up already," her husband ordered. "You annoyed them, and now look what you've done..."

Daniel listened to every word, even as he kept his cover story in mind. His main concern was the young woman. His fate was now in her hands. There was no doubt that she was scared and not thinking clearly. Her husband, he knew for sure, was a local agent cooperating with the Mossad. He knew nothing about her and hoped she had no idea who he was.

"Please stay calm," he said to her in English, hoping she understood, but she just kept sobbing. He concentrated on his story. There was no reason to worry, he reassured himself. I'll get through this if I just stay calm and collected.

After a short drive, the vehicle turned, slowed, and stopped. Outside he heard the creaking of a gate and a rapid exchange of words in Arabic that he couldn't catch. The engine was turned off. The front doors slammed. Gravel crunched underfoot, and then the back door of the van opened. Daniel squinted, blinded by the bright light.

"Move it." One of the soldiers pulled him out roughly. Daniel reached for his backpack, but the soldier pushed him forward. Behind him, he heard the woman still wailing and her panicked husband trying to calm her down. On the short walk from the driveway to the building, he noted that they were in a small compound surrounded by rusty, dented sheets of metal. Worn-out armchairs sat at the entrance to the building under a canopy of dried palm fronds, and a faded sign in Arabic announced that the single-story building was a headquarters. A remote outpost, Daniel thought, not an interrogation facility. There was little chance that anyone spoke French.

A guard escorted him to a windowless room with a few chairs, a Formica table, a telephone, and a photo of the president. Next door, he assumed, was the situation room – every few minutes he could hear bursts of garbled speech from the radio base station. The guard handcuffed him and left him seated on one of the chairs. Again, Arik's mantra echoed in his head; ninety percent of the time is waiting. This time, he was waiting to be interrogated. But he was surprised that what he felt was mostly anticipation, not fear.

The door swung open, and a tall man entered the room, dressed in civilian clothes and wearing a black leather jacket. He looked around 70 years old, with a full head of carefully combed gray hair, a trimmed mustache, and the fresh scent of cologne. He set Daniel's passport on the table and dropped his backpack on the floor. Secret service, Daniel thought, wondering about the man's age. He stood and greeted him in French. The man looked surprised. He gestured at Daniel to sit, took a seat facing him, and offered him a cigarette. Daniel politely declined.

"Abu Suleiman," the man introduced himself, patting his chest. "What are you doing here?" he asked in Arabic, lighting a cigarette.

"*Français?*" Daniel bluffed.

The interrogator repeated his question in Arabic. Daniel explained in French that this was his native language, but he also knew a little English. He hoped that would help him understand the depth of the hole into which he had fallen.

"What are you doing here?" Abu Suleiman asked in heavily accented English.

"Traveling," Daniel answered, also in English.

"Here, in the desert?" Abu Suleiman picked up his passport, "We have more interesting and beautiful places to visit."

"Yes, and I plan to see them too. I'm interested in archaeology; I studied your ancient kingdoms at university, so I thought it was an opportunity to visit the ruins."

Abu Suleiman gave him a skeptical look. "When did you arrive?" he asked, flipping through the passport.

"Two days ago."

"Alone?" Abu Suleiman took a drag of his cigarette.

"*Oui*," he nodded.

"And where did you sleep?" He threw the passport on the table.

"Yesterday, I slept in my tent near the archaeological site," Daniel pointed at the cylindrical bag tied to his backpack.

"And the day before?" Abu Suleiman tapped his cigarette on a small glass with the dried dregs of coffee at the bottom.

"I arrived late at night. I stayed at the border crossing until morning and then hitched a ride to..."

The door opened. A soldier stormed in and leaned down to whisper in the interrogator's ear. Abu Suleiman got up and left the room, taking the passport with him.

On high alert, Daniel turned to the soldier who had stayed to guard him, pointed to the backpack, and mimed drinking from a bottle. The soldier shrugged, and Daniel pulled a transparent dark blue bottle from the side pocket with his cuffed hands and took a few sips.

Fifteen minutes later, the door opened, and Abu Suleiman entered. Daniel looked at him closely, searching for a clue as to what was happening.

"So, where did you get a ride to?"

"The ancient ruins. I walked a bit and stayed there overnight."

"I see," Abu Suleiman's expression was unreadable. He emptied the backpack on the scratched Formica table, leaving the tent bag tied to it.

"COMBAR," Abu Suleiman read the brand name on the multi-tool handle out loud and examined it from all sides. "What is this?" he asked, opening the spade, "To steal artifacts?"

"It's a tool I use when I'm in the field to help set up the tent, clear stones... you know." Daniel remained impassive, the image of the hidden camera in his head.

Abu Suleiman continued to examine the tool. "And what is this?" He pointed at a different part that was folded inside.

"That's an axe," Daniel explained. "I travel around the world and sometimes need wood to make a fire."

"An axe, eh?" the interrogator mumbled, "Are there other tools that can kill here?"

Daniel tensed at the word kill. There's no point in hiding anything, he thought. "There's also a knife and saw." He pointed at the small flap at the bottom of the handle.

Abu Suleiman opened the flap and pulled out a hunting knife and a folding saw. His eyes widened when he saw the knife. He clucked his tongue loudly. "Just for this, you should sit in jail." He waved the knife.

25

Daniel knew that the threat was just a bluff, an intimidation tactic. Intelligence officers in the Mossad, otherwise known as the Office, had researched and validated the legality of every item he carried. "They saw it in their search at the border crossing and told me there was no problem," he insisted.

The interrogator scoffed, "So they told you. So what! Now I'm telling you! You want to argue with me?"

"Sir," answered Daniel, "If there was a misunderstanding, you can keep the tool."

The interrogator nodded to himself and put the tool aside. Then he picked up the video camera that Daniel had used as a night vision device.

"Did you film anything?"

"Yes, a little bit," Daniel answered, hiding his unease, "the ruins that I visited."

"Show me!" the interrogator ordered.

"Of course," Daniel said and explained how to operate the player. Daniel had never visited that site yet knew there was no way the interrogator would know the difference. The video was downloaded from the internet at headquarters and edited to add Daniel's voice describing what he saw. It looked authentic.

The interrogator put the camera down and continued rifling through the items he'd spread out on the table: wrinkled clothes, a gas camping stove, a jar of coffee, books in French, a Lonely Planet guide, first aid kit, black baseball cap, toiletries, comb, hair gel, and a towel. He glanced at the items, stuffed them in the backpack, and threw it on the floor.

"Did you sleep well?"

"*Oui.*"

"Liar!" Abu Suleiman roared in Arabic as the woman from the red pickup entered the room crying, escorted by a soldier. The soldier closed the door behind her and stayed outside.

Daniel, who pretended not to understand a word of Arabic, looked back and forth between her and the interrogator and remained silent.

"Liar!" the interrogator barked, this time in English, and then turned to the woman, speaking in Arabic, "Tell me what you said before! What's your connection to him?"

"We got an order to pick him up," she replied in Arabic, her eyes on the floor.

Daniel felt as though a rug had been pulled out from under him but remained calm and alert. Now there was no doubt; she was also in the know and maybe an informant herself.

"Did you hear?" the interrogator shouted in English. "You are Mossad!"

Daniel muttered something in French and gestured that he didn't understand what the woman had said.

The interrogator slapped his face hard. The woman pointed at him and continued to sob. Shocked at the slap, Daniel cursed in French and faced the interrogator. "Why did you hit me?"

The interrogator pushed him down into the chair. "Israeli!" he yelled.

Stunned at the man's strength, Daniel muttered in French that he didn't know what he wanted from him.

"Israeli! Mossad! Israeli! These stamps are fake!" The interrogator waved his passport. In the background, the woman was still crying. "We checked the records, and no Pierre Denis entered the country."

"I don't understand," Daniel pretended to look confused, "What do you mean fake? Of course, I entered the country... how else did I get here?"

"That's what you're going to tell us!" the interrogator yelled and ordered the woman and the guard to leave the room. He told the guard to take Daniel's things.

They all walked out. The door closed behind them, and Daniel heard the snick of the lock. He couldn't believe that he'd been captured on his first operation. Everything had gone so smoothly, and now it was going downhill fast. Even if they had detected the plane, why did they suspect him? Maybe a wandering Bedouin had seen him with the parachute? He remembered hearing the rock hit the ground. My name is Pierre Denis. I don't know who that woman and her husband were supposed to pick up and from where – I just hitched a ride. Let them search the desert for their suspect. I was resting next to a boulder when I heard a car stop. I climbed up to the road and asked if I could get a ride. If they're spies, that doesn't mean I am too – just an unfortunate coincidence. And the passport stamps? I have no idea. Maybe someone forgot to register my entry – mistakes happen. That's the truth! He focused on his story. Let them prove differently – I have nothing to lose!

Except for the radio with its sporadic bursts of chatter, he didn't hear a thing. He put his ear to the wooden door. Silence. Daniel surveyed the room, now certain that this wasn't an interrogation facility. He lay down on the floor and tried to fall asleep. It was important to rest, even if just for a few minutes. He fell asleep quickly, but not for long. He heard the rattle of a key in the lock, and the door flew open. Abu Suleiman walked in holding a piece of paper and kicked him with his black moccasins. "Get up!" he ordered in English.

Daniel got up and sat in the chair.

"Take this, sign it!" He held out the document.

Daniel grabbed it with both hands and read to himself: I, the undersigned, confess that... "I don't know Arabic, and I'm not signing," he handed the paper back.

The interrogator smirked and slapped him again. "Don't you understand that you have no reason to refuse? You idiot! We know exactly who you are!"

Daniel was helpless, and it was driving him crazy. He felt like a volcano about to erupt, that if he could get in one punch, it would be enough to end the interrogator. But he suppressed his anger. "This is your mistake!" he grumbled in French, not hiding his impatience, "what do you want from me!"

The interrogator didn't understand a word he said. He continued to ask questions in English, and Daniel answered in French until finally, he'd had enough and gestured for Daniel to be quiet. Abu Suleiman opened the door and ordered someone to bring the woman in. He heard her whimpering even before she appeared escorted by a soldier, her husband protesting in the background.

"Last chance!" The interrogator pushed the confession document into Daniel's hands.

"I told you I don't know Arabic, and I won't sign." Daniel lowered his arms but kept hold of the paper.

"So that's the way it's going to be?" Abu Suleiman gave him a dark look. "No problem!" He jerked his chin to the side and turned to the woman. She looked down, and Abu Suleiman ordered her to kneel. Trembling, she went down on her knees. Abu Suleiman pulled out a black pistol, cocked it, and held it to her head. Her whimpers turned into cries of anguish.

Daniel was boiling with rage, close to exploding. The woman's wails echoed off the walls; her desperate gaze seared him. He looked back and forth between her and Abu Suleiman, who gave a sly, victorious smile.

"Are you crazy?" Daniel shouted in English and pushed himself between the woman and the gun. He realized his mistake immediately and tried to think about how to reverse it. The woman took advantage of the situation and crawled behind the desk as if to hide.

"Where do you think you are? The Champs-Élysées?" Abu Suleiman sneered, "You're risking your life for this traitorous bitch?"

Daniel glared at Abu Suleiman. He didn't have a single intelligent thing to say and didn't know how to get out of the situation. He had given his interrogator ammunition and exposed a vulnerability.

"You're that much of a gentleman? Sign, and I will release them."

"I won't sign anything that I can't read. You wouldn't either!"

"And if I bring you this in French?" Abu Suleiman raised a gray eyebrow. "You will sign it?"

"Depends on what's written. If it isn't the truth, then I won't sign... This is ridiculous! It's a violation of my rights... you're arresting a tourist for no reason – I haven't done anything wrong."

Abu Suleiman ordered the soldier to take the woman out of the room. "Let's see how you feel after spending a night here! Dammit!" he cursed as he left. Daniel remained standing and analyzed what had just happened. He wondered why the interrogator didn't continue to pressure him, threaten the woman or torture her in front of him. Something felt off.

Despite the anxiety, he tried to fall asleep again. He lay on the dusty concrete floor in a fetal position, closed his eyes, and fell into a fitful sleep for several hours. Like a guard dog – his body was relaxed but senses remained sharp, hearing steps, the radio, doors slamming, fragments of conversation in Arabic, and the couple pleading. His captors left him his watch, so every time he opened his eyes, he checked the time.

He awoke to the roar of a fighter jet in descent. It was five am, and the floor was hard and cold. He didn't have a blanket. He dozed off again and suddenly felt hands lifting him into a seated position. Daniel opened his eyes in panic and saw one of the soldiers standing over him. He stood, and the soldier pushed him down into a chair, this time with his back to the door. He heard the door open and footsteps. Two large hands settled on his shoulders.

"Hello, Eran." He heard his Hebrew code name, recognized the voice immediately, and jumped up as if bitten by a snake.

"Arik? What the hell is this?" he asked in Hebrew.

"What do you think?" Arik smiled at him, his voice quiet and authoritative.

"Son of a bitch!" Daniel shouted and shoved his instructor angrily. "How could you do this to me!"

"Sit down, Eran. Take a deep breath. You learned the most important lesson of your life in the past 24 hours."

"I don't understand... how did you get here?"

"In my car."

"Where...?"

"We're in the Negev."

"I don't believe this." He held his hands to his head. "This is insane! We're in Israel?"

"We'll discuss everything."

"But how?" Daniel was in shock. "All the maps I studied and the navigation app..."

"We switched out parts of the maps. The same with the app's database. It wasn't that complicated."

Daniel stared at his instructor and thought how convincing deception could be.

"This was the final exercise," Arik announced. "Now you've really completed your training."

The door opened, and the interrogator and the couple from the truck entered, smiling. Daniel gave them a sheepish look. The elderly interrogator patted him on the shoulder. "Nice to meet you," he said with a big smile, shaking his hand. "Forgive me for the slap, eh?"

The driver came up to him next, held out his hand, and winked. Then the woman, giving him a shy smile. He barely recognized her without the head covering and long dress. She wore tight jeans and a hoodie, but he was most surprised by her brunette hair in a pixie cut that framed her delicate features. It wasn't how he'd imagined her face under the hijab. She held out a delicate hand, bit her lower lip, and introduced herself. "Hi, I'm 'Roni'," she said, making air quotes. "Nice to meet you, and I'm sorry for what I did to you."

Daniel held out his hand and looked into her eyes, this time without a mirror between them. The touch of her fingers felt nice and strangely calmed him. "No need to apologize," he said, with a touch of the French accent that came out when he was emotional. He let go of her hand. "You probably went through the same thing."

"You don't know the half of it," she rolled her eyes and whispered, "That was crazy, what you did, and you'll be reprimanded at the debriefing, but you should know it meant something to me."

Daniel looked at her in amazement and wondered what her real name was. Something sparked within him. He was fascinated by the disparity between the hysterical sobbing woman he'd been ready to strangle just a few minutes ago and the confident woman standing before him.

"Let's go, people," Arik called out, "We have an early breakfast waiting for us and a long ride home."

PART ONE

A Vision of the Homeland

Five years later

1

Daniel locked the door behind him. It was twenty to eight; he could hear his neighbors up and about, getting ready to start the day. The small studio apartment he rented was at the end of a narrow corridor on the third floor, overlooking one of the main streets of Bethlehem. Like the other apartments in Abu Elias' stone building, his apartment was well maintained and simply furnished with everything he needed: kitchen appliances and sofa all in the same space as the bedroom, with a separate bathroom. His neighbors were young people who studied or worked in the city. The apartment he shared a wall with was fortunately empty most of the time; sometimes tourists stayed there, and sometimes Arab Israelis who came for the weekend.

He walked down the stairs to the entrance. The door to Abu Elias' small office was wide open so that he could keep an eye on the tenants' comings and goings.

"*Sabah al-kheir.*" Daniel knocked on the green door to say good morning.

"*Sabah a-noor,* Frenchman!" Abu Elias peered at Daniel from behind his copy of Al-Quds and took off his reading glasses. He was long past seventy and lived in a nice house adjacent to the apartment building he owned. He had a few stores that he rented out in town and spent his days peacefully sitting in the tiny office, always wearing wide cotton pants and a jacket over a vest with a white button-down shirt underneath.

"Here's another month's rent." Daniel handed him a small white envelope.

"It's been a month already?" Abu Elias sounded surprised and took the envelope. "How long will you be staying, Jalal?" he asked, absently patting his cross necklace.

"Another month for now," Daniel answered. "We'll see how things go at the hospital. I hope that's okay with you?"

"If you keep paying in euros, then no problem!" Abu Elias' laugh turned into a cough. "I hope you stay another year! It's not easy finding tenants as nice as you. Our young people... you see for yourself..."

"You exaggerate, Abu Elias. Everyone who lives here is very nice," Daniel said and turned to go. Behind him, he heard the landlord grunt and shake out the pages of his newspaper. Daniel assumed that Abu Elias informed Palestinian Intelligence on his regular tenants and certainly on out of the ordinary ones like him. His warm relationship with the owner, especially with the owner's wallet, was an effective incentive to Abu Elias to vouch for his integrity.

Daniel went out to the main street, and just like every day over the past month, he walked to the bakery before hailing a taxi. The familiar smells of the Middle East mingled in the air; the sweet aroma of baking, spices, freshly ground coffee, hookah smoke, and exhaust fumes. He loved that unique imprint; it heightened his senses and the thrill of being in the field. The essence was the same, although the circumstances were completely different – for the past month he'd been undercover in the heart of an Arab city, this time for a greater cause. He'd never done anything quite like this before, and his burgeoning self-esteem ignited the spark of hope.

As soon as Daniel entered, the baker wrapped up two *manakish*, Daniel's favorite pita bread topped with red pepper and onion. He ate one of them with a glass of sage-infused sweet tea, different from the typical North African mint tea he had grown up on. The other he put in his messenger bag, for his ten-thirty coffee break at the hospital.

He went out and hailed a passing taxi. After giving the driver the address, he stared out the window to avoid conversation. It was a short drive to the hospital and the roads were still empty. The landscape in Bethlehem was no different than any other West Bank Palestinian city, and even East Jerusalem. The streets came to life late; in an hour or two they would be bustling with cars and people. Old stone buildings stood alongside modern construction and crowded shops displayed their colorful wares on the edge of the sidewalk, close to the street. One thing differentiated this city – bell towers competed with minarets for the skyline; crosses and crescents, bells ringing and the call of the muezzin.

Two miles and twenty minutes later, the taxi stopped at the gates of Bethlehem's psychiatric hospital. Daniel paid the driver and walked toward the arch in the limestone wall surrounding the compound. On each side of the gate, on a background of whitewashed stones, were enormous portraits. On the right, Yasser Arafat, and on the left, Abu Jihad. The latter was assassinated in Tunisia at the end of the 1980s by commandos in Sayeret Matkal, the IDF's elite special operations unit. The former was poisoned by

Israeli intelligence, or so the Palestinians believed. The walls were covered with slogans of struggle and heroism. Daniel greeted the guard and entered the wide inner courtyard. At the center stood an impressive stone building with many arches – the administration and main offices. The wards were in smaller, plain buildings throughout the large compound. Behind the main building was a wooded area with pine and cypress trees, a pearl at the heart of a walled island of insanity. People from the open wards, each living in their own world, wandered about. It could be intimidating for anyone who wasn't used to it. But the truly difficult sights were in the closed wards, where the more problematic patients lived.

Daniel walked across the cracked asphalt to the courtyard and went straight to the staff room in the main building. Some of his fellow aides were already there getting ready for their shift. He greeted them and went to his locker to get his white coat which was hanging on a cheap plastic hanger. The others greeted him back politely and got on with what they were doing. The hospital had many staff members and therapists, and he only knew a few of them personally. But every single one of them had heard of him, the son of French immigrants who came to volunteer at a Palestinian psychiatric hospital in the West Bank. Some respected him, others thought that he was crazy himself.

"What's up, Jalal?" Rashid, his co-worker, entered the room and patted his shoulder. "Hurry up, let's go, shift changes in five minutes."

Rashid, a young, bearded man with glasses, was the son of an established Bethlehem family. One of Daniel's first friends at the hospital, Rashid had been working there for almost two years, and they bonded immediately. He was well-versed in the social politics of the place and loved to gossip. This trait served Daniel well, but also made him keep their friendship mostly to work hours. As a rule, he politely declined social invitations that crossed the boundary of the yellowing limestone walls. "I'm writing a book," he would say, "I work on it whenever I have spare time." It was also a plausible cover for all his note taking.

They left the main building and quickly walked up the narrow path to their department. The men's ward had permanent patients, but their conditions were relatively mild. They were allowed to wander around the hospital compound with few restrictions, and sometimes, at first glance, they seemed perfectly healthy. Only conversing with them revealed, sooner or later, the disturbances they suffered from. Unlike the seriously ill patients, who gave off a somewhat stressful vibe with any contact, conversations with these patients could be amusing.

Daniel and Rashid entered the stone building, two stories completely devoid of character. Blank faces peered out of windows barred with white security bars, their eyes squinting against the glare of the sun. The other aides stood in the entrance hall, wearing their white coats, waiting for the routine shift change. The tenseness that Daniel had felt during his first few days was almost forgotten. He had been undercover for almost a month, and every day he became more Jalal and less Daniel. He'd never thought about it before coming to the psychiatric hospital, but lately he'd wondered about the parallel between the mentally disabled, who in some twisted way had lost touch with reality, and undercover agents – intelligent and rational people who had to immerse themselves in their fake identity to be convincing.

The shift handover ended, and the aides dispersed. Cold fluorescent lighting, some flickering and buzzing, illuminated the corridors and rooms. The smell of fresh paint and new furniture lingered in the air from a large renovation project that had just been completed several months earlier, thanks to an international humanitarian organization. That same organization had been seeking volunteers in Europe who were interested in working as aides at the hospital for a small stipend. It was a perfect fit for the operation that Daniel had taken upon himself. When he saw the advertisement online, as part of his preliminary intelligence gathering on the hospital, he couldn't pass it up. It was the opportunity of a lifetime. He had nothing to lose – he had nowhere to go but up from his job in the warehouse of his father's chain of grocery stores, and if his plan succeeded, everyone would hear about it.

"Jalal! Jalal! *Bonsoir*, Jalal!" one of the patients called out, a man in his early twenties.

"*Bonjour!*" Daniel corrected him, as he did every morning. "You remember, right? *Bonsoir* means good evening. How are you today, my friend?"

"They hit me in the head and tortured me," wailed the young man in Arabic, "Here, look." He lifted his shirt and displayed a healthy body with no signs of injury.

"Who did that to you?" Daniel gave him his complete attention.

"The army," he continued in tears.

"Which army?" Daniel asked gently.

"The Israelis! May Allah take them!" The patient started walking around in agitation. "They caught me last night and beat me with metal poles. Look! Look!" He lowered his head and buried his fingers in his hair. "I'm all bloody!"

Daniel embraced the young man and tried to calm him down. "You're already healed, it was a long time ago, and now everything is okay."

The man wrung his hands nervously. "Not true! It was last week... The police. They caught me and tortured me with electric shocks... for no reason, I didn't do anything!"

"Look at how strong you are! You're not afraid of them, are you?" It was almost the same story every time he saw the man, except for the changing identity of the attackers; Israel, the Palestinian Authority, Hamas, the Jordanians. "There's your bicycle," Daniel pointed, "go ride for a while, you'll feel better."

With a childlike smile on his face, the young man jumped on the bike and rode off around the compound.

The patients liked Daniel, and some even preferred him over the other therapists, the locals. Daniel was patient and compassionate, listening to their stories with undivided attention. Rashid kept saying that one day his patience would fade. "You're new at this... we all felt sorry for them at first, but after a while you get tired and become indifferent."

Daniel knew that his time there was limited. He couldn't stay in Bethlehem for too long. His volunteering was a cover story that

43

allowed him to investigate freely and maybe succeed in exposing what he was searching for. But his cover could be blown. Feeling that things could fall apart at any minute, he was always the first to volunteer to switch shifts, work overtime and at night – anything that would let him visit all parts of the hospital. In his modest apartment at Abu Elias' house, he cross-referenced the data he collected under the pretext of writing a book. The hospital was not an exceptionally difficult operational arena, but like in any undercover operation, he faced sudden challenges. One time he'd managed to avoid being interviewed for a story by a team from the Palestinian Al-Watan television channel. The director of the hospital begged him to do the interview, but the last thing he needed was a public record of his face under a fake identity. His excuses were based on numerous drills in the Mossad that trained him for every possible situation. In another incident, a few days after he'd arrived, Israeli military forces, to the extreme annoyance of the Palestinian National Security Forces, pursued a wanted man who'd tried to escape to the hospital in the middle of the night. Daniel had been terrified, but it was over quickly with no negative impact.

Daniel enjoyed the warm sun as he observed the patient riding in circles around the small plaza near the department, an ancient olive tree at its center.

"Hi Jalal," a shy and gentle voice called from behind him.

"Hi, Ibtisam *ukhti*," he replied, noticing the pretty woman's disappointment at being called 'sister.'

"How are you?" She stopped beside him, holding a stack of medical files.

"I'm fine..."

Ibtisam was small and fragile looking. She wore a black hijab, a sharp contrast with her crisp white uniform. Rashid had already mentioned that she was interested in Daniel as a way out, an escape to a peaceful life in France. He kept his distance, but Ibtisam didn't give up. She was always around, and Daniel was uneasy having sharp, observant eyes on him, watching his every move.

"Okay, so I'll see you at ten thirty by the espresso machine," she said with a shy, hopeful smile and went on her way.

Her understated way of flirtation almost always made him think of Yael. It had been a while, but he still missed her. He longed to hear her voice, if only for a minute, but still couldn't get up the courage to call her. And even if he did call, what could he tell her? She wouldn't believe him anyway and would think he'd gone totally off the rails. Everyone would, and that was why no one could know anything until he completed his mission. Even then, he'd have to find a way to reveal the story convincingly without being accused of being delusional.

He heard the bustle of patients gathered at the entrance to the ward. It was time for occupational therapy. He joined the rest of the staff. Walking a group of seventeen patients along the hospital paths toward the main building was not easy. They had minds of their own. Some were older and it was hard for them to walk. Others were childlike and boisterous. A mix of different types and unexpected behaviors. The senior staff members joked about the patients' oddities. Daniel still tried to avoid that, but completely understood the need for humor in this depressing and dreary place. Sometimes it seemed that his colleagues tried to joke at the expense of the patients even more when he was around, to see his reaction. But maybe it was just his imagination.

The group safely reached the main building and responsibility was handed over to the therapists. Rashid and Daniel left the crafts room and escaped to the kitchenette. Rashid got to work on the espresso and sent Daniel to bring the *manakish* from his locker in the staff room. Ibtisam followed him.

"Jalal?" She came up to him after making sure they were alone.

"Yes, *ukhti*?" He stood at his locker without turning to her.

"Can you do me a favor?"

"Of course." He shut the locker and turned to her, holding the bag with the fragrant bread.

"Can you please stop calling me sister? It's a little insulting."

Daniel felt sympathy for the offended young woman. "I'm sorry, but why? I respect you as if you were my little sister."

"That's just it. I'm embarrassed to say this..." she hesitated and then gathered courage, "but I would be happy if you saw me as a woman, you know... and not like a sister or cousin."

That bastard Rashid knew what he was talking about, Daniel thought to himself, and very briefly even considered it. He had been alone for too long. As a woman, Ibtisam certainly intrigued him, and more than once he'd thought about what was hidden beneath her conservative clothes. But only very briefly. There was no chance, nothing good could come of it.

"I don't want to hurt you, but I don't think it would work between us." He saw her frown. "Sooner or later, I will return to France, and then what? This isn't my home!" The double meaning in his words echoed in his ears.

"It's been known to happen," said Ibtisam. "It's too soon to speak of this, of course, but I wouldn't be the first to leave Palestine for Europe."

Bingo, Rashid. A smile spread across Daniel's face. "Okay, now I'm embarrassed too... it's really too soon to speak of such things."

"Is there someone waiting for you at home, Jalal?"

The image of Yael flashed through his head. "*Ukhti*, I'm not comfortable speaking about this... and Rashid is waiting for me." He ran off toward the kitchenette.

"May your house be destroyed," he cursed in Arabic at Rashid, whose round, full face greeted him with a look that said, 'what took you so long?'

"It was destroyed more than once already because of my dead brother; may he rest in peace," Rashid responded, a sad look in his eyes behind the rectangular frames.

"Forgive me, my brother. That was inexcusable." Daniel was angry at himself for the momentary lapse.

"It's okay," Rashid sighed, "I never supported his path. I just feel sorry for our parents. What happened?"

Too bad your brother didn't feel the same way, Daniel thought. "You were right about Ibtisam."

"Huh! Of course I was right! I'm always right about these things. But what happened? Tell me!"

They sipped their espresso and shared the cold pita bread. Daniel told him and Rashid, who was very pleased with himself, punctuated each sentence with an "I told you so."

"What are you going to do?" Rashid asked finally.

"Nothing, man, that's the last thing I need! There's no future in it!"

"They say she's not as religious as you would think by the way she dresses," Rashid said suggestively, "that she's influenced by the Christian girls in town. Go for it, who knows... have some fun. Why not?"

Daniel laughed. "Keep your fantasies to yourself and leave me in peace."

Rashid raised a fist in the air. "Yes, I will, *inshallah*, when I come visit you in Paris."

"Absolutely. God willing, as you said," Daniel affirmed. And dream on, he said to himself, a hint of a smile on his face.

After the therapy session, the patients went back to their building for lunch and then to nap. Daniel wandered through the rooms, stopping to smile and say a few words to those who were awake. His real target was Ibrahim, the most senior resident of the hospital. He hoped to find him alone and in the mood to chat.

Ibrahim was in his late seventies, and unlike the other residents, he had never suffered from a mental illness. It was hard to say that he was entirely healthy after so many years among people with mental health disorders, but he had never received any psychiatric treatment. Back in the days of Jordanian rule, when he was thirteen years old, his brother brought him to the hospital, which in its previous incarnation had been an orphanage. Ever since, for more than sixty-five years, he had lived there without anyone taking any interest in him. If there was anyone who knew the secrets of the place, Daniel had very early on figured it would be Ibrahim.

His seniority entitled Ibrahim to special treatment, and he lived in his own room at the end of the corridor on the first floor. When Daniel peeked in, he found him sitting on a plastic chair facing the space heater, the hot coils casting an orange glow around his folded hands. He wore faded black sweatpants, a threadbare green sweater, striped socks and rubber slippers, and a baseball cap with the symbol of the IDF Golani Brigade – an olive tree. It was Ibrahim's signature cap; he was never without it. Many clothes gathered for donations in Israel found their way to the West Bank and some were sold, but a baseball cap like that was a rare sight in the hospital.

"Uncle Ibrahim, how are you?" Daniel called him uncle as a sign of respect. He sat on the bed and laid a warm hand on the old man's stooped shoulder.

"What can I say, Jalal..." Ibrahim sighed and waved away an annoying fly.

"Let's go outside. It's cold in here and you're sitting in front of the heater when it's so nice out in the sun." Daniel supported the elderly man and helped him to rise. He handed him his cane, took his other arm, and slowly led him across the hospital paths. They made their way in silence. Ibrahim struggled with every step, and Daniel felt compassion for the gaunt, frail old man. When they reached the woods, he led Ibrahim to a bench under the pine trees and sat next to him. The tops of the trees swayed in the light breeze, spreading their aromatic fragrance. Ibrahim took a deep breath and asked Daniel to give him one of the dry pinecones that were on the ground.

"Here you go." Daniel handed him the hard shell, and Ibrahim started to pick off the dry scales, one by one.

"You know, Jalal," he said after a few moments of silence, "I love these woods. I spent my childhood here among the trees. They used to look taller. I'd escape here with my friends, and this is where we used to play. The smell of the trees reminds me of those days."

Daniel nodded silently with a smile. His heart felt heavy. The smell of the pines reminded him of a different childhood – family vacations in Provence. He felt the same way in the Carmel mountains, the Galilee, the Jerusalem hills, or any other forest in Israel. Only the desert, which France didn't have, brought up more adult memories of Israel.

"But everyone is gone and only I remain here," Ibrahim added. "No one comes to visit me or asks about me. Not even my friends who were orphans with me here. When the mentally ill people came, I wanted to run away. They scared me. I think I've also become a little crazy."

"How could you not be?" Daniel sympathized. "Uncle Ibrahim, you are just fine. You aren't crazier than any other average old man." Daniel patted the old man's thigh.

"Good thing I discovered the 'sadaa'... I used to hide there for days."

Daniel didn't know that word. It could have been the dialect, or maybe just that Arabic wasn't his native language. "What do you mean *sadaa*?" Daniel asked without hesitation. Ibrahim did not pose a threat. "Where did you hide, Uncle Ibrahim?"

"In that split in the ground, where it opens..." Ibrahim explained, his eyes unfocused. "It was winter, a lot of rain, and there was a hollow in the ground with piles of pine needles that fell inside."

"And that's where you hid? Sitting in the mud?" Daniel went along with the story, but it sounded like Ibrahim was making things up.

"There was a kind of tunnel there, made of stone..."

"A tunnel?!" Daniel's heart started racing. "What tunnel?"

"It was so much fun," Ibrahim continued his storytelling, "like in a fairytale. And all the other tunnels that led from it... I crawled down there a lot with Zaki's flashlight that I used to steal. Once, I even got lost there..."

Daniel felt a rush of excitement, "Who's Zaki? What flashlight?"

"Zaki - may he rest in peace!" Ibrahim tore the last scale off the pinecone. "The caretaker. He didn't understand where his flashlights kept disappearing to."

"When was this?" Daniel looked around as if fearing that someone was listening to their conversation.

"Oh... it was a long time ago... when the Jordanians ruled." The old man slid his rough palms up and down his emaciated thighs.

"Please tell me about it, it sounds interesting," Daniel said, his eyes gleaming. "The Jordanians. So..."

"It was my secret for around four months... no one knew until Zaki saw me with the flashlight and followed me. He told the principal and that was it."

"What do you mean?" Daniel encouraged him to continue. "What did the principal do?"

"He threatened me. Told me it was dangerous and that if I went into the tunnel one more time, he'd throw me out of here! So that was it. I never went there again."

Daniel raised his eyebrows. This was incredible information! "And you've never gone back there since? Where is it?"

"After they found out, people came to dig with shovels."

Daniel's eyes threatened to pop out. "They started digging? Who? Archaeologists, you mean?"

"*Aiwa!*" Ibrahim nodded, pointing at Daniel with a trembling hand.

"And... did they find anything?"

"They were there for maybe two or three days, and then the war started." Ibrahim pointed his cane at another pinecone, and Daniel quickly picked it up for him.

"What war?" Daniel was confused and started to doubt the whole story.

"The 1967 war."

The Six-Day War? Daniel wondered, "Are you sure, Uncle Ibrahim? How old were you? You weren't a boy anymore!"

"I was twenty-something when the Jewish came." Ibrahim stared off into the distance as if seeing it on an imaginary screen. "Let's go, Jalal, it's cold here in the shade. I want to go back to my room."

Daniel stopped pushing him. He helped the old man stand up and supported him as they trod on the crackling bed of dry pine needles. Before they reached the asphalt path, he decided to ask one last question, "And where is this tunnel today?"

"Allah knows!" Ibrahim threw down the pinecone still in his hand. "The woods once spread across almost the entire area, so they must have built over it."

Daniel was overwhelmed. He'd spent quite a bit of time with Ibrahim over the past month and heard many stories, but this was the first time he felt close to a breakthrough. He escorted Ibrahim back to his room and promised to take a walk with him again. Out in the courtyard he met Rashid.

"What's up, Jalal?" he asked. "Where did you disappear to? Meeting up with Ibtisam?"

"Don't be an idiot. I took Ibrahim to the woods. He loves it there."

"So why are your eyes shining? What happened?"

"Nothing much. He went on about caves, ghosts, Ali Baba and stories about some crazy old man."

"Allah help him. You got plans this weekend? Working?"

"No. I'm free until Sunday."

"Come with me to the mosque tomorrow for the Friday sermon?"

"I was planning to go to Al-Quds to pray at Al-Aqsa. Maybe next time."

"You lucky dog," Rashid griped. "You and your French passport! I have to stand for hours at the checkpoint and that's only if I can get an entry permit," he grumbled and went back inside.

For the remaining three hours of his shift, Daniel tried to tamp down his excitement. He kept coming up with more questions and tried to remember all of them until he got home so he could write them down in a safe place and make sense of them. When his workday was over, he rushed out through the arched gate and walked down the main road, lost in his thoughts. A horn honked twice behind him. He waved down the taxi and got in. The traffic was heavier in the afternoon and the ride took longer. Daniel stared out the window, but all he could see were images of the young Ibrahim playing in the woods and discovering this mysterious opening, Ibrahim crawling through the underground passageway, and images of Zaki the caretaker. Despite the patience and discipline that had been drilled into him – this time, maybe for the first time in his life, he felt on edge, anxious. He was impatient for the weekend to be over and to pick up the conversation with Ibrahim.

2

Daniel was up early the next morning. The exciting revelations from Ibrahim occupied his thoughts, on top of the anticipation for his trip to Jerusalem. He showered and shaved, got dressed, styled his hair with gel, and headed out for his daily stop at the bakery. Inhaling the mouthwatering aroma of freshly baked bread, Daniel drank a cup of fragrant tea and ate savory pita with melted goat cheese. Ten minutes later, he went out to the main road and hailed a taxi to the Rachel Border Crossing at the northern end of Bethlehem.

The square outside the Crossing, enclosed on one side by a tall concrete wall, was chaotic with merchants, taxis, and masses of people milling about, mostly men from Bethlehem and the surrounding area on their way to Friday prayers at the Al-Aqsa Mosque. Daniel made his way through the crowd. They swarmed together, shouting, pushing and shoving at the bottleneck – the entrance to two long lanes separated by steel bars. Palestinians on the right, and everyone else – tourists, Israelis, the elderly, and humanitarian cases – on the left. Daniel, who went through as a tourist, was spared the crowding, sweating, and strong body odor the others had to suffer, herded like cattle through the lane to his right. The glares he got from the other side of the bars revealed precisely what they thought of him. Like everyone else in the privileged lane, Daniel walked quickly with his eyes on the dusty concrete floor to avoid the glares. At the end of the lane, a turnstile opened into a hall for the security check. He felt conflicted by the sights of Palestinians squashed into the lane next to him but forced himself to ignore them. He had to stay focused. In just a moment, he would present his fake French passport to the Israeli Border Police. Unlike the Christian tourists, his name and Palestinian appearance automatically made him suspicious to Israeli security.

On the wall, a large yellow sign in three languages instructed visitors to prepare documents for inspection. Since this was his first time crossing Rachel Border Point, he observed the young Muslim woman who passed through Border Control ahead of him. Fully confident in himself and the quality of the forgery in his hand, he went up to the booth and presented his passport to the sharp-eyed Border Control officer. She sat behind a thick security window and signaled him to press his passport against the bulletproof glass. Daniel smiled and did as she asked. The young woman leaned forward, narrowed her eyes, glanced back and forth from him to his photo, and then gestured for him to push his passport through the opening at the bottom of the window. No matter how many times he'd done this before, his heart always skipped a beat when he presented fake documents to government officials. He slid his passport through and silently waited. The officer rifled through the thin book, examined the page with his photo and personal information for anything suspicious and then turned to the computer. She quickly typed something and waited. Daniel assumed she was validating that he wasn't listed as a wanted person, or maybe she was checking when and how he entered Israel before arriving in Bethlehem. He had no reason to worry. He had used this passport to enter Israel at Ben Gurion Airport on a direct flight from Italy, where he had arrived from France by train. A few seconds later, time that felt much longer to Daniel, she returned his maroon passport.

Relieved, Daniel entered the small hall decorated with landscapes carefully selected by the Israeli Ministry of Tourism. Just a few short steps and it was like landing on another planet: the Israeli side of the border crossing. It was also crowded, but people who had already crossed over were in better spirits. He wandered between the taxis and found a taxi van going to East Jerusalem. It was second nature to get in the front seat – close to the door and apart from the other passengers, alert and listening to every word and sign, aware that he never knew who might be following him. As the taxi drove off, he noticed a man standing on the sidewalk. His purple shirt stood out in the drab surroundings. Daniel kept his eyes on him through the sideview mirror, and at the last moment, just before disappearing from his field of vision, the man got into a car and drove off.

A few minutes later, they were in Jerusalem, and the traditional laid-back atmosphere of Bethlehem gave way to a more cosmopolitan one. The roads were wider, the buildings, shops, and cars looked modern, and the street signs displayed a combination of Hebrew, English, and Arabic, reflecting the diverse population residing in the city. So near and yet so far. It reminded Daniel of his army days in the Duvdevan undercover unit. Going deep into Palestinian territory and quickly getting out. One minute here, the next minute there. A tricky, shifting reality.

Behind him, two passengers were having a loud conversation and the others were silent. Prayer beads hanging from the rearview mirror clinked on the glass as they swung from side to side. The large taxi sped down Hebron Road. The Gilo neighborhood on the left, Ramat Rachel on the right, Arnona, Talpiot, and then east on the narrow, slower roads whose names carried such weight, loaded with meaning and history from Biblical times: Valley of Hinnom, City of David, Derech HaOphel Street. The taxi continued around the eastern walls of the Temple Mount and the Muslim Quarter until reaching its destination – the Damascus Gate. The area was teeming with cars, people, market stalls, men and women rushing around, and young porters pushing gaudy green carts. You couldn't tell the sidewalk from the street.

The passengers got out. Daniel crossed the busy street and entered the Old City through the gate. The crowd surged toward the Al-Aqsa Mosque on their way to Friday prayers, and Daniel along with them. When he reached Ala-e Din Street, which led to Bab al-Majles – one of the main gates of the Temple Mount – he noticed an increased presence of heavily armed police officers and Israel Border Police. They were on high alert after another stabbing attack in the Old City just a few days ago, with yet another innocent civilian killed. He decided to go through the Muslim Quarter and enter from a different gate. It didn't look very different from the narrow alleys of Bethlehem's Old City, but he felt hostility and tension in the air. Or maybe it was just his imagination. He walked along the colorful covered alleyways past the many stalls and small shops. Mountains of brightly colored spices competed for the attention of passersby, and juice vendors called out to them. Young men who made a living transporting goods here and there pushed through the crowd like industrious ants among the locals and tourists. It was the hustle and bustle so unique to the Arab street. Daniel stopped by a falafel stand and took his overflowing pita to a small round table. Alternating bites with sips of tart lemonade, he watched the crowd. He always wondered why Arabs carried everything in plastic bags. Rarely any other kind of bag. Amused, he looked for people who had backpacks. Most were tourists. Suddenly he saw the man in the purple shirt from Bethlehem. Daniel observed him, thinking he was undoubtedly an Arab, maybe from East Jerusalem.

After eating, he set out for the Cotton Merchant's Market. The closer he got, the faster his heart thudded. There were fewer people around. At the end of the old covered market, daylight streamed in from the top of the stairs, piercing the crypt-like darkness as if from a mysterious source. Daniel was mesmerized, although it was just an everyday sight for the people around him. Each step closer revealed more of the imposing view. Behind the large cypress trees gleamed the golden exterior of the Dome of the Rock. He eagerly climbed the stone stairs, worn smooth from the many thousands of pilgrims over the centuries. The police officers stationed there gave him the same suspicious look they gave everyone else.

"Where are you coming from?" one of them asked.

"Bethlehem," Daniel answered in fluent Arabic that didn't reveal his background.

"Permit," the officer asked to see the Friday prayer permits given to Palestinians by the Civil Administration in the West Bank.

Daniel gave him his passport.

"Muslim?" he asked, flipping through the passport.

Daniel nodded.

An official of the Waqf, the Islamic religious authority that governs the Temple Mount, approached them. "*A salaam alaikum!*"

"*Wa alaikum salaam,*" Daniel greeted him in response.

"From where?" the Waqf representative asked.

"France. But I work and volunteer in Bethlehem. At the hospital there."

The police officer returned his passport, and he entered. His heart pounded with excitement as he strode across the vast stone plaza. For him, this was *the* Temple Mount. More than ten thousand Muslims milled around. Although it was the most volatile historical landmark in the world, it felt like being at a major tourist attraction. That was exactly how most of the people there were acting, like tourists. He decided to wander the compound. He really was a tourist, and this was his first visit. Daniel didn't feel threatened at all. No one gave him a second look. He stopped at the ancient fountain at the center of the compound to purify himself as required before entering the mosque. He walked through the engraved stone arch, left his shoes at the entrance, and entered through the large green doors left wide-open for visitors.

The mosque was jam-packed. Thousands of worshippers sat on rows upon rows of red prayer rugs decorated with beige designs, listening to the Friday sermon that blared from speakers across the entire compound, waiting for the prayers to start. Enormous marble and stone columns, crowned with artist-rendered decorations, supported the high ornate ceiling. Huge crystal chandeliers hung above their heads. After a few moments of taking in the impressive beauty of the building, Daniel went out and put his shoes back on. This was standard procedure. Many thousands filled the compound inside and outside the mosques. Some were satisfied with a quick visit inside, then prayed outside under the open skies.

He walked past the crowds of Muslim faithful who gathered outside and made his way to the place that really interested him, the turquoise building with the golden dome. As he got closer, the butterflies in his stomach went wild. Removing his shoes again, he entered the octagonal building and was immediately overcome with emotion. Right there, in front of him, surrounded by a brown wooden fence, was the sacred Foundation Stone, an enormous ancient rock in its natural state. Yet, it was more breathtaking than the surrounding marble columns, stone engravings, and mosaics. Daniel was not a religious man, and even his visits to the synagogue which had stopped when he moved to Israel, were just for the sake of tradition. But he was awestruck by the thought that he was standing where the Temple had stood thousands of years ago. He didn't hear the commotion around him; it was as if he were alone.

He walked around the stone, passed through an ornate entryway, and descended the stairs to a cave-like chamber, the floor covered with a bright wine-red carpet. There were a few other worshippers there. He sat in one of the niches and leaned against the smooth stone wall. A shiver ran up his spine as he contemplated the fact that this was the only way he could see and experience this extraordinary place. It also angered him. Here, where everything started, was so much a part of the Jewish consciousness and yet so absent in Israeli awareness. That sudden realization saddened him. He wasn't thinking about the Third Temple at that moment, and not about the Kohanim's sacrifices, consumed by fire on the altar; he thought that most of the Israelis he knew were not interested in this place, which was identified with the extreme right and messianic movements. But it should interest them. And if not, he thought angrily, this entire country shouldn't interest them either.

Daniel's thoughts turned to his grandfather, Rafael. He never got to visit the Temple Mount, but he had been down in the depths of the earth, feet below where Daniel was now sitting. What he might have found there with his colleagues, beneath the sediment and stubborn layers of mud, before an angry Arab mob attacked them, would forever remain a mystery.

The Islamic call to prayer brought him back to reality. "I bear witness that there is no god but Allah," the Imam recited, "I bear witness that Muhammad is the messenger of Allah!"

Daniel hurried back up from the cavern and quickly left the Dome of the Rock. He had no desire to kneel like a Muslim there. He joined the crowd outside and followed them while his thoughts wandered. He noticed the man in purple appear once again a few worshippers away from him. The short prayer ended, and Daniel went along with the crowd back to the Muslim Quarter. He wandered around the alleyways for an hour, ate lunch at a crowded restaurant frequented by locals, and then made his way back to the taxis waiting near the Damascus Gate. He took a shared taxi to the At-Tur neighborhood. The taxi passed by Gethsemane and slowly climbed up to the Mount of Olives. He asked the driver to stop when they were close to the Al-

Makassed Hospital. Fortunately, no one else got off there, but he decided to make a short stop to be sure he wasn't being followed.

Twenty-five minutes later, after stopping for coffee at the hospital cafeteria, Daniel walked to the promenade beneath the Seven Arches Hotel at the top of the Mount of Olives. Carefully he made his way between parked buses, their diesel fumes overpowering the scent of spring in the air. He strolled with his hands in his pockets. A group of Israelis got out of a tour bus and went to the observation point to see the panoramic view. Some of them lingered behind and took pictures with a camel which was a permanent fixture there. Their tour guide, holding a voice amplifier, gave an overview of the historical landmarks and Daniel listened: "Below us is the ancient Mount of Olives cemetery. Down on the right is Gethsemane – the Church of all Nations. The gilded onion domes just above Gethsemane belong to the Church of Mary Magdalene. And right across there, you probably recognize the Old City, and the mosque with the golden dome. Who knows what it's called?"

"*Al-Aqsa!*" shouted a chorus of tourists, as if the answer were obvious. Daniel was amazed by their ignorance. "Wrong!" The guide sounded delighted as if he had expected their response. "It's the Dome of the Rock! The dome above the Foundation Stone. Where Abraham nearly sacrificed Isaac, remember? Later, of course, Solomon built the Temple there. The mosque on the far left, with the gray dome, *that's* Al-Aqsa, which literally means "the furthest mosque" in Arabic. Over to the left, you can see..."

The tourists oohed and aahed as he spoke, taking pictures with their cellphones. Daniel watched and wondered if any of them, like him, were trying to peel back the layers of time from the unchanging landscape. Were they, too, imagining the wonders of the past, a vision of their ancestral homeland, of two thousand years of longing? Maybe only a handful of them, he thought. This is where they were born. Their homeland was here and now: a path on the kibbutz, an orchard on the moshav, the Sea of Galilee, rivers in the Golan Heights, forests in the north, the Negev, Tel Aviv... each person and their own childhood. They did not have the exiles' collective yearning for an ancient past they could only imagine.

The group gathered by the bus and the promenade emptied. Daniel sat on a stone bench and viewed the thousands of gravestones below. There was no chance of identifying the grave from this distance, yet he felt closer to his grandfather than he had in a long time. He spoke to him in his head, telling him how much he missed him, about his new discoveries in Bethlehem, his emotional visit to the Temple Mount, and how he missed Israel. He took a deep breath, filling his lungs with mountain air, and slowly exhaled. He was overcome with conflicting feelings. The life he had left behind when he returned to France seemed within his grasp again. He lay down on the bench and shut his eyes, listening to the sounds around him and breathing it all in, recalling the last Saturday in the very happy life he'd had with Yael before everything went wrong. The images were burned into his memory; the peaceful Saturday morning, a car starting, the laughter of children playing in the backyard next door, and Yael's father's footsteps downstairs.

The winter three years ago had been dry, just like it was now. The winter sun streamed through the narrow slits of the blinds. Bright rays of light trailed along the folds of the down comforter wrapped around their bodies. He wore black boxer briefs, she wore a flannel nightgown and tiny gray panties. The window was cracked, letting cool, fresh air flow into the room. He remembered how he gently ran his hand up and down her thigh. Yael moaned and pressed her backside into him; he nuzzled her short hair and breathed in the lingering scent of her sweet perfume. She tilted her neck and shivered when he nipped behind her ear. His hand moved between her legs and into her panties. Yael pushed back into his groin, and he hardened as she leaned into him. When he felt she was ready, he pulled off her panties and thrust inside. Yael crossed her arms over her chest, and Daniel wrapped one arm around her as they moved together in a hard and fast rhythm until they climaxed, first her and then him. When they came down, he kissed her flushed cheek, and Yael snuggled in his arms. He woke to the sound of water running in the bathroom, jumped out of bed, stretched, and started to do pushups. Daniel was in top physical shape – his body lean and ripped. The water stopped as he finished his third and final set. He went into the bathroom. Yael stood in a thick cloud of steam wrapped in a white towel, wiping the mirror.

"*Bonjour*, Monsieur Ben Atar."

"*Bonjour*, soon to be Madame Ben Atar." He gripped her hips from behind, "Why did you shower so quickly?"

"Not so quickly. I woke up twenty minutes ago."

"You're still wet," he stroked her hair, "come on, shower again with me."

"Stop it! I don't have the energy to go again," she said, looking down at his erection.

"Hey," he pretended to be insulted.

"Oh, come on, don't make that face," she said. "My stomach hurts, and I'm nauseous."

"Really?" He got into the shower and adjusted the water. "Maybe it's something you ate?"

"I don't think so." Yael dropped the towel and walked naked into the room to get dressed.

"Maybe you're excited about the flight tonight?" he shouted at her from the shower, looking at her as she walked out.

"Yeah, right!" She returned to the bathroom, pulling on a pair of blue sweatpants. "I think I'm way past getting excited."

"I hope you feel better by this evening," he mumbled through a mouth full of toothpaste.

"I'll be fine." She went back into the bedroom and slathered on scented hand cream.

Daniel remembered how he finished his shower and got dressed, and they went downstairs to her parents' living room. Her father was reading the weekend paper at the dining table. Her mother was sitting across from him doing the crossword. The large window behind them had a magnificent view of Haifa Bay. It was a beautiful clear morning after two days of stormy weather, and you could see all the way to the border with Lebanon.

"How much can you sleep?" her father grumbled, peering at them through his reading glasses. "We never get to spend enough time with you when you visit."

"Good morning to you too, Dad." Yael blew him a kiss, and Daniel lifted his hand in greeting. They went to the kitchen – Yael to the coffeemaker and Daniel to the electric kettle.

"I got you fresh mint leaves," Yael's mother called out to him, "they're in the fridge."

"You're the best," Daniel said, and made himself a big mug of sweet tea with the green and fragrant leaves. He usually started the day with a cup of espresso but kept to the Saturday tradition from his childhood. He sat next to Yael's father at the table.

"Anything interesting in today's paper?" he asked, taking a sip from the glass mug.

"A lot of nonsense!" her father grumbled.

"So why are you so fascinated by it?" Yael sat next to her dad and hugged him.

"Habit," he said and pushed the paper to the center of the table. "So... how are the wedding plans coming along? Did you decide where? What about the menu? You remember I told you that I know the owner of –"

"Dad!" Yael lifted a finger in warning. "Don't start. We're handling everything and we'll let you know when we have any updates."

"Three months go by quickly, Yaeli. And you're both busy with your work. There's no reason to drag things out..."

"Why don't you leave the kids alone!" his wife scolded, and Daniel's lips twitched at being called a kid. He wasn't sure that the people sending him around the world would agree with that definition. But her father's concern was heartwarming. His father never showed much interest in him.

"Alright, alright," her father said with a wave of his hand. "Tell me, Daniel, will you at least shave your beard before the wedding?"

"Why? Doesn't it look good on me?" Daniel smiled and stroked the rough black beard he'd been growing for several weeks.

"Actually, it suits you," his future mother-in-law said without lifting her eyes from the crossword, "The beard makes you look more mature."

"My bearded babyface!" Yael kissed his whiskered cheek.

"You said it, not me," her mother muttered.

"I love that Middle Eastern look on you." Yael picked up her coffee cup. "And that's what's important," she said firmly, taking a sip.

Daniel shook off his thoughts, stretched his arms and sat up. The sound of the wind whispering through the tree above him blended with the laughter of small children. Two little kids were chasing one another. Their mother called to them in Arabic, telling them to stop running. They ignored her pleas and ran even faster until they hit the stone wall of the promenade. Their father caught up to them and stopped them from climbing it. Daniel watched them and his heart ached. With no relatives in Israel, the Barak family had been like his own. They had a close and warm relationship. To him, they were the personification of Sabras, native-born Israelis. Yael's brother was a deputy squadron commander in the Israeli Air Force, her father was a former battalion commander, now on reserve duty, and her mother was a school principal. They were so different from the family Daniel had left behind in France. Sadly, his family didn't feel the need to move to Israel despite the increasing difficulties at home. His father's chain of grocery stores meant everything to him, and his mother and sister wouldn't leave him behind. Only Daniel's grandfather, an academic who had devoted his life to the archaeology of Israel, moved there in his late seventies after frequent visits over the years for research and excavations. Daniel had joined him many times as a child, then every summer as a teenager. Sometimes he thought his father preferred to stay in France to keep his distance from the old man. But as Daniel grew up, the distance bothered him. As soon as he could, he left for Israel and joined the army.

The snores of the camel in the parking lot attracted the two children like a magnet. The camel's owner pulled at the reins and tried to move it away from the middle of the road. Daniel yawned, stood up and started walking back to At-Tur. The climb was short and not too steep, but the emotional stress of his memories exhausted him. He couldn't shake them off, not even for a day – the events that had brought him to the lowest point of his life. But this time was different. Now he had a spark of hope that his journey would lead him to a new future. Just like back then, when he'd believed in a future with Yael, right before the operation that ruined everything.

That same Saturday at noon, Yael had reminded them that they had to go back to Tel Aviv early, and they'd better set the table for lunch. Her dad again complained that they "never had enough time," and wondered out loud what was so great about this job of theirs that kept them busy with frequent business trips for someone else. "Why don't you just go into business for yourselves," he used to say. They both had no intention of explaining. Yael's brother, who was the only one in the family who knew exactly what they were doing, shut her father down, saying that at least they got to see the world – "I don't fly anywhere much except for training in the Negev. And when I do go somewhere more interesting, it's always a nighttime operation!" Even now, Daniel smiled thinking of it; a wonderful Saturday spent in the company of people who were dear to him. Nothing about it gave the slightest hint of what was about to happen.

'Eran,' 'Roni,' and the others disembarked the El Al flight in Copenhagen for the start of another operation. It was not something they ever took for granted, but just like so many times before, they quickly got through passport control and went their separate ways as if they were strangers. Outside the terminal, Daniel saw Yael get in a taxi. A minute later, he also hailed one and went to the hotel that had been booked for him, tired from a sleepless night and looking forward to a soft pillow beneath his head.

He woke up in the late morning after only a few hours of sleep and got ready for the day's activities. He showered and sat at his laptop. He had to send a few emails to real estate agents with whom he'd already scheduled meetings in two days' time, supposedly to check out commercial rental properties for a fictitious company – a logical reason for his visit to Copenhagen. When he was done, he dialed the front desk from the hotel phone and asked them to book a taxi for him in fifteen minutes. A few minutes later, he walked across the lobby wearing jeans, a gray sweater and black jacket, with a green canvas messenger bag slung over his shoulder. He was dressed casually, but his clothes were chosen deliberately to blend into the background that evening. His beard, the Middle Eastern appearance he'd inherited and his fluent French and Arabic, would allow him to walk around the immigrant neighborhoods as if he belonged there.

To maintain as convincing and authentic an identity as possible, he not only had to keep up his native French, but he also had to get to know the French Muslim immigrants and stay up to date with social trends, even adopt their cultural and religious traditions. He made sure to improve his fluency in the Arabic he'd heard at home and often contemplated unhappily on the fact that his entrance ticket to the Mossad, a symbol of the Israeli identity, was based on the characteristics that defined him as a "non-native." He almost idolized his Sabra brothers in arms. "I don't need to work hard to become an Arab," he confessed to Yael once, "You guys, who have to learn everything from the beginning, are amazing!"

The taxi arrived. Daniel sat in the back seat and asked the driver to take him to Nyhavn. A twenty-minute drive through the streets of Copenhagen took him to the entertainment district. He paid the driver a little above the fare and then walked along the colorful waterfront; new sailboats next to wooden ships, buildings with harmonious colored facades lining the canal, and at the edge of the pier, close to the water, young people sat drinking from green bottles of local beer. Across from them, people sat at outdoor restaurants and cafes, enjoying the winter sun shining in a blue sky dotted with white clouds.

Daniel reached the meeting point, entered the café, and ordered lunch. The chatter was so loud you couldn't hear the music playing in the background. Fifteen minutes later, exactly on time, the courier entered, wearing an elegant suit. They shook hands like old friends, and while they talked and ate, the courier rummaged through the black briefcase he carried with him and pulled out a book. A casual

71

observer might have thought he was recommending a novel he had just finished. Daniel picked up the book, looked at the blue cover and read the blurb, written in English, on the back. He seemed interested. He also took out a book and suggested they swap. The courier nodded and like Daniel, stowed the book in his bag. Daniel looked around for the waiter, and his eyes caught two local police officers entering the café. The two walked toward them, and Daniel felt his heartbeat accelerating. He told the courier what was going on behind him. They froze. Both had in their possession a book that hid within its pages a passport with Daniel's photo. Same man, different personal information, different passports. In one, he was Eran the Israeli. In the other, Jalal the French citizen. There was no plausible legal explanation. The courier stood, shook Daniel's hand, and went to the restrooms at the back of the café where he could hide Daniel's Israeli passport in his bag without raising suspicion. Daniel signaled the waiter for the check. After looking around and exchanging a few words with one of the employees, the police officers left. The courier came back out, walked past Daniel and went on his way. Daniel left five minutes later, strode down the street, got into one of the taxis that waited at the side of the road, and went to the train station.

An hour and a half later, Daniel was in Malmö, the Swedish coastal city across the Öresund Bridge. He rented a car with his new identity as a French Muslim, picked up Yael and two other field agents at the meeting point, and the team made their way to the outskirts of Rosengård. The neighborhood, which over the years had become a Muslim ghetto, was one of the most violent and dangerous districts in Sweden. Crime and terrorism ran rampant, with many weapons out on the streets. Even the police avoided the area.

Daniel and Yael left the car in a side alley and walked to the closest bus stop. Yael wore a black hijab. A long, dark blue dress covered her lithe body from neck to ankles, with a black coat on top. She and Daniel, in his inconspicuous clothes and hair slicked back with gel, looked like any other married couple who just happened to be in the area.

Near the bus stop stood a rowdy group of young men who spoke in various dialects; four immigrants from different Arab countries whose circumstances tied them to a common fate. Yael clung to Daniel, holding his hand. The bus arrived, and the two of them squeezed in among the passengers. They got off four stops later, together with a few others, and walked down the cobblestone street to the heart of the neighborhood. Satellite dishes in different sizes and colors hung from the balconies of the housing projects, blocks of tall and drab apartment buildings. Wearing miniature hidden earpieces, Yael and Daniel heard reports from a team following their subject into the neighborhood. He was an ISIS terrorist, an Arab Israeli who came to Malmö to meet with members of a local terrorist cell that was planning to carry out a major terror attack. Shabak, Israel's internal security service, suspected that the preparations were at an advanced stage. However, they were still missing critical details that would enable thwarting their plans. The Shabak preferred to continue following the subject and gather more information before they arrested him. When he made plans to leave the country, the Mossad then took over the surveillance.

The couple reached the hub of the neighborhood – a busy shopping center – and Yael went into a supermarket. Daniel, who had been provided with information on the location, went to a building that served as the local mosque for evening prayers. He took off his shoes at the entrance, hung up his coat and entered the crowded prayer hall. It didn't look like a mosque from the outside; it didn't have the typical tall minaret or dome. But inside it had the familiar elements: wall-to-wall carpeting and signs with verses from the Quran. The worshippers were organized in rows on the red carpet. It was prayer time and Daniel, like the others, repeated the movements of the prayer leader, praised Allah and muttered verses from the Quran that were part of the ritual. Every few minutes in his right ear, he got whispered updates in Hebrew on their subject who had landed an hour earlier and was on his way to the neighborhood. He was being tailed by a surveillance team that had "welcomed" him at the airport.

The short prayer was over after the ritual of kneeling three times, and Daniel hurried back to Yael to prepare for the next stage of the operation. Suddenly, a strong hand gripped his shoulder from behind. His heart skipped a beat.

"Brother," said a young man with a thick beard who was wearing a large white skullcap, speaking in the Iraqi Arabic dialect, "Why don't you stay for the lesson?"

"I wish," Daniel replied in his North African Arabic accent, "But my wife is waiting for me outside. Maybe another day," he added, turning toward the shoe stands – rows and rows of shelves that were once white.

"Where are you from?" The young man sounded skeptical.

"From France," Daniel answered. "We came to visit my aunt who lives here," he added, guessing the next question. "They're waiting for me, and I don't want them to worry, you know…" he explained as he glanced at his watch. "But thank you for inviting me."

Distrustful people, Daniel thought as he put his shoes on. They notice every stranger. Yael sat on a bench outside the mosque, a large bag from the supermarket next to her. She stood when she saw him.

"What did you buy?" he asked in Arabic.

"This and that… it's rude to go to your aunt's empty-handed."

Daniel feigned appreciation with a smile. "She'll be angry. But good idea!"

Yael hugged him and hid under his coat a gun with a silencer that she had carried while he was in the mosque. Daniel furtively adjusted the gun in his waistband when she let go. She picked up the bag, a thin glove covering her hand, and they crossed the main road back to the shopping center. They heard in the earpiece that the subject was fifteen minutes away. Daniel went up to a shawarma stand that overlooked the main street. A red sign in green Arabic letters certified that the meat was "halal," slaughtered according to Muslim law and therefore permissible to eat. Daniel ordered two, and Yael called out that she didn't want to eat. Just a diet cola. "The wedding," she whispered to him in Arabic, reminding him that she was watching her weight ahead of the most important day of her life. Daniel smiled and whispered back that she looked fantastic, and that one pita wouldn't change that. Yael insisted and Daniel shrugged. Their cover and reality merged for a few seconds; they were like a married couple, and really would be married in just a few months.

Daniel finished his shawarma and thought it was an excellent time to let the people around them know why they were there. He pretended to call his aunt.

"*Bonsoir*," he spoke to his fictional aunt and continued in Arabic with a touch of French. "We're here. Are you home already?... What happened?... How is he?... Never mind, we'll wait for you... okay... Allah help you... everything's fine... Allah help you... we ate shawarma nearby... yes... excellent shawarma." He made sure the owner of the stand heard him praising him because you never knew when you might need to be on someone's good side. "Allah be with you. We're waiting here."

"What happened?" Yael pretended to be worried.

"Hassan broke his leg at school. They took him to the hospital," explained Daniel, aware that the owner was listening.

"Oh no." Yael put her hand to her cheek.

"Got off the bus," they heard through the earpiece, "red coat, black roller bag. He's climbing up the stairs in your direction."

Daniel looked over Yael's shoulder at the stairs from the street. "Let's go." The man's upper body appeared, and then the rest of him as he walked up. The two of them left the stand and Yael reported that they were "on him" through the mouthpiece hanging from the inside of her coat collar.

The man walked a few feet and stopped at the small plaza in front of the shopping center. He called someone on his cellphone. Three minutes later, two young men with scruffy beards arrived. One wore an outsized rapper's cap and the other a wool beanie. They shook the subject's hand and gave him a hug and a traditional cheek kiss. The three of them started walking. Daniel and Yael followed them from a safe distance. Two other team members, who'd cut off contact earlier at the bus stop, came from a side street and followed the couple between the tall buildings. After a few hundred feet, the terrorist trio turned left and crossed a deserted playground. Daniel and Yael stopped there, and the two others took over. When they were out of sight Yael sat on a bench and put the bag down at her feet. Daniel sat next to her.

It was a little after eight in the evening and fewer people were out on the street. They got an update that the subjects had entered a building. One member of the surveillance team followed them and saw where they went. He confirmed the floor and the apartment number. Yael slid her hand into her black bag and fiddled with something. When she finished, she took Daniel's hand, and they walked toward the large apartment building. Their teammates walked past them and away from the area. Daniel opened a white metal door, and they entered the lobby. It wasn't as cold inside. The light in the stairwell was on and they walked up to the second floor. Yael scanned the hallway with an experienced eye and quickly decided on a plan of action. She went up to the door of apartment number twenty-three, deftly pulled out of her bag what looked like a wad of chewed gum and stuck it on the lower part of the gray Formica door. She walked down the hall a bit and took out the can of diet cola she had poured out earlier. While Daniel covered her, she slipped something that looked like string cheese through the opening of the can, carefully crushed the thin aluminum and placed it in a plastic pot of artificial flowers. They walked up another flight and then took the elevator down to the entrance and sat on a concrete bench across from the building, waiting, if anyone should ask, for Daniel's aunt to return with his cousin from the hospital.

Their fingers were freezing. Yael pulled the hood of her coat over her hijab and adjusted the earpiece. The miniature microphone she had attached to the door picked up voices in the apartment and transmitted them with the help of the amplifier in the can of cola. Daniel sat next to her and waited. Minutes went by and Yael occasionally updated him with the details she managed to pick up. So far, the most important were the names of the local hosts.

Daniel saw a woman walking alone down the main street. When she passed under the streetlight, he noticed that she was young, and judging by her clothes and light-colored hair, she wasn't an immigrant. This isn't a good place for her to be, he thought to himself. Loud whistles from the dark pierced the air. Yael was focused on listening through her earpiece, but Daniel looked around. The whistles continued and two young men burst out of the shadows. They hurried after the blonde, adding lewd comments in Arabic to their whistles. Observing the unfolding incident, Daniel felt his heartbeat accelerate. The men had caught up to the woman and were blocking her way. She tried to ignore them, but they were persistent.

Daniel's heart threatened to explode. Everything came back to him at that moment as if it hadn't been two decades since that damned Saturday in his childhood that changed his life.

The woman tried to walk around the men, but they grabbed her. Daniel stood up, rocking back and forth uneasily.

"I think they're getting ready to leave the apartment," Yael said.

"Uh-huh," Daniel mumbled, concentrating on the incident in front of him. Their body language was aggressive. He started walking toward the shadows, trying to understand what was happening. Yael called to him quietly. He continued walking and motioned her to wait a minute. She didn't understand what was going on. The men were dragging the woman toward the back of one of the buildings. She tried to resist and kicked one of them. "Shut up, you stupid bitch," Daniel heard in Arabic and ran after them. He heard Yael call him to come back – their subject was planning to leave – but he didn't answer. The images that had tormented him since he was ten years old came back in full force. He was trembling. Back then, it was from fear and helplessness, but this time, it was something else. He felt like a volcano about to erupt, spewing out the anguish of that fateful Saturday.

"Leave her alone!" he shouted and shoved one of them.

The men looked at him in surprise. The blonde woman was sobbing. Under her torn coat, on her shirt, Daniel saw the logo of the humanitarian organization that she belonged to.

"Go fuck yourself!" one of the men cursed and tried to shove him back. "What do you care? She's just a Christian whore!"

Daniel pushed him away. "You're bringing shame on our religion!" he said, amazed at the words coming out of his mouth.

The other man tried to get closer and attack him.

"They've opened the door," Yael reported. She stood up and spoke into her mouthpiece. "Jalal, where are you? They're coming down the stairs," she whispered as she searched the darkness around her. Two orange bursts and the muffled sounds of silenced gunshots answered her.

3

In the afternoon, Daniel crossed back into Bethlehem. Entering Palestinian territory was quicker and easier than leaving it. He got into a taxi and asked the driver to stop two blocks away from Abu Elias' building. He always made sure the taxi drivers didn't know where he lived. And every time, he felt the absurdity of it. There was no way to stay out of sight of the watchful eyes that every undercover agent knows are always there. It was habit, that was all. Daniel crossed the street, walked between two buildings through a narrow alleyway that smelled like damp clothes and came out on the other side facing the neighborhood supermarket. At the corner, not far from the entrance, stood the man in purple. Daniel started to believe he was under surveillance, but since there was nothing incriminating in the man's actions, he decided to ignore it.

It was six thirty in the evening and his stomach was growling. He leaped up the three stairs to the store, grabbed a black plastic bag and filled it with the ingredients for a simple dinner: fusilli pasta, tomato sauce and a jar of anchovy fillets. He returned to his apartment, and three-quarters of an hour later – in a sink that had seen brighter days – a bowl sat with the remains of congealing tomato sauce. He lit the burner on the black marble countertop and put the ceramic coffee pot over the blue flame, a heap of Turkish coffee floating on top of the water. The aroma filled the room, and just before it boiled over Daniel removed it from the heat and shut the gas off. He went to the sofa, set the coffee pot and a small ceramic coffee cup on the round table inlaid with a brown mosaic and sat down with his notebook.

Daniel flipped through handwritten pages of French and reread his notes – some from the past month, others from before. No one would understand what they were really for. If asked, he would explain that these were notes for an action novel he was writing – his first novel, set in a psychiatric hospital in Bethlehem.

When he got to the last page, he summarized his discoveries from the day before, circling keywords and drawing lines to the questions that he would ask Ibrahim on Sunday, to try and get more information. He reread what he wrote a few more times and then got up, went to the suitcase stored in the closet and took out a leather file folder holding a single piece of brittle, yellowed paper. All his hopes were there—his last chance. Daniel smoothed the page out carefully. He had looked at it more times than he could count since Yael sent all his personal belongings from the apartment they had shared in Israel to France. Among them were boxes of his grandfather's notebooks and binders that he'd never gone through. Daniel held the sketch by his grandfather to his nose and tried, like always, to catch a fleeting scent and glimpse of memory.

Daniel turned his head at the sound of sharp knocks on his front door.

"Jalal?"

Daniel quickly folded the fragile sketch and put the folder back in the suitcase in the closet.

"Jalal?" The knocking got louder.

Who could it be? Daniel wondered and quickly undressed, wrapped a towel around his hips and cracked open the door. "What's up?" he asked his next-door neighbor.

"Hey Jalal." His neighbor looked embarrassed. "Is this a bad time?"

"You can see for yourself," Daniel answered with a friendly smile.

"Some friends from the university came over. We're going up to the roof to barbeque, you want to join us?"

"Thanks, brother... too bad you didn't tell me an hour ago. I already ate and was just about to take a shower. Next time."

"Okay, next time!" His neighbor waved goodbye and turned around.

Daniel closed the door and heard him walk away. He yawned and decided he might as well shower now. After a long hot shower, he put on underwear and a t-shirt, took his notebook and got into bed under the leopard-print blanket Abu Elias provided to every tenant. The television on the wall was quietly tuned to a talk show on the Al-Jazeera channel. Daniel grabbed the remote. For a split second, Hebrew voices filled the room from the Channel Twelve news, triggering a wave of longing. He channel-surfed until he got to Rotana – the Arab equivalent of MTV. He turned up the volume a bit and went back to his notebook, but his thoughts kept wandering back to his experiences that day until he fell asleep.

When he woke up a few hours later, still groggy, light from the television screen flickered in the room. Someone was banging on the door. Daniel wondered what time it was but couldn't find his watch. The knocks got louder and more forceful. Daniel got out of bed and went to the door, thinking that it was his annoying neighbor bringing him a plate of grilled meat.

"Jalal?"

Daniel opened the door, his eyes barely open. In the doorway stood the elderly landlord wearing a tracksuit and slippers. Two other men were with him; the man closest to him had a mustache and wore a black leather jacket. The other stood slightly behind and was cut from the same mold.

"Abu Elias!" Daniel said in surprise, tamping down his fear. "Is everything alright?" he asked, glancing at the two hulking strangers.

"I'm so sorry," Abu Elias said, "These men will explain everything. Stay strong, son!" he blurted and walked away.

Daniel stared in shock at Abu Elias, who had disappeared down the stairs, and at the two men.

"Preventive Security," the man with the mustache introduced himself in Arabic after they entered his apartment. Daniel saw the bulge of a gun under his jacket. "Get dressed and come with us quietly."

4

Daniel couldn't think until they took the black hood off – he was trying not to throw up. The stench inside the hood indicated that others hadn't met the challenge. The moment they slipped it over his head he knew that horrible smell would haunt him for the rest of his life. His eyes slowly adjusted to the fluorescent lighting, and he looked around him: four bare walls, sloppy paint job, no windows. A metal door, a chair facing him and a simple desk with an office phone. The hood was still there, maybe on purpose, and he was still handcuffed.

He was alone and had no idea where he was. From the time it took to get there, Daniel figured they had left Bethlehem. Maybe they drove to Ramallah. The loud objections in his apartment and in the black Pajero SUV parked outside Abu Elias' building didn't help. The Palestinian Security weren't being aggressive, but they also didn't talk to him and weren't about to back down – they politely insisted he come with them. Daniel preferred to keep quiet and assess the situation when they started asking him questions. The first thing that came to mind was the interrogation exercise at the end of his Mossad training, and that brought up the emotions, the mistakes, the lessons learned, and even the hope that this was just another exercise. He dismissed that last thought immediately. There was no chance, he thought to himself. I'm on a personal mission, and no one knows that I'm here. As opposed to last time, there is no doubt that

I've been arrested in Palestinian Authority territory and not in Israel. He noted a camera in the top corner of the room. He pushed the hood to the far end of the desk in disgust and tried to nap while sitting.

An hour passed before Daniel heard the click of the lock. The moment the man entered, Daniel knew he would never forget his face. It wasn't scary or intimidating, just dead ugly in a way that couldn't be ignored. He wore a light button-down shirt tucked into dark dress pants, shiny black dress shoes, and emanated an overwhelming scent of cologne.

"Do you know why you're here, Jalal?" the man asked in a Palestinian dialect as he paced the room. The tap of his shoes on the floor sounded like a woman's stiletto heels.

"No," Daniel shrugged.

"That's what they all say," he smiled, revealing a perfect set of teeth in complete contrast to the rest of him.

"I don't know what everyone says," Daniel responded. "I also don't know who you are. I'm just a volunteer at the psychiatric hospital and I'm not looking for any trouble."

"Excellent," the man clasped his hands. "If you don't want trouble, tell me what you're really doing here and why. Good for you, volunteering at the hospital – but we don't buy it."

"Sir," Daniel tried to display irritation, "I am a French citizen."

"Hah!" the interrogator jeered, sitting on the desk.

"And I came here with only good intentions. There is no reason for you to act this way. What did I do?"

Daniel felt his fake identity melting away.

"Listen, pal, we're not in Europe. You'll rot here until you tell me what we want to know. We won't even notify your consulate."

That was good news – apparently his identity wasn't in question.

"I really want to get this over with as quickly as possible and I don't understand what I'm doing here. I'll answer your questions, but you've not asked me anything."

"I asked you!" Mr. Ugly raised his voice. "But I'll repeat: what are you really doing here in Bethlehem?"

"I was tired of my aimless life in France... so I decided to do something meaningful. You know, turn over a new leaf." So far, this was all true, Daniel thought. "Friends suggested different places in the world where I could volunteer. I did some research and decided to come here."

"Of all places you decided to come to Bethlehem?" The interrogator sneered and just looked uglier. "And to a psychiatric hospital?"

"Why not? I get a stipend – it's not much, but better than in other places. And I have no problem with the language. I understand the people around me and they understand me. In other places that were looking for volunteers, I thought I'd find it more difficult to communicate and my English is bad." He wasn't improvising. Daniel methodically related his cover story, exactly as he had devised it.

"Your Arabic accent isn't exactly what we're used to," the interrogator commented.

"That's how I speak," Daniel explained. "I was born in France and that's what I heard at home and in the neighborhood."

"Where are your parents from? North Africa?"

Daniel nodded.

"They'll worry when they don't hear from you." The interrogator got up and stood behind Daniel. "Too bad, no? Come on, confess and you'll be able to talk with your mother today."

Daniel felt the interrogator's hands on the back of his chair and was glad he was behind him and not looking him in the eyes. "My father died when I was a baby, and I don't have a relationship with my mother. She remarried and her new family was more important to her than me."

"Heartbreaking," the interrogator said in mock sympathy and went back to pacing the room. "So, who do you have in France that's important to you? Who is waiting for you?"

"No one," Daniel responded in a subdued voice, trying to gain sympathy.

"Excellent!" The interrogator yawned and glanced at his watch. "No one will be looking for you and now we have all the time in the world," he said and left the room.

Daniel's eyes burned with exhaustion. He estimated that it was five o'clock in the morning, maybe six. There was no telling when the interrogator would return. He assessed his situation. He had drawn someone's attention. Maybe the man in purple? A nurse at the hospital? Someone who lived in Abu Elias' building or a passenger in one of the taxis? But that didn't matter now. His story was unusual, and it was only a matter of time before he was investigated. According to their questions so far it didn't seem that they were suspicious of his identity. His identity was in fact his only problem. Apart from that, he had done nothing incriminating. His cover story was also convincing so far. They had no interest in notifying the

French consulate and he certainly didn't want that either. On the other hand, why was he being interrogated if they weren't suspicious of his identity and had no evidence against him because he hadn't done anything?

He kept dropping off and jerking awake sitting in the cold room with artificial lighting, which just made him feel more tired. Daniel got up and walked around the room, his hands handcuffed in front of him. He sat back down, tried to guess why they'd arrested him and methodically retraced his steps since he first arrived in Bethlehem. Hours passed. How many? He didn't know exactly, but he was getting hungry again. He didn't consider asking for food. If he did, they would use it against him – no free lunch. He went to the desk, lifted the hood, and sniffed it. For a split second the hunger was replaced by nausea. There's a good side to everything, he thought. Just then the door opened. A new face appeared and, without saying a word, set a plastic tray down by the smelly hood. On it was a disposable plastic plate with hummus, two pita pockets and a cup of water, also disposable. He looked at the tray with disgust and just drank the water. Shortly after, the door opened again, and the ugly interrogator came in. The stench from the hood together with the congealing hummus and the cloud of cologne were too much, and Daniel threw up on the floor, splashing the interrogator's shiny black leather shoes.

"You son of a whore!" the interrogator hissed and angrily left the room.

Daniel stood with his back to the camera, a hint of a smile in his eyes that were still tearing from vomiting. You motherfucker, he cursed silently and moved away from the puddle. The door opened, and the man who had brought the tray appeared holding a green plastic bucket. He set it down by the door, signaled Daniel to mop the floor, and left. Having no choice, Daniel picked up the bucket. It was two-thirds full of water with some detergent that smelled like bleach, a tattered floor cloth at the bottom. Daniel knelt near the puddle of vomit and wiped up the remains of yesterday's dinner – undigested pasta. and red bits that looked like crushed tomatoes. When he finished, he placed the bucket back by the door, and wiped his damp sticky hands on the outside of the hood – maybe some of the bleach smell would rub off on it and lessen the stench. Then he sat down and took deep breaths. The nausea had gone and he felt better, despite the sour taste in his mouth. He heard the lock turning behind him and the door opened. He didn't turn around.

"Take that disgusting bucket away," he heard in Arabic, and from the exchange of words, he knew that two people had come in. The door closed and he heard someone walking toward him. The voice and the sound of the footsteps indicated that a new player had joined the party. Daniel kept his eyes on the wall and didn't lift his gaze until the new interrogator sat on the chair facing him. A pleasant-looking man in his mid-seventies, perfectly shaved with a trimmed mustache and carefully combed gray hair surveyed Daniel, starting with his shoes and slowly upward until their eyes met. Daniel's brown eyes threatened to pop out of his head. His breath hitched and his heart beat like a jackhammer. It was the same man that had interrogated him in his last exercise of the training course. He was sure of it.

The interrogator immediately noticed Daniel's strange reaction. He adjusted his wool jacket over a blue button-down shirt and observed him for a few seconds before opening his mouth.

"How are you?"

"Confused," Daniel answered hesitantly, keeping his eyes down.

"Of course," the interrogator said, sounding sympathetic, and cleared his throat. "I completely understand, but you know – if you play with fire, you get burned."

Daniel looked up, still looking shocked. "I think you're wrong. I'm not playing with any fire and my intentions were good... to make a fresh start, do something good for others and then go back to France."

"Why do you have to do something good in a new life? Did you do bad things before?"

Daniel thought carefully. Either he was imagining things, or this interrogator still hadn't realized who he really was. Maybe he had but was a great actor. Before he responded, he gave a sheepish smile, completely intentional, and then asked, "Sir, if it isn't rude to ask, how should I address you?"

"Abu Suleiman." The interrogator smoothed his gray mustache and added in French, "*Enchanté!*"

That did it. Now there was absolutely no doubt. It was the same interrogator from his final training exercise. Daniel felt the blood drain from his face, and questions ran through his head at the speed of light. What was going on here? Why the pretense? Was this another exercise? But what kind of exercise would it be? He wasn't part of the Mossad anymore, and what was the point of sending someone he knew and who knew him, and, on top of that, pretending that he didn't recognize him? The questions piled up and Daniel felt even more confused. "Abu Suleiman, I've never done anything wrong. I just decided to do something. To leave my boring life in France and go to a new place, to try something new and go back to France a different person with a future. Hopefully, I will find a woman, get married and have a family."

"And this is how you chose to do it?" the interrogator asked, as if impressed.

"*Oui*," Daniel asserted, an innocent expression on his face.

Not even the tiniest muscle in Abu Suleiman's face twitched when he got up suddenly and walked out, slamming the door behind him. Daniel listened to his footsteps walking away. *Merde!* What the hell just happened? There was no mistake; it was him for sure! Daniel got up and restlessly paced the room, trying to calm down and think clearly. He had to carefully weigh every word that came out of his mouth. Until he knew what was going on he had to consider the most dangerous outcome for him.

The footsteps were coming back in his direction. Daniel tensed. The door opened and Abu Suleiman walked in, no jacket, sleeves rolled up. "Sit," he ordered, and Daniel sat down immediately. Abu Suleiman dragged over the other chair and sat facing Daniel, close, with no space between them.

Daniel stayed silent and looked at Abu Suleiman, not revealing the storm inside him.

"What's your name?" Abu Suleiman fired at him.

"Jalal."

"Where are you from?"

"Bethlehem."

Abu Suleiman snorted, "Answer the question and don't be a smart aleck!"

"Paris," he answered.

Abu Suleiman scratched his head irritably. "What are you doing here?"

Daniel hesitated before responding. He was baffled and didn't know what was going on. Reality was playing tricks on him again. There were a few possible explanations for this new development, but he couldn't be sure about any of them. There was no choice but to stick with his cover story, he decided, and repeated what he had said just moments ago, but this time in more detail.

Abu Suleiman closed his eyes and seemed to be concentrating. When Daniel finished talking, he opened them, leaned forward and said quietly, "We've met before, haven't we?"

Daniel looked at him, his face blank. Yes or no were the only two possible answers. Both complicated things, each in a different way. He tried, like an advanced algorithm, to scan all possibilities, and after a few seconds of feigning surprise at the question, he answered, "I don't think so, sir."

Abu Suleiman leaned toward Daniel again and said even more quietly, "Son, I think we've met before. If so, you can tell me. Don't be afraid." He emphasized the last words. He leaned back. "Take a minute and try to remember."

What the hell was going on? "I think you're wrong, sir," he said with an awkward smile, "You must have mistaken me for someone else. I came to Bethlehem a month ago and have never been in trouble. I'm sure that this whole incident is one big mistake."

"You try to remember. I'll be back!" Abu Suleiman promised and left the room.

Despite his exhaustion and apprehension, Daniel's senses sharpened. He remained seated and assessed the situation. If Abu Suleiman was who Daniel thought he was, and if he did indeed recognize him – why the hell was he still speaking to him in Arabic? What was he doing here, at Palestinian Security? The thoughts nagged at him.

Hours later, the door opened again, and even before Daniel saw who it was, the cloud of cologne gave him away. It was the ugly interrogator again, holding an ink pad and a piece of paper. He ordered Daniel to sit and took his handcuffs off. When he rolled his finger in the dark ink and stamped his fingerprint on the paper, Daniel knew that things just got more complicated. The interrogator left and the guard came in carrying a tray with lunch: chicken breast, yellow rice, pita bread, and a glass of water. This time Daniel decided to eat. He was starving. They didn't give him utensils, but his inky fingers didn't bother him at all. In between bites he continued to evaluate the situation. So, Mr. Dead Ugly was still in the picture. Where was Abu Suleiman? Maybe he knew who Daniel was, knew that Daniel had recognized him, and decided to keep it to himself. There was only one logical reason, and that got him agitated: Abu Suleiman was an informant for the Palestinians! Or maybe he was undercover with the Palestinians? His age disqualified the second option, so Daniel concluded that Abu Suleiman was working for the Palestinians – he was a traitor!

After eating, Daniel curled up on the floor at the side of the room and closed his eyes. The floor was warm compared to the cold wall. His ear pressed to the worn tiles amplified, like a sensitive microphone, the sounds, murmurs, and even his own breaths and pulse. Hours passed and he drifted into a deep sleep with vivid dreams, one after the other, like movie trailers: at kindergarten in France, at the synagogue, his grandfather smiling at him, Rashid sipping coffee, the shots fired in Sweden, Yael, Ibrahim, his father being slapped, night detention in the army, and a voice whispering: Eran... Eran... Eran...

The whispering got louder, and he felt his body being shaken. He opened his eyes and for a few seconds stared straight ahead. His face and fingers felt swollen. Above him stood Abu Suleiman holding a small glass of coffee full to the brim.

"Eran, get up!" he said in Hebrew. "Game over, my friend!"

Daniel stared at Abu Suleiman for a few more seconds, then pulled himself together and stood up.

"Sit!" Abu Suleiman gestured with a sharp nod.

Daniel took a few steps forward and sat. He felt the blood coursing back through his body. Abu Suleiman sat across from him with a look that Daniel couldn't read and slammed his glass down on the table.

"You know, 'Eran,'" Abu Suleiman started. He lit a cigarette, took a drag and continued as he blew out the smoke, "as you can probably imagine, I've been retired for a while. And in this profession, I thought I'd seen everything. But, sometimes, I still find myself surprised. So, as long as it's up to me, I'll continue to volunteer until the day I die. And now I'm curious to hear what you have to say."

Daniel stared at him in silence. The elderly interrogator, who spoke fluent Arabic, also spoke Hebrew with no trace of an accent. The words were clear and sharp. "Sir," Daniel replied in Arabic, "I don't understand that language."

Abu Suleiman took a deep drag. With a serious expression on his face, he narrowed his eyes, and after blowing out a cloud of smoke in the windowless room, he smiled, picked up the telephone on the desk and pressed a button set to speed dial. "Come in," he said in Hebrew to whoever answered.

Thirty seconds later, the ugly interrogator entered the room. He glanced at Daniel and then spoke to his colleague in Hebrew. "What's up?"

"Our friend here, 'Eran,' doesn't understand Hebrew," Abu Suleiman jeered.

"Oh! Is that so?" he answered in fluent Hebrew. "You know, it's interesting. For some reason our guests here suddenly forget or don't understand all sorts of things. He'll get over it, you'll see." He waved his hand dismissively and left.

"Convinced?" Abu Suleiman asked. He crushed the cigarette butt in a disposable cup on the table. "I understand you're confused and don't know what to believe. But you can relax. There are no Palestinians here."

Daniel glared at him. There was no end to the conspiracies, he thought and realized he didn't have too many options left; the fingerprints they took confirmed his identity. Abu Suleiman was not a traitor and wasn't anyone's informant. The Israel Security Agency had arrested him, impersonating Palestinian Security, and there was a reason he called him Eran.

"When you came into the room, I didn't know what to think. The truth is that I still don't know," Daniel replied, speaking in Hebrew for the first time in a month. His French accent sounded especially heavy to him.

Abu Suleiman lit another cigarette, took a deep puff, and exhaled. "What in the hell are you doing in Bethlehem?"

Daniel took a moment to consider his response. If he told the truth no one would believe him. "I already told you," he said finally.

Abu Suleiman took a loud sip of coffee and sneered at him. "I think you don't understand just how bad your situation is! Even the Prime Minister has been briefed on your arrest. A former Mossad field agent who is now spying for someone else... that hasn't happened in a very long time. So please spare me the stories."

Spy? For someone else? The possibility that his actions would be interpreted that way had crossed his mind in the past, but the enormous gap between such an accusation and the truth drove the thought out of his mind every time it popped up. "You must be crazy! You think I'm spying for someone else?"

"If anyone's crazy it must be you!" Abu Suleiman laughed. "Tell me, 'Eran,' so I won't confuse you with all these names; what do you want me to call you? Your bosses must have given you a new name."

The accusation infuriated him. "Call me Daniel!" he shouted, "That's who I am! That's who I've always been! And you can stop with your Arabic nickname already. Enough!"

"My name is Shlomo," Abu Suleiman said. He appreciated that Daniel was truly insulted.

"I feel a lot of anger toward the Office," Daniel took a deep breath. "They betrayed me. But I would never betray my country! Never!"

Shlomo raised his eyebrows, deepening the wrinkles in his forehead. "The Office betrayed you? What are you talking about? You executed two innocent men in the middle of an operation, endangering your entire team. It was a miracle that we didn't get entangled in a scandal with Sweden. They betrayed you? What did you want them to do? Give you a medal? You should be thankful they kicked you out and didn't put you in jail!"

Daniel got even angrier. "Listen, Shlomo! I see you know all the details. I have nothing to say to you. Do what you want with me! You don't understand anything, just like you didn't understand back then! Traitor. Spy. Terrorist. Whatever. Because you all know everything, right? So why all the questions if you don't like my answers?"

Shlomo chose his words carefully. "Look, Daniel. I'm objective. I'm not part of the Office, you know that already," he said softly. "Put yourself in my shoes and think logically how this looks from this side. You're angry at the Office, you left the country and all of a sudden you appear in Bethlehem with a fake identity. What do you want us to think? If the answer is more complex, please, explain it to me. You can be sure that everyone will be happy to hear that there's been a mistake. Our biggest nightmare is discovering that a former field agent has become a double agent. The very thought makes me shudder."

Daniel listened in silence.

"I have a lot of respect for you from way back, since that exercise in the desert. I'm going now and we'll continue in the morning. I'll make sure you're given food and allowed to shower and sleep. Rest, son, and we'll talk tomorrow." Shlomo didn't wait for a response. He stood, gripped the back of Daniel's neck for a moment, and left the room.

Daniel trembled. The touch of Shlomo's warm, comforting hand overwhelmed him, and despite his suspicions, he couldn't hold back the emotion. It felt just like so long ago, when he went with his grandfather on digs in Israel, a young boy in a group of students, digging, sifting dirt or removing the layers of time from shards of pottery with a small brush. Suddenly he would feel his grandfather's hand gripping the back of his neck, and then he'd kiss his head and say, "*Bravo, mon chéri!*"

Daniel quickly ate the dinner that the guard brought him. This time he also got hot coffee. He was not handcuffed again, and the young guards escorted him to a different room. Now he realized that he was in a house that had been converted into an interrogation facility. The three of them climbed the stairs and entered a room that was empty except for a simple bed with a metal frame, a mattress, pillow, and blanket. The windows were covered with thick sheet metal, the walls were white, with holes where the wall sockets should be. The daylight bulb on the ceiling was protected by a metal cage. Adjacent to the sparse bedroom, through a doorless opening with just a frame, Daniel saw a shower stall and toilet.

"There are clean clothes for you in there," said one of the security guards. "Go shower and bring us the clothes you're wearing now."

Daniel didn't respond. He entered the bathroom, got undressed, wrapped a towel around his hips and brought them the pile of clothes, with his shoes on top. The guards left the room and slammed the heavy door behind them. Daniel looked around him and saw two security cameras at opposite corners of the room. He saw another camera in the bathroom at an angle that enabled some measure of privacy. He got into the shower, shut his eyes and stood under the hot water that came directly out of the curved pipe – there was no shower head. He let the water rinse away the past 24 hours. He felt unsettled. The questions hovering in his mind since his arrest remained unanswered. He preferred to put his thoughts aside and surrender to the hot water and smell of cheap soap.

Five minutes later the stream of water suddenly stopped. Daniel got the message and reminded himself where he was. No free lunch, he thought. Everything was calculated, and everything had a purpose. He dried off with the scratchy towel, which softened as it absorbed the drops of water on his body. He put on the clothes he'd been given, faded underwear and a shiny brown, synthetic tracksuit. Before going to bed he searched the walls for the light switch and realized that there wasn't one, but as soon as he lay down on the thin mattress and covered himself with the rough blanket, the light went out.

Daniel lay on his back, hands behind his head, and stared at the dark ceiling. It was silent. The sheets were clean, but they had no fragrance. To his surprise, he missed the smell of the sheets from his apartment in Bethlehem, not his apartment in Paris. He wondered what time it was. Was it the middle of the night already? Early or late evening? Once again, he assessed his situation: he was in no immediate danger, and no one would torture him or cause him pain. His identity had been revealed and there was no need to pretend. That was the positive side. The only issue on the agenda was to clear himself of suspicion. Daniel understood why they thought he was a spy, and also knew that they wouldn't believe him if he told them what he was looking for at the psychiatric hospital. His cover story would be easier for them to swallow, and that's what he would tell them. And yet, there was a problem: how to continue what he'd started in Bethlehem. They'd never let him go back there.

This last realization disturbed him more than his own fate. His personal quest was his only hope of returning to a meaningful life. He still didn't know how he was going to do it but was determined not to let anyone take away his hope – which had only increased with Ibrahim's revelations.

5

A long, irritating buzzing sound woke him up. When he opened his eyes the ceiling light was casting a gloomy shadow on the white walls. One of the guards from the day before came in carrying a tray with breakfast. "Eat quickly and get ready," he ordered. "I'll be back in a few minutes to take you downstairs."

Daniel sat on the bed, the tray on his knees. He didn't usually eat breakfast so soon after getting up, but he took the pita bread and stuffed it with the cold hardboiled egg and slices of cucumber and tomato, flattened it into a sandwich, and alternated bites with sips of tea from a plastic cup. As he'd expected, the two guards came in the minute he finished eating; the cameras didn't miss a thing. He put on thick socks and rubber slippers that were part of his new wardrobe and was led to the familiar interrogation room. Outside the door he saw a small digital screen at eye level. He was ushered into the empty room. He walked around and did some stretches. A glance at his feet in the rubber-soled slippers reminded him of the patients at the psychiatric hospital. There was a buzzing sound and the door opened.

"Good morning." Shlomo entered the room. He was perfectly shaved with every gray hair in place, in gray dress pants and a blue button-down shirt. "Please," he nodded toward the chair and sat down, holding a cup of coffee.

"Good morning," Daniel replied, his face impassive.

"I hope you slept well. It's going to be a long day and we have a lot of work to do," the interrogator said, sipping his coffee.

"Yes, I slept," Daniel responded in a strong voice, "but today doesn't have to be long and tedious. I get your suspicions, but you can relax. I'm on my own mission. I'm no one's spy, and it's absurd you would even think that. Do whatever you have to do and ask whatever you need to be sure. I started something in Bethlehem, and I want to finish it. You know what, I don't just want to, I have to! Otherwise, my life will never get back on track. So, get on with your investigation, clear me of this ridiculous accusation and let me be. I didn't commit a crime."

Shlomo looked at Daniel's blank face, but he was clearly listening closely to the words he was speaking in Hebrew, now with no trace of an accent. Daniel looked sharp and calm, yet his body language showed his agitation. "I'm glad," he said. "As I told you yesterday, we all hope that you come out of this clean."

"Where do you want me to start?"

"At the heart of the matter! What made you decide to go to Bethlehem under a fake identity and 'volunteer,'" he said with air quotes, "at that psychiatric hospital?"

Daniel took a deep breath and exhaled slowly. "When I returned to France, I was at a low point in my life. A very low point. I had to do something bold, different, that would get me back on track; to believe in myself again."

"Wait a minute. Back up a bit." Shlomo sat up in his chair. "Why so low? Because of Sweden?"

Daniel nodded.

"What happened there?"

Like every other time he recalled that night, Daniel's heart stuttered. He knew what Shlomo was looking for. "I guess you already know."

"I know what others chose to tell me. But I want to hear it from you."

Daniel's eyes scanned the floor. He looked up at Shlomo and scratched the stubble on his cheeks. "I guess I was in the wrong place at the wrong time. But I did the right thing."

"You still think that today?"

"I have no regrets. I couldn't stand there and do nothing. If I hadn't gone up to them, I would never have been able to forgive myself."

"Forgive yourself for what? I don't understand."

"For not doing anything!" Daniel explained. "What should I do when I see two lowlifes grab a young woman, a girl, and call her a 'dirty bitch'? I knew that they were going to rape her. How could I just stand there and not do a thing?"

"I'm sorry, but I don't understand," Shlomo questioned. "Why was it your business? You're in the middle of an operation. It's not like you're in Israel, on the boardwalk in Tel Aviv, and you suddenly see an attempted rape and decide to get involved."

Daniel knew that Shlomo was right, but at the foundation of his actions were deeper motives that he didn't want to share with anyone, especially not a stranger. "What's the difference? If I was witness to something like that in Israel and I'd got involved, I'd be applauded. I'd even be *expected* to get involved."

"Daniel, even in that final exercise, you failed at that same situation. You saw a woman in trouble, and you lost it."

He remembered Yael's smiling face as she came up to him. "Those are two completely different things. It's not about a woman in trouble."

"You shot two unarmed, innocent people, and killed them! And that's before we talk about all the others you endangered. A field agent doesn't let emotions affect his actions. Maybe you shouldn't have been recruited from the start."

"That's how you see it and there's nothing I can do about it. I saw something completely different."

"What did you see?"

"I already told you. I couldn't just stand there and do nothing. I didn't plan to shoot them. I thought they would run away, but their pride wouldn't let them. When they moved to attack me, I had no choice."

Shlomo considered what Daniel said. "But you could have just wounded them."

"And really endanger the team? You know the police would have investigated them because they were immigrants."

Shlomo got up and left the room. He came back with a pitcher of water and two glasses. He filled one and offered it to Daniel.

"Thanks," Daniel said after drinking it all.

"Do you hate Arabs?"

Daniel lifted his eyebrows. He was surprised by the question. "What do you mean by Arabs? When I was a child, I only knew the immigrants in France, and I was afraid of them. But when I got older,

I understood that 'Arabs' is something much more complex than what I was familiar with. When I came to Israel and served in the army, I got to know more of those you call Arabs: Palestinians and Arab Israelis, and of course Druze and Bedouins – brothers in arms that I met in different places. And in Office operations I also encountered Arabs of all kinds, each one had his own story. So no, I don't hate them and I'm not afraid of them anymore."

"I hear a 'but,'" Shlomo said.

"But... I know them, I know what to watch for and how to act with them, and even more so now I've actually lived among them for a month already. Just like everywhere else there are all kinds. I don't have to teach you about Palestinians."

"I was afraid that I was going to hear politics."

"That doesn't really interest me," Daniel replied. "But in general, I'm pretty sure that there will never be a love story with them. There will only be quiet when there's a mutual interest, when both sides have had enough of the conflict."

"And what does that have to do with Bethlehem?"

"Like they must have told you, they decided that I couldn't stay in the Office, so –"

"So, they threw you out, you were going to say."

"Fired, dismissed, thrown out – take your pick," Daniel retorted. "I have nothing to say about it and it's not something I dwell on anymore."

"But you must have been angry."

Daniel looked at Shlomo and laughed.

"Why are you laughing?"

"Because I would have expected you to be a bit more subtle. You're looking for reasons for revenge?"

"Listen, son, I go home at the end of the day and you're the one staying here. I don't need to be subtle or play word games. I'm being as direct as possible."

"Of course, I was angry. Who wasn't I angry at? At myself, at God, that stupid Swedish girl wandering around at night…"

"And?"

"And in the end, I was the one who pulled the trigger, no one else. I'm responsible enough to understand that. But I think that the Office came to hasty conclusions and things could have been different."

"So, you just went back to France?"

"It wasn't as simple as you make it out to be, but that was the end result," Daniel replied, his chest tight. "You have to understand, Shlomo, this is the only place that felt like home. When I'd hear Israelis fantasize about living abroad and complaining about Israel, it drove me crazy. They're crazy. I was born in France but always felt like a foreigner. Let me tell you something; when I was around fourteen, living in France, I went to Poland with a delegation of Jewish children from the community. To the camps. They showed us everything and told us about the horrors done to our people."

"I was on one of those delegations with the agency," Shlomo nodded, a blank look in his eyes as if recalling that visit.

"And I," Daniel continued, "I felt ashamed… I couldn't understand it all, you know? I thought that something was wrong with me. On the last day, we visited Birkenau. I stood there with the guide, right at the entrance where the trains would come in, and the guide was talking to us, explaining, and then I heard the sound of marching. Everything went silent. No one spoke. Only the sound of marching, coming closer. Stomp, stomp, stomp. My heart was beating with the rhythm, and I was afraid. I think I even heard a trumpet... that echo, I'll never forget it. I was shaking like a leaf, like at any minute the Germans were going to come. We were all looking at the gate, and then suddenly we saw a long line of soldiers. Israel Defense Forces officers in dress uniform and wearing berets, marching in step. An old man with a flat cap on his head was leading them. They passed by us, right by me, and I watched them, hypnotized, shaking, as if I were in another world. I looked into the old man's eyes, so blue, so deep, I don't know how to describe it, but his gaze looked like he was holding back tears. His eyes held both despair and hope, sadness and joy, and even though his back was hunched, he held his head high. Suddenly, the soldiers stopped. The old man turned to them, and they all saluted him. And he started to cry." Daniel leaned forward, "Shlomo, that day something changed in me. I knew exactly where I had to live and what I had to do for my people. Even though I was just a boy."

Daniel's eyes glistened with tears. Another memory came up, a different one, difficult and painful. "I left my family. My father, mother, sister, aunts and uncles, and came here. I was planning a wedding... May I?" Daniel stopped and pointed at the pitcher. Shlomo nodded, and Daniel poured a glass and drank. "After Sweden, I felt like a nobody. Yael, my girlfriend, she was a field agent, like me. Her family is as Israeli as it gets. So where do I go from here? What will I do now? This was my purpose. I couldn't stay here anymore. As part of the Office, I felt on top of the world. Without that, I was just another new immigrant."

Shlomo just looked at Daniel for a beat and said, "But there's something else, right?"

Daniel knew that the man sitting across from him could see right through him. Maybe it was his tone of voice, maybe his body language. "Yes," he admitted. He closed his eyes for a few seconds, and then opened them.

Shlomo also looked pensive. After a moment of silence, he asked Daniel to continue.

"My father and I... we didn't have a good relationship, but when I came to Israel and joined the army, and later the Office, our relationship was the best it had ever been, even from a distance. I think he was even proud of me. But when..."

"They knew you were in the Mossad?" Shlomo asked, surprised.

"I never said anything. But people in the community talk. People aren't stupid. I think they guessed."

"And when..."

"When I was dismissed?"

Shlomo nodded.

"Yael was pregnant when all this happened. It wasn't planned... it was before the wedding... and I asked her to get an abortion, I told her that I didn't want to get married and didn't want children."

"And that's the real reason you escaped to France?" Shlomo leaned back and glanced at Daniel, who wasn't hiding his anguish.

"When that baby grew up what would I tell him or her? I was ashamed... also, Yael's family, they were like my own, even though they didn't know that we were both in the Mossad. Don't you see? Everything I'd thought about myself burst like a balloon and there was nothing left. I couldn't live with being disgraced. She was still a field agent, that was her career, how could I be with her? She was insistent, said she loved me and that nothing would change. But I knew that if I didn't disappear, she'd keep the baby."

"And what happened? Did you stay in touch?"

"No." Daniel thought of all the times he wanted to call her but didn't have the guts. "After a while, she sent the things I'd left behind in our apartment to my parents' address, with a letter, and that was it. I didn't hear from her again."

"And in France, you went back to your parents?"

Daniel shifted uneasily. "Only at the beginning. Then I left. Let's just say that my father and I didn't get along."

"How did you explain that the wedding was canceled?"

"I let them believe that I'd discovered Yael was cheating on me. They knew how much I loved her, so they never asked questions. But when I told them that I wouldn't be going back to Israel they understood that something big had happened. You have to understand, I had always been a Zionist. I was angry at them because they didn't want to move to Israel, I argued with them, and suddenly I do an about-face? They realized that it was something traumatic."

"And why didn't you stay in France?"

"It didn't take long before the situation with my father deteriorated. I started working with him. He has a few supermarkets in Paris... Shlomo, can I get a cigarette?"

"Sure," he said, and left the room.

Daniel took advantage of the break to collect his thoughts. He felt relieved. These things had weighed heavily on his soul. The trajectory of his life had turned around overnight, and the repercussions continued. Suddenly, in this unreal situation he found himself in, he felt comfortable letting it all out. Yet he didn't forget for a moment that Shlomo was an interrogator, not a psychologist, and every word was measured and analyzed in one respect. He was giving Shlomo the background that completed the picture. In the end he hoped everything would seem logical to him, much more than the truth would be.

Shlomo returned, holding a small glass filled to the brim with fragrant coffee, and in the other hand a pack of Marlboro. He lit one for himself and another for Daniel and pushed the glass toward him.

"*Merci.*"

"Cheers," Shlomo replied, and poured water into the coffee cup he had drunk from earlier. He mixed the muddy dregs with the cold water in front of Daniel's astonished eyes.

"Habit," Shlomo explained without being asked. "My first cup of the day I prepare as usual, and the others – I just keep diluting with cold water."

Daniel took a couple of drags, sipped his coffee, and thought about the closeness that had developed between them. He very rarely smoked.

"What kind of work did you do there, in the supermarkets?"

Daniel looked embarrassed. "I worked in the warehouse and stocking. 'You have to start from the bottom,' my father used to say. Even if that's true, I think he had a different reason."

Shlomo seemed to understand, so there was no point in saying anything more. "And you didn't stay there very long?"

"One month was enough," Daniel took another drag of the cigarette, and exhaled into the room, watching as the smoke was sucked into the ceiling vent. "I moved in with a childhood friend who went on frequent business trips, and I started working as a security guard at Jewish schools during the day, sometimes at clubs at night."

"And were you in contact with anyone from home?"

"Mostly my mother and sister. Sometimes I'd go for a short visit on Saturday."

Shlomo glanced at his watch. "So, what's the story with Bethlehem?"

Daniel tried to hide his tension. He was on the boundary between truth and fiction. Everything he'd said up until now could be corroborated. From this point he'd twist the truth to serve his purposes. You're not lying, he repeated to himself, as he'd been trained, it's your inner truth and it's what you believe. The essence isn't a lie, only the facts are distorted.

The corner of Daniel's mouth twitched, a small, involuntary move, and Shlomo raised an eyebrow. Many years and hundreds of interrogations had taught him to notice even the smallest of facial tics.

"None of my friends knew what I was really doing in Israel. These are people I grew up with, who knew me. I always stood out, everyone said I had potential and didn't understand what happened; how Daniel, who was a combat officer in the IDF and a businessman traveling around the world, was suddenly stocking sardine cans in the supermarket and working as a security guard for schools and clubs. They didn't get it. And this friend that I lived with used to say to me, 'Daniel, you've got to pull yourself together, believe in yourself. You were born to do great things. Go. Don't stay in France.' He didn't let up, drove me crazy. Suggested I go volunteer in some African country." Daniel took a sip of coffee. "I started searching the internet for UN organizations, and I found this humanitarian organization that was looking for people to work at the psychiatric hospital in Bethlehem. That interested me. I played around with the idea for a couple of days. I couldn't stop thinking about it. Volunteering somewhere else wasn't a problem; in Bethlehem it would be a challenge, it would put all my skills to the test. If I succeeded, that would be amazing. But I couldn't go to the Palestinians as Daniel Ben Atar. I started to imagine how I could do it, build my cover, live there for a few weeks. What did I have to lose?"

Shlomo searched Daniel's shining brown eyes, clearly looking for what he was trying to hide, "Were you excited about being in the field again?"

Daniel was relieved. Excellent, it was going in the right direction. "Listen, it was like they threw me off a cliff. Before, I had fulfilled my dream of being just like a native-born Israeli, then I was in the

Office, and I was going to get married and raise a wonderful family – I truly believed in myself, and in a split second, it was all gone. They told me: you're not suited to be an undercover field agent, you lack judgment, you let your gut make the decision."

"Those are serious accusations. Sounds to me like a perfect reason to offer your services to a foreign organization, to prove to yourself that you can and on the way get your revenge on those who didn't believe in you."

Daniel hesitated for a second before answering. "Maybe, but that isn't my story. I didn't come to Israel, join the Duvdevan Unit or join the Office for recognition, to be James Bond; I did all that to be an Israeli and live in my homeland."

Shlomo burst out laughing with a dismissive wave of his hand, "What's this about Zionism now? Your generation joins the Mossad or Shabak for Zionist reasons? What are you talking about? Zionism is just a facade, a decoration. It's all about self-worth, prestige, the challenge, wanting to feel more special than others. Don't bullshit me."

A smile spread across Daniel's face. "Your friends at the Office wouldn't like what you just said, but I think you're right. I already told you about people who were born here. Look at their recruitment advertisements: come be the spearhead, part of an elite group, do the unimaginable just like in the movies. And what hooks do they use for those of us with foreign citizenship who don't live in Israel? Zionism, homeland, the Jewish people. But I don't judge. Everyone has their own reasons. To answer your question – being a spy is not my purpose in life."

"Come on, give me a break," Shlomo persisted.

Daniel sobered. He knew that Shlomo was goading him, but he was still offended. "Believe me or not – this is who I am."

Shlomo said somberly, "I'm sure you know that when we finish with the questions, you'll have to take a polygraph test."

Daniel had known that was coming, but his heart started racing. "Wonderful," he shrugged.

"I'd like to know how your 'playful' thoughts became a reality. When did you decide to go for it?"

For a split second, Daniel considered telling him about the real watershed moment, but he was ashamed. "I couldn't get it out of my head. I thought about it constantly. A few days later I decided to try and get a fake passport. I knew that was the key. Without a passport there was no Bethlehem. I said to myself, let's see if I succeed and then decide what to do. I wandered around the immigrant neighborhoods. Honestly, it was easier than I thought. I went to the mosque a few times, went to lessons, got to know people, asked questions here and there – and got to the right person. On the way I built my cover story, worked on my Arabic, walked around, heard some gossip, names of places, some stories... you know."

Shlomo shook his head in disbelief. "Let's say everything you're telling me is true – you realize *that*, in itself, is a very serious criminal offense. What else did you get mixed up in before you even set foot in Bethlehem?"

"I understand perfectly well! Don't be a hypocrite, Shlomo. When I did these things as a field agent, were they less dangerous?" Daniel laughed. "Actually, this isn't so bad. They'll only charge me with forgery, not espionage. How do you get to decide when it's okay and when it isn't? And what if a retired field agent does almost exactly the same thing in the private sector? Here I'm only endangering myself, no one else, so you have no right to say anything!"

Shlomo didn't push it. He tried to move on, "I'm talking about the danger of being exposed to the Muslims there. They would have slaughtered you!"

You're transparent, Shlomo, Daniel thought. "I have enough experience and they're the last ones who concern me," he said confidently, "I didn't do anything that I haven't done before."

"So, you got a passport. Then what?"

Daniel told him how he'd applied to the volunteer organization, filled out forms, the interview – exactly how it happened. He had nothing to hide and there was no harm in telling him everything. Then he went on in more detail about the flight to Israel and the drive to Bethlehem, about the psychiatric hospital, the apartment he rented and his daily routine over the past month. Everything – except the things that touched on his real reason for being there.

"And then you people showed up, and you know the rest."

Shlomo remained silent for a few minutes, scratching his forehead. "So how long did you plan to stay there? Seems like you managed to establish yourself. Isn't that enough? Haven't you proved to yourself that you can do it?"

Daniel hesitated. "Maybe a few more weeks," he shrugged. "I'm starting to feel that it's really doing me good. The daily stress helps keeps back that person who I don't want to be anymore."

"Every day that passes only endangers you more. What if it was really the Palestinians that had arrested you?"

"So, they would have interrogated me. Apart from my fake identity, which I think I did a good job with, I'm not doing any harm. I go to the hospital in the morning and back to my apartment in the evening. I think it's a calculated risk."

"I think otherwise but let's say you're right. Is there anything else that you need or want to tell me?"

"Why did you arrest me? Why did you wait a month?"

"You know what? Maybe you're right. We should have arrested you at the first opportunity."

When was the first opportunity? Daniel nodded. "I think we've covered everything."

"I still don't understand," Shlomo said, "why Bethlehem?"

"Like I said, it was just by chance. If they had been looking for volunteers in Hebron I would've gone there."

"That remains to be seen." Shlomo stood. "They'll bring you something to eat soon. I'll see you later," he said, and left the room.

Daniel spent the time after lunch in his room. He lay on the bed and stared at the ceiling, his hands behind his head. It was very quiet. He heard the occasional faint sound of doors slamming, but that was it. For the first time since he was arrested, he thought about what he'd left behind in Bethlehem. Today was Sunday and he hadn't shown up for his shift with no advance notice, without calling in. He assumed that someone would try to call his cellphone, which was now in the hands of the Shabak. At some point someone would come to check out his apartment. Probably Rashid. As far as he could remember, no one from Abu Elias' building had witnessed his arrest except for Abu Elias himself, and from his reaction, the Shabak must have told him some story. And even if someone had been there, all they saw was Daniel leaving the building with two other men and getting into a black SUV. He knew very well that anyone who suspected a security incident would most probably prefer to keep their mouth shut. On the Palestinian street people were reluctant to get involved in anyone else's business when it was related to security. At the most, there would be whispers in coffee shops around the hookah pipe. With no control over the developments, he decided to let that go for now.

His next thoughts were of people from his past. Which of the Mossad field agents who had served with him were involved in the arrest? Was it a compartmentalized security incident? Did he know any of the people downstairs who were pulling the strings of the investigation? And most important, did Yael already know? "The universe is perfectly balanced," his grandfather used to say to him, "it takes something from you and gives back something else. In the end, everything works out the way it was supposed to and it's not always the way you planned." The first time Daniel heard that he was a young boy and didn't really understand. Now, he hoped his grandfather was right.

In the afternoon, the security guards came in and shook him awake from a deep and relaxed sleep. Daniel sat up groggily and looked at them. They asked him to come with them. He nodded, got up, and put his head under the faucet in the bathroom. His escorts looked somewhat uncomfortable this time, as if they knew what he'd done in his previous life. They were both young, probably students with combat experience who put undercover field agents on a pedestal.

Daniel accompanied them to the interrogation room, which wasn't empty this time. A man, who looked to be around forty-five, sat at the desk. He had gray eyes and a buzz cut, and wore jeans and a striped shirt, the top buttons undone. Instead of the regular chair, which had been pushed to the corner, there was a very large, brown, vinyl high-back chair with wide armrests. Daniel had previous experience, but he was still nervous. He didn't know anyone who hadn't felt anxiety at a polygraph test.

He sat on the strange chair and the examiner explained the procedure in detail. Then he read Daniel the questions he was going to ask, told him how to answer several of them, and finally checked the equipment. Daniel lifted his arms to let the examiner attach the sensors: black tubes with a beaded chain taped to his body, one around his stomach and one around his chest; two perspiration monitors attached with black Velcro strips to two of his fingers; and last – a regular blood pressure cuff around his other arm. When the examiner inflated the cuff, just like at the doctor's office, Daniel shifted his arm in discomfort. The pressure made him feel like his blood flow was cut off.

"Sit up straight," the examiner asked calmly, "and put your hands on the armrests, fingers spread wide."

Daniel did as he was asked and took a few deep breaths. His immediate association was the electric chair.

"It's uncomfortable, I know, but try not to move. Let's begin. Is your name Daniel Ben Atar?"

"Yes."

"Do you plan to lie to me during the test?"

"No."

"Is today Sunday?"

"Yes."

"Were you born in France?"

"No."

"Are you married?"

"No."

"Is there a cat in the room?"

"Yes."

"That's the first stage," the examiner said, and turned the laptop around to Daniel. "Can you see? The graph indicates the questions I asked you to lie about. Now, let's start the real test, and don't lie this time on those questions. Ready?"

"Uh-huh," Daniel nodded.

"Is your name Daniel Ben Atar?"

"Yes."

"Do you plan to lie to me during the test?"

"No."

"Is today Sunday?"

"Yes."

"Were you born in France?"

"Yes."

"Are you married?"

"No."

"Is there a cat in the room?"

"No."

"Did you lie during the interrogation?"

"No."

"Have you ever contacted a foreign intelligence service on your own initiative?"

"No."

"Has a foreign intelligence service ever contacted you?"

"No."

"Are you currently working for a foreign intelligence service?"

"No."

"Were you sent to Bethlehem by an organization other than the one you spoke of in the interrogation?"

"No."

"Are you hiding anything from us?"

"No."

"Have you lied to me during this session?"

"No."

The examiner, who didn't take his eyes off the screen during the test, waited for a few seconds more and then turned to Daniel. "We're done," he said, and got up to remove the sensors. Daniel's escorts came in to lead him back to the room upstairs.

6

Daniel's sense of time was off. Without a watch or a window to the outside world, his meals were the only indication of the time of day. He thought that it was now late evening, and wondered when they'd bring him another tray, and if they'd finished their questioning for the day. Dinner was served, offering the same menu: tea, two pita pockets, cottage cheese and freshly cut vegetables. Now what? Will they continue today? Tomorrow? During the polygraph test he used a different technique for response than would be expected. Instead of trying to remain calm he did the opposite – he tried to get overly excited at each question, regardless of the answer. Did it work? Time would tell. He felt good about the results; that was something to hold onto. The rest of the interrogation would be based on his performance. He got into bed and tried to sleep. The lights turned off thanks to the people watching him through the camera, but he just kept tossing and turning. Random thoughts kept racing through his head. Had Rashid gone through his things already? What else would Ibrahim reveal? Was his mother okay? Would he miss the annual memorial service for his grandfather in two months? Was Ibtisam worried? Where was Shlomo now? At home with his wife? Did he even have a wife? Maybe with his grandchildren? Would Daniel ever return to Bethlehem?

The light suddenly came on. Daniel sat up. The guards entered. "Wash your face and come with us." He did as they asked. It was probably going to be an all-nighter, and he prepared himself as they walked downstairs. If everything was okay, they would have waited until morning. Shlomo or that baboon would bark at him that he was lying, or at the very least not telling them everything, and then they would start their tactics. They wouldn't let him sleep, maybe keep him hungry. Out of habit he turned toward the interrogation room, but the guard pulled him in the other direction. "Downstairs," he ordered and pointed at the stairs.

The routine of the past two days and the familiar places were his safety net, and now suddenly they were going someplace else. Where? Why? Who was there? How long would they keep him there? When would he go back to his room? Oddly, he missed Shlomo.

One floor below the interrogation room the guards led him through what must have once been a living room with an open plan kitchen. The three of them walked past a few armchairs scattered around the room and stopped at a large glass sliding door. Outside, it was completely dark. Their blurry, shadowed faces reflected on the glass. Daniel concentrated on his own face, which disappeared when one of the guards slid the squeaking door open, pushing hard. "Out!" he ordered. Daniel was surprised. Maybe they were finally letting him out for some fresh air? Too bad it wasn't in the sun, he thought, as he took two steps forward.

Coming out from the brightly lit room, he couldn't see a thing in the dark. He heard the squeal of the sliding door closing behind him and took a few more steps into what looked like the villa's backyard. The shadowy bushes became clearer the deeper he went into the garden, as did the tall privacy fence covered with a tarp. He heard the muffled sound of cars. The night air was cold. Under different circumstances, he'd bundle up in a coat, but now he was just glad for the opportunity to be outdoors. He straightened, looked up at the stars shining in the clear sky, filled his lungs and slowly exhaled. Inhaled, exhaled. Dogs barked in the distance. The quiet was hypnotizing. Daniel stood there for a few long minutes and wondered about the previous life of this strange facility.

In front of him, from behind a dense growth of bushes that revealed the edge of a bench, he noticed movement. Shlomo? He hoped it was for a second, and then, without warning, she appeared.

His heart started racing. The brick wall he had put up to forget came tumbling down so hard that he started shaking. She stood unmoving and Daniel, his legs weak, came closer. Each step revealed more of her lithe body, short wild hair, her face, and finally, her almond-shaped eyes. And then, enveloped by the scent of her signature sweet perfume, the deeply buried memories surfaced, flooding him like a dam breaking.

Yael faced him, just inches away. She wore black leggings, a thin fleece jacket and sneakers. In all the possible scenarios he'd imagined where they might meet some day, he never imagined this. They stood there for a few seconds, and then Yael took a step forward, lifted her arms and held him tightly without saying a word, resting her head on his chest. Daniel lifted his arms automatically and held her close. They stood there, as if fused together, for a long time. Daniel, a head taller than Yael, breathed in the scent of her shampoo and kissed the top of her head. She leaned away from him and kissed his stubbled cheek.

"How are you?" she whispered in a choked voice, still standing close. Daniel hesitated before answering, fighting to control his emotions. He struggled to fill his lungs with air, and when he could take a deep breath, he responded, "They don't waste time, do they?"

"I insisted," she clarified.

"How did you know? They told..."

"That doesn't matter now," she cut him off firmly.

Daniel held her cold hands and felt a ring on one of her fingers.

"I'm sorry, Yaeli. I'm so sorry you were dragged into this."

"Let me help, Daniel."

"I don't know if you can."

She let go of his hands, and he wondered about her ring. Had she gotten married?

"Come with me!" She held his arm and led him to the rough wooden bench. She sat on the edge of the seat, facing him. The darkness blurred their expressions, easing the awkwardness a little.

"How are your parents? Your brother?"

"Everyone is fine now. But it was very difficult for them... they loved you like a son, you know."

Daniel was silent.

"And they didn't understand what happened."

"I can imagine. What did you tell them?"

"What could I have said? They don't know anything about the Office. I could share a little with my brother."

"I don't know how you can ever forgive me..." He thought about the abortion he'd demanded she have and didn't dare ask. "Yaeli, you're the love of my life."

Yael looked at him with a tight smile. "It didn't seem that way when you left. But I don't want to talk about that now. That's not why I'm here and we don't have much time. What's the story Daniel? What's the reason for all this?"

"It's complicated. I don't want to get into it."

"I don't think you understand the mess you're in. They believe you're working for someone else now, that you're a traitor. Even the Prime Minister was briefed about you!"

"The Prime Minister," he muttered, "Yes, Shlomo mentioned that. Just forget it, they'll let it go in the end. They'll realize that it isn't true." He punctuated his words with a wave of dismissal. "They have no evidence and won't find any, because it simply isn't true."

Yael laughed. "Who cares about the truth if they don't have convincing answers? What's the matter with you, Daniel? They don't need evidence to keep you under administrative detention. They'll hold you here for months. Even Palestinian prisoners have more rights than you do – there's the Red Cross and other organizations. And what about you? Does anyone know you're here?" she ranted. "Does anyone even know you were arrested? Does your family know that you're in Israel? Can anyone make any demands to visit you or see you? No one knows! Fortunately for you, I'm also here by chance."

"What do you mean by chance?"

"It means what it means! By chance! I'm not sure what I'm allowed to say, but you're here by chance and that means so am I."

"So, you're here because they sent you."

"Daniel, I'm here with their permission. They might think it's for them, but it's for me. I think I can help."

"Why would you?" he blurted, and immediately chastised himself. It was obvious, wasn't it? She was implying that he was the love of her life, too. That was enough. There was no need for other motives.

"I think you know. I didn't want you to leave! I still don't understand why you did it. It didn't make me stop loving you. I was disappointed, angry, but I didn't stop loving you. I chose you to be my partner and to be the father of my children. That's not something I can just erase! Does that answer suffice, *Monsieur* Ben Atar?"

Her words hurt. He tried to act like an undercover field agent, stone cold and sharp, in survival mode. But the emotions churning inside fought for his attention. Daniel looked at her silently.

"Why aren't you saying anything?"

"I don't understand what you mean, by chance?"

"Because they've been surveilling the hospital for a long time," she explained. "Something is going on there, I don't know exactly what. Somehow, they received intelligence of a French Muslim who came to volunteer. It looked suspicious to them... maybe an ISIS or Al-Qaida operator. And then they arrested you."

Daniel didn't know if that was the truth or some cover story. "You mean to tell me that I really was arrested by chance?" He leaned toward her. "That they didn't know it was me?" Despite the dark, there was no doubt that Yael could see his wild eyes.

"Didn't you realize that yourself?"

Daniel stood and started muttering in French.

"What did you say?"

"That bad luck keeps following me," he said quietly in Hebrew. "That's what I said. I simply can't believe that this was a coincidence."

"What's that thing you say about the universe?"

He sat back down next to her. "The universe is perfectly balanced. What's mine is mine and what isn't, isn't, and everything works out the way it was supposed to… that's my grandfather's old expression, it's not mine." He stared at some random spot in the darkness for a while, and then turned back to her. "But what's going on? Nothing's happening at the hospital. I mean, the place really is bizarre, but it's a mental hospital, so that's a given."

"Believe me, something's going on. Otherwise, they wouldn't have made such an effort to put on this show for you. What and why – that's Shabak's business. If they want, they'll tell you."

If that was true, Daniel thought, then it all made sense. It also meant that they had someone on the inside. Well, not necessarily. The intelligence on Jalal could have come from different sources, and maybe only someone in the Shabak had put the pieces together.

"I get that you don't believe a word anyone says," Yael said, "But in the end you'll have to decide what's true and what isn't."

Daniel shrugged. "It's hard for me not to believe you."

Yael remained silent.

"But I don't get something. I've been there a month. I didn't notice anything suspicious. Now, clearly if you all suspect that I'm a spy for someone else –"

"Daniel, stop! Don't put me in the category of 'you all.' I don't believe that you're a traitor. But yes, the circumstances are questionable, and you have to explain them. And stop with the convoluted logic. You'll dig yourself into a hole. You can suspect, you can doubt, but find an objective truth to hold onto, or just give them one. Because so far, you haven't done so great on the polygraph test!"

Daniel felt his chest tighten. "So that's why they called you?"

"They sent the Mossad a picture of you and your name. And they suspected that I was involved too. After they spoke with me and realized I didn't know anything, I offered to help. They know that I know you better than anyone!"

"So, they sent you?" Daniel ignored her last comment.

"They sent Arik. And it seemed very strange to him, too. He watched you on camera and listened to the recorded interrogation. He didn't want to believe it. Logic says it's you, but he was still uncertain because it really doesn't make sense. So, he suggested that they take –"

"Fingerprints," Daniel interrupted. "I got that. And then they got you involved. And Arik was here."

Yael nodded and looked at Daniel, who started laughing. "What?"

"If Shlomo hadn't been here – if it were some other interrogator – they wouldn't have had any idea. What rotten luck."

"Maybe they wouldn't have had any idea, but they wouldn't have just let you go easily. They initially wanted to recruit you as an informant, so you'd think that you're working for the Palestinians on the inside."

Daniel waved it off. "Nah, I would have agreed and then given them nothing or just disappeared. They would have given up and gotten off my case. Honestly," Daniel stood up, "I wouldn't have helped the Palestinians. But if I had realized that it was Shabak – then gladly! Think about it. They couldn't have found anyone better."

"You have a point." Yael looked pensive. "But don't play 'what if'. You're not in a great place right now."

"I don't know what you meant when you said I didn't do so great on the polygraph test. I wouldn't have failed the treason question, it was the truth!"

"But you didn't answer other questions truthfully! And now they can't decide. You know what this kind of situation is like – neither here nor there, a gray area. And now they have doubts, but they're sure of one thing, that you're hiding something. What? They won't release you until they investigate. Do you get that?"

Daniel paced back and forth, breaking off bits of a dry twig he had picked up. He had no choice, he thought. He believed Yael had his best interests at heart, but he assumed everything they said to each other would be reported to Shlomo and interpreted one way or another. Maybe they were being recorded right now, with or without her knowledge. The location for this nighttime meeting was intentional; Shlomo and his people wanted him to feel comfortable, unthreatened, in an environment other than the interrogation room, so he wouldn't feel he was admitting to something. More like a confession, and in the role of the priest was Yael. It seemed his only option, and he had to play his hand. Anyway, he couldn't sink any lower.

He sat down next to her, "Yaeli, did anyone ever call you a dirty Jew?"

"That again?" she replied impatiently, "We've talked about it before."

"We talked. But not about everything."

"Daniel, enough! So there's antisemitism in the world. There was and always will be. What does it matter and what's it got to do with anything now?"

"It matters! Don't you see?" He raised his voice. "It doesn't bother you! I don't think it bothers anyone who was born here. You'll never feel that fear. Maybe your grandparents told you stories of being called dirty Jews, about the fear of walking around with a yarmulke or a Star of David necklace. I," he pounded his chest, "I lived that every day. Walking down the street scared to death!"

"I know, and I'm certainly not downplaying it. I'm also happy that I only heard stories and didn't experience it myself. But what's that got to do with Bethlehem?"

He looked at her hesitantly. "I've never told anyone this," he said quietly. "But now I don't care what anyone thinks. I'm not ashamed. And anyway, you deserve to hear it. It'll answer a lot of your questions. You'll understand things."

"I'm listening."

"When I was ten years old, in Paris, we were on our way home one Saturday after synagogue – me, my sister, mother, and father. We walked through an underpass to cross the street, and at the other end were some Arabs. Three immigrants. They immediately saw that we were Jewish. They came up to my father, slapped him, called him a dirty Jew, pulled his yarmulke off and threw it in the street."

"What?!" Yael looked shocked.

Daniel continued, his voice shaky, "They called my mother a dirty bitch, spit on her, and then stepped on my father's yarmulke. They touched my little sister... you know... and they shoved me. And the native Parisians walked by as if they didn't see anything. Didn't want to get involved! I looked at my mother and saw the spit sliding down her face. And my father... like a coward... stood there paralyzed, crying. Didn't do a thing! Didn't fight back! My father, who an hour earlier at the synagogue wrapped me in his tallis during the priestly blessing and protected me, now stood there crying like a little kid! If police officers hadn't just happened to walk by, those Arabs would have killed us. That's what I saw in front of my eyes in Sweden!" Daniel was almost shouting. "Now do you get it? That's why I came to Israel, joined the army and the Mossad! So I wouldn't be scared anymore! And I was never scared, not in any operation! But what can I do when I see two bastards grab a girl and call her a dirty bitch? How can I stand there watching and not do anything? Like I hadn't gotten over it? Like I'm a coward like my father? No way! Let them die! They're not innocent in my book. I didn't plan to shoot them; I just got involved and tried to help. But when they came at me, I pulled the trigger."

Yael looked at Daniel, horrified. She shifted closer to him on the bench hesitantly and finally hugged him. "You never told me..."

"I buried that day," he whispered in her ear as they embraced. "I can't even explain the feeling. It's fear, helplessness, shame – all together! I never forgave my father for that Saturday."

"Did he ever explain why he didn't do anything?"

Daniel laughed and leaned back. "I asked him on the way home. He didn't say a word. I called him a coward, and he told me I was disrespectful. We never spoke about the incident at home. But it was always the elephant in the room."

"And I always felt so awful when I thought about the tragedy with your grandfather. I could never imagine something like that happening."

"My grandfather was the only one I could talk to. And he said that my father had always been a coward and that I was nothing like him."

"I don't know what to say."

"You don't have to say anything."

"And that... that still haunts you?"

"It used to. Until that trip to Poland. You already know what happened there. Everything changed. I knew I'd get past it."

"But that belongs to the past. You got over it, came to Israel, served in the army, and became someone else. Didn't you? It's horrible, Daniel... but I don't understand how it relates to what's happening now."

Daniel avoided her eyes and stared at the ground. His movements suddenly made him look like a young boy. He was silent for a while.

"After that Saturday... I... I started to wet the bed." He looked up at her, his eyes moist. "I'd wake up in the middle of the night sometimes, screaming, sweating, scared. My mother would come to me and calm me down. It went on for years. And after Poland, it stopped. That was it. I was absolutely sure where I had to be and what I had to do with my life! And a few years later, my grandfather died in front of my eyes when the dig collapsed over him... I felt like the sky had fallen, but I also felt strong. He stayed with me, inside me, supporting and encouraging me like he always had. There was a reason I went with him to every dig in Israel on my vacations. I loved him so much."

Yael looked shocked and sorrowful. Neither said a word for a few minutes. Then Daniel told her, as he had Shlomo, everything that had happened since he left her and returned to France.

"Daniel, now I'm confused," she stopped him. "I saw you talking with Shlomo. But what of all that is the truth, and what isn't?"

"You saw everything? Also what I said about you?"

"Yes." She took his hand. "The day you left, I understood without you telling me. I understood why you didn't want to get married. I understood that you couldn't stay with me when I was still a field agent and you weren't; that I couldn't share my experiences, maybe because they were covert and maybe because it would just cause you pain, and that you wouldn't feel comfortable hanging out with our friends from the division. I also knew that you were afraid I'd want to leave the Office for you, and you wouldn't want that on your conscience. I thought that you were wrong, but you decided on your own and left. You didn't give me a chance."

Daniel exhaled slowly. "I'm sorry."

"That's in the past," Yael said brusquely. "Let's look forward. What haven't you told Shlomo?"

"When I went back to France, things didn't work out so well – working with my father and also in security. I started to feel like I did back when I was a boy, when I was afraid I'd end up like my father. It drove me crazy, and I started to fall apart. I stopped believing that I would ever get over it. Everything I'd achieved over the years was gone, and I was back at square one. I even started wetting the bed at night, and that was the breaking point, you know? At my age? Don't get upset, Yael," he stopped a minute to take a deep breath, "but I was afraid to start anything serious with other women because what would happen when they found out at night? Who would want to be with me?"

Yael looked at Daniel in shock. "I never would have imagined..."

"Yes, unfortunately, that's the story," Daniel hung his head. "That's why I did something so extreme. I'm no spy. When you sent my things to my parents and the boxes with my grandfather's work, I sat and read everything. Like you suggested in your letter. You knew I'd wanted to do that for years and never got around to it. All his notebooks, his articles, everything. Every single word. And that gave me strength. He was the most important person in my life, you know?" Daniel gave a small smile. "Sometimes when I came to visit him here in Israel on vacations, when I was just a little boy, instead of reading me stories about Mickey Mouse, he'd tell me about history, wars, and how momentous it was that we returned here after two thousand years. I didn't always understand, but I was fascinated. I'd wait for bedtime. He'd lie next to me and tell me stories until I fell asleep."

Daniel's tone became more and more excited. Deep inside, the suspicion that Yael might be wired remained, but he felt a strong need to finally tell someone the truth, and there was no one better than her for that. "Among all the folders, there was one that looked the same, but what was inside was shocking! I don't know if anyone from the university knew what he was working on, what he was really looking for. I don't even know how to tell you... you'll probably think that he was crazy."

"Try me."

Daniel's heart was racing. "The Temple treasures!"

Yael raised her perfectly sculpted eyebrows. "Artifacts from the Temple?"

"*Oui*! Exactly. Hundreds of pages, dozens in his handwriting – I read every word – and the others were photos of historical documents in different languages. He describes the route of the treasures since the Romans took them. Exactly like an intelligence report... convincing facts. The entire journey, how they passed from hand to hand, from empire to empire, and finally, after hundreds of years, some ended up back here."

"Where is here, Daniel? What do you mean by some?"

"Here! To Israel! At first, they were hidden in Jerusalem under some monastery, then they were transferred to another monastery in Bethlehem. And there's a sketch he made. It's the last place he went to, and that's also where it all ended up."

"And that's what you're looking for?"

"The hospital where I volunteer is built over the remains of that monastery! Now do you understand? I found my purpose, something to act on! Something that will pull me out of all the shit I drowned in! It was driving me insane! It's the most meaningful thing I've ever done in my life! The most important! Imagine if it's all really there!"

"Temple treasures? Are you serious?"

Daniel couldn't tell if she was surprised or just being condescending. "Yes! What's so strange about that? My grandfather was an archaeologist, a well-known and esteemed academic. He did research and uncovered quite a few sites in Israel. Why does it sound strange when it's about the Temple? Wasn't it real? Didn't it happen? You think it's just a myth?"

Yael scratched her head. "Of course it isn't a myth, but... I don't know, it sounds so... mystical."

Daniel sighed and threw his hand up in despair. "You see? That's why I didn't tell Shlomo the truth! I just don't get it! Everyone goes to the Western Wall, millions of people visit the City of David and get all emotional. But just mention the Temple or the Temple Mount and people get riled up. Automatically it goes hand in hand with extremism, Messianism, a world war with the Muslims and the destruction of Al-Aqsa. Why the fear? What's so mystical about it?"

"I don't understand, why are you so upset?" She started playing with the ring on her finger.

"Because that's exactly how people react to antisemitism! I never understand how it goes right over people's heads. The same with our history. The British dug in every corner of Jerusalem to find the remains of the Temple. The British, okay? Were *they* crazy? Did they care more than us? But we only do it in secret. Only private individuals. Not the government. It interests the Christians more than it interests us. That's absurd! I totally understand why my grandfather did his research under the radar."

"Daniel, what are you talking about? You understand that you're playing with –" the ring slipped off her finger and fell onto the paving stones with a clink.

Daniel bent down and started feeling around for it. He found the ring, stared at it for a second, and handed it to Yael. "That's our engagement ring, isn't it?"

"Yes. I love it and still wear it. I lost some weight and it's too big, but I couldn't bring myself to resize it. I wanted it to stay the same as when you gave it to me."

Daniel felt awkward. "And you didn't..."

"I didn't get married, Daniel. Let's put that aside for now and get back to the issue at hand, please. You're playing with matches next to a barrel of explosives! Do you understand that?"

"I understand perfectly! You don't have to explain Muslims to me. I see what's happening even in Europe. People have gotten used to this shit all over the world. Let's not get them upset. They're dangerous..."

"Okay, we're not going to solve all the problems of the Middle East right now."

"And I'm not trying to! My views aren't new to you. I guess you have to live abroad for that. But that isn't the issue right now. I'm talking about something else entirely and it's got nothing to do with volatile places like the Temple Mount; it's about the hospital in Bethlehem – my grandfather's last stop."

"Your enthusiasm is amazing, Daniel, it reminds me of when we were just starting out. Every operation was the most important thing in the world to you. But, and don't get me wrong... your enthusiasm is also a little naïve."

"Because I've had it! I've had it with the alienation I felt after I was kicked out of the Office! Yes! I want to be naïve again. It gives me hope. Yaeli, look at where we are. How did I get here? I know that there's a reason you're here. I'm not stupid. Everything will get back to Shlomo and his pals and maybe they're listening to us right now, or you're recording – I don't know. What I do know is that I want all of you, you and them, to understand everything. I didn't feel comfortable talking about this with Shlomo face-to-face. I've known him for all of two days."

"I'm not recording you."

"Okay, but I know that it will get back to them. This meeting between us isn't a humanitarian gesture by the Shabak." He lifted his hand toward her but then pulled it back. "Yaeli, discovering my grandfather's secret work brought me back to life! I'm not going back to the way I was even if this is the last thing I do!"

"So, what treasures are you talking about? Did your grandfather know?"

"Candle holders and trumpets. Made of gold and silver. That's what he thought. Maybe even the menorah."

Yael turned toward him, her eyes dreamy even in the dim light.

"What?"

"Nothing," she said quietly. "This conversation reminds me of why I chose you. These things that move you, your infectious enthusiasm... you're so different from everyone else."

Daniel remained silent. He didn't know what to say to her. Their conversation had taken a turn that, up until an hour ago, he couldn't have imagined.

"So, what now?" she asked, putting her hand over his.

"It's bigger than me. I'm in so deep that I have to find a way to continue. It's not just rumors, Yael. This research is real. It has huge significance, and I'm sure this country would want to have it. Not just want to – has to!"

After he'd shared Ibrahim's story, Yael looked thoughtful for a few minutes, and then suddenly said, "I have an idea…"

7

The next morning Daniel woke up in good spirits. Yael's idea was sound. Win-win. Everyone benefited, but only he was taking a risk. When he entered the interrogation room again, the polygraph examiner was there. He assumed that the Shabak wanted to verify his latest input. He was relieved. He had nothing to hide anymore. It was all out there. And of course, there was a new batch of questions.

The test ended and the examiner left with his equipment. Daniel stayed in the room, waiting. Now what? It was Monday morning. With every passing day, the chances grew of someone sniffing around his disappearance.

The electric bolt lock buzzed, and the door opened. Shlomo came in with a younger man who wore light-colored cotton pants, a green t-shirt, and blue hiking sandals.

Shlomo sat down. "Good morning, this is Jonathan."

"Nice to meet you," Jonathan extended his hand.

"Hi." Daniel took his hand, surprised at the firm handshake.

Jonathan put a laptop and a thick hardcover notebook on the table. Shlomo got straight to the point. "We want to ask a few questions about the hospital. You want to help, right?"

"Of course." Daniel shrugged.

"Excellent. Let me give you some background," Jonathan explained, "I coordinate the special intelligence team on Hamas activities in the psychiatric hospital in Bethlehem."

"You're a case officer? Intelligence officer?" Daniel tried to assess how open they were being with him.

"Intelligence officer. I can't reveal everything we know. I'm sure you understand."

Daniel nodded. "That's fine. Ask whatever you want."

Jonathan glanced at Shlomo and then said to Daniel, "Right. So, we've been monitoring the place for a few months now. Hamas is up to something there and making extreme efforts to hide it. We believe that even Palestinian Intelligence has no idea."

"I've got to tell you," Daniel interrupted, "that seems very strange to me. I've been there every day for a month and didn't notice anything suspicious. The place operates normally. Just a psychiatric hospital."

"I don't know if you were there when it happened," Jonathan said, "but around a month ago, we were there with the army at night and..."

"I was. It was my first week there."

"I can tell you that according to the intelligence we received, it really had the Hamas worried. They were afraid that we'd discover what they were doing, but they finally calmed down, thinking it was just a spontaneous raid to search for wanted persons."

"Really?" Daniel furrowed his brow. "So, you're sure?"

"Daniel, listen," Shlomo cut in, "You already know that we arrested you by accident. We didn't know it was you."

"So I've been told." Daniel leaned back and crossed his arms. Shlomo nodded in admission.

"Imagine," Shlomo continued, "the efforts we made to grab you from the middle of Bethlehem and make you think we're Palestinians so that you would cooperate with us. Something big is going on there. We wouldn't have made the effort if we weren't convinced."

"It was very convincing," Daniel nodded, staring at a random spot on the table. He lifted his head. "Okay, just ask me, because like I told you, I haven't noticed anything unusual there."

Jonathan opened his notebook and laptop and turned it so Daniel could see the screen. Daniel recognized a clear and sharp aerial image of the hospital.

"Tell me," Daniel asked, "don't you have sources there? Informers?"

Jonathan's body language gave him away, but his answer was vague. "We have access," he said, "but we aren't sure that's going to get us answers."

"Okay." Daniel understood that Jonathan couldn't reveal more than that.

"Let's start with mapping the structures in the compound," Jonathan requested.

Each structure in the aerial photo was numbered. Daniel patiently detailed what he knew about each one, what it was used for, how many floors, where the openings were located, who worked there on a regular basis, whether there were surveillance cameras, basement floors, and security bars. He told them about the staff members, shifts, and routine activities. From Jonathan's questions, Daniel assumed that the Shabak was very familiar with the hospital. He enjoyed every minute. The investigation reminded him of debriefings after intelligence-gathering operations in which he had participated.

Unlike Jonathan, whose notebook filled quickly with notes, Shlomo appeared to be incredibly bored. He walked out of the room several times, each time returning with something else; fruit, coffee, water. When lunchtime rolled around, Daniel wasn't hungry anymore and Jonathan and Shlomo didn't seem anxious to eat either. They drank coffee with him and chatted about Bethlehem. When they were done, Jonathan asked a few more questions, then packed up his things, thanked Daniel, and left. Shlomo went with him and said he'd be right back.

Daniel walked around the room and wondered if they were examining the extent of his willingness to cooperate or just getting what intelligence they could from him.

Shlomo came back holding a cellphone and asked Daniel to sit. He set it on the table.

"What now?" Daniel asked, recognizing his phone.

Shlomo folded his hands. "Listen, nothing's been decided yet, but I want to leave all options open."

"I'm listening." Daniel spread his hands on the table.

"Our first thought was to recruit you."

Daniel nodded.

"Your sudden disappearance might have raised questions, and that was a concern. We didn't know how things would develop and how long it would take. So, we went to your landlord and presented ourselves as representatives of the Palestinian Authority's Ministry of Foreign Affairs. We told him that your mother had died and your family in France asked the French consulate in Jerusalem to locate you."

Daniel nodded. "Now I understand why Abu Elias told me to 'be strong' when I opened the door."

Shlomo continued. "We also sent a WhatsApp message from your phone to Rashid, from you, of course. We wrote that you had to visit France for a week or two and that you'd be in touch. Short and to the point. Here, look," he pushed the phone toward him.

Daniel's eyes widened. "To Rashid? That gossip?"

"We did a little digging and saw that he was the one you had the most contact with. We knew he's your colleague at the hospital. It seemed logical. Anyway, call him now on WhatsApp, so he won't see that it's a local call. Tell him that your mother died, and you took the first flight to France. Ask him to let the hospital know and that you'll be in touch."

Daniel felt like a weight had lifted off his chest. He was happy the Shabak had solved the problem that had burdened him more than anything else. He did as Shlomo asked, called Rashid and told him that on Friday night, representatives from the French consulate had come to his apartment to tell him that his mother had passed away. Rashid expressed his condolences and promised to keep in touch.

"Excellent," Shlomo said, and took the cellphone. "Let's go to the backyard for a cigarette."

After their cigarette break outside, Daniel was escorted back to his room. He was tired but hopeful. After days indoors, the sun lifted his spirits. He spent the afternoon lying on his back, napping and waiting. What was next? Would someone take Yael's idea seriously? Their meeting continued to run through his mind. The memory of her scent lingered. When would he see her again? There were so many things he wanted to ask and learn about her life. The fact that she still wore their engagement ring surprised him, but he was afraid to delve into what that could mean.

Supper arrived, but Daniel wasn't hungry. He hoped that something would happen today, and every muted step or sound raised his hopes that the security guards were coming to get him. How he wished it would be for another visit with Yael. When the hours passed and no one came, he gave up and fell asleep. But not for long. The door opened and this time only one guard stood in the doorway, "I'll be back in 15 minutes. You have time to shower."

Now what? Daniel asked himself as he hurried into the adjacent bathroom. I hope it's another meeting with Yael.

The guard kept his word and came back on time. He escorted Daniel to the interrogation room. So, it isn't Yael, he thought, disappointed. Probably Shlomo with the results of the polygraph. Or maybe Jonathan with more questions. They entered the room. But there was no one there. Daniel sat down and ran his fingers through his hair, which was still damp from the shower.

The buzzer sounded and the door opened. He lifted his head and looked at the two guests in utter shock. He stood up awkwardly. One of them he knew well, and the other just from the media.

"Eran!" The director of the Mossad greeted him with a nod and sat down.

"Hello," Daniel answered and remained standing. He looked at the two high-level figures and sat down only after the director of the Shabak did.

"What's the matter? Why do you look so surprised?" Amos, the head of the Shabak, looked at Daniel impassively. He looked younger in pictures, Daniel thought, as he looked from Amos to David, the head of the Mossad. "You're the last people I expected to meet here," he replied.

"Same here," said David.

The Shabak director didn't say a word, just rolled his eyes in blatant annoyance as if he'd been forced into this meeting.

"What's the deal with the Temple?" David got straight to the point and folded his hands on the table.

Daniel didn't like his tone of voice. He still held a grudge against the man for his sentence after the incident in Sweden. "I have nothing more to say other than what I told Roni," he replied, making a point of using Yael's code name.

Amos' tone was milder. "It's important that we understand the credibility of the material you're basing yourself on, your grandfather's research."

"Very credible, as far as I'm concerned. I don't know what you've analyzed so far, but my grandfather devoted his life to it. Everything is documented and explained. He was a well-known authority."

"According to the information we have, in the summer of '81, he and others were part of an unauthorized dig under the Temple Mount. If they hadn't been stopped in time, who knows what would have happened."

"Unauthorized?" Daniel retorted, "Enough people knew about the dig and their silence implied consent. They even encouraged him, including a former senior member of the Office and a few other decision-makers. You know exactly who they are. Problems with the Arabs started after there was a leak. And instead of dealing with them, who did you take care of?"

"And you?" David interrupted. "Are you crazy? Don't you have anything better to do? Couldn't you find a less volatile place to do your digging?"

Daniel stared at him. "That's exactly the issue! This country has the best covert capabilities in the world. Why don't you use them for these types of operations, too? That's why we have them, to do things you can't do openly in volatile places."

"You want the Mossad and Shabak to start digging for artifacts?" David snapped at him.

"That doesn't sound logical?"

"Of course not! Since when were these security issues?"

"And since when do we only deal with security issues? Are you that inflexible?"

The two directors looked at each other, shocked at Daniel's nerve.

"I have a question," Daniel continued, "Ancient Torah scrolls that the Office helped to smuggle into Israel many times – that's a security issue? What about smuggling Jews from Arab countries into Israel? Did you know that in World War II, the Americans had a special unit that searched for works of art stolen by the Germans, to rescue them?"

"What's your point...?" David said impatiently.

"My point? Why can't we search for our own? What's so strange about what I'm saying? We have extraordinary capabilities. Use them!"

The Mossad director's response was a mocking laugh and a cold look. "You're criticizing us? Do you even know how these things work? Even when there were incidents of smuggling Torah scrolls, it didn't come from us. Someone asks for help, uses connections, and that's how things get rolling. It's not like the operations that the government decides on."

"*Merde*! That's what drives me crazy! Why *doesn't* the government support these missions? Someone just has to make the call to get involved and it will suddenly become legitimate."

"You're right; the intelligence community has incredible capabilities," David replied. "But do you really expect undercover field agents to start looking for pottery? As though we don't have any other problems to deal with? If we told you when you were a field agent to take risks for some broken piece of pottery, what would you say to us?"

"If there are sites with significant artifacts that archaeologists can't get to – then yes! We've done more dangerous and far less important things."

"Your guy lives in an alternate reality," Amos said to his Mossad colleague.

"What are you talking about? I admit, I get excited over ancient pottery! It's part of my identity! That's what nations go to war over – identity!"

"Don't we have enough wars? Not everyone gets excited over pottery. And anyway, what do you need it for? We're here now, right? We have a country. A homeland. We have our identity. It's called the

State of Israel!" David replied. He started to blink, showing fatigue and glanced at his watch.

"A country isn't an identity –" Daniel started to say passionately, but Amos cut him off.

"Okay, we're not here for a philosophical discussion. I think we all understand that your adventure, Eran, is based on solid information. We have an offer for you."

PART TWO

Come to Zion

1

The skies of Bethlehem were clear and blue as though summer had come early. All the signs heralded a heatwave more typical of mid-August. The taxi stopped at the gate of the psychiatric hospital, and Daniel hopped out enthusiastically. Two weeks had passed since he'd disappeared, and people were naturally curious. He had kept in touch with Rashid, mostly text messages, and assumed that the story of his mother's passing had circulated. But his return was sure to draw attention.

Walking past the guard at the gate, he was already proven right. Daniel expressed gratitude for his condolences and continued to the imposing stone building, straight to the staff room. His colleagues immediately gathered around him. He saw Ibtisam out of the corner of his eye, outside the circle. Each member of the staff offered condolences. Some shared their experiences of personal losses and assured him that time healed. Daniel went to his locker and felt Ibtisam coming up behind him. He recognized her perfume.

"Jalal?"

He turned to her with a half-smile. "Hello, *ukhti*."

She adjusted her head covering over some loose strands. "May she rest in peace."

"Thank you, *ukhti*."

"How are you?"

"I'm fine."

"I thought about you all the time," she said softly, lowering her eyes shyly. "I worried about you."

"*Merci*!" he thanked her. "You're a good woman."

She looked into his eyes. "I'm here for you, you know that, right?"

Daniel nodded. "Thank you!" He put his hand over his heart and bowed slightly.

"J-a-l-a-l!" a loud voice called him from the other side of the room. "My brother!"

Daniel looked over Ibtisam's shoulder. Rashid was walking toward him quickly, a big smile on his face. The two hugged and exchanged three cheek kisses, inadvertently pushing her aside. "Allah give you strength," she said, and Daniel nodded at her in response, his arm around Rashid's neck.

"I'm so happy to see you, my brother." Rashid patted Daniel on the back. "I missed you. How are you?"

"Thanks, I missed you too. I missed everyone."

"I was afraid you weren't coming back to us."

"No way! Now it's even more important for me to be here. I'm in no hurry to go back to France. We'll talk later. Let's go up!"

Daniel put on his white coat and closed his locker. The two left the main building and walked up the path to their ward. On the way, a few other staff members stopped them to pay their respects. Being undercover as a Muslim gave Daniel the rare opportunity to see another side of those he'd considered his bitter enemy – an opportunity he'd never had before. He'd never operated so deeply and for so long within the Muslim community. The compassion they demonstrated wasn't surprising but not something he had necessarily expected. And yet, Daniel remained realistic. He'd seen enough of the often very ugly sides of the culture into which he was now trying to assimilate.

At the entrance, the two went their separate ways. Rashid went up to the second floor, and Daniel was interested in only one thing – a walk in the woods with Ibrahim to continue where they'd left off. But first, he had to visit each room, show interest, listen, and help whoever needed assistance. He walked down the long, cool corridors, stopping to exchange a few polite words with colleagues. Some of the patients looked at him as they always had, as if he hadn't been away at all, and others brightened when they saw him. As usual, he paid extra attention where it was needed. He came closer to Ibrahim's room, and with every step, his anticipation grew. Ibrahim's revelations had given him hope and strength while he was detained.

He finally entered the room. The fluorescent lights were turned off, and the window blinds were halfway down. The space heater stood in the corner of the room, the electric cable coiled behind it.

"Uncle Ibrahim," Daniel called quietly, lifting his hand to the body covered in a blue cotton blanket.

"Ahhhh." The back facing him stretched.

"Uncle Ibrahim! Wake up! How are you?"

The bed creaked under the man's efforts to sit up. He turned his head toward Daniel with a gap-toothed smile. "Ibrahim isn't here anymore." A man Daniel didn't know sat on the edge of the bed and put the cracked soles of his feet on the tiled floor.

"So where is he? Did he move to another room?"

The man stood up and swayed. Daniel hurried to help him sit back down on the bed.

"He's dead. May Allah have mercy on him."

Daniel's heart sank. "Dead?" he cried out, his hands on his head. "How? When?"

"Two days ago!" the man answered, lying back down and struggling with the thin blanket.

Daniel was devastated, about Ibrahim and the missed opportunity. "But... how? What happened to him?"

"I strangled him!" the stranger replied and turned his head.

Daniel's eyes widened.

"You bastard!" Daniel heard a voice behind him. "Get out of my bed!" Ibrahim leaned on Daniel with one hand, and with the other struck the man with his cane. "Get out!"

The strange man tried to get out of bed, crying, "I'll kill you! I'll strangle you tonight!"

Ibrahim kept whacking him. Daniel pulled himself together, sat Ibrahim down on the bed, and dragged the other man out of the room. He motioned to one of the aides to take him away and then went back into the old man's room and sat next to him on the bed.

"Did you see that?" Ibrahim asked and threw his cane on the floor.

"Yes," Daniel replied, patting him on the shoulder. "I also saw how strong you are. May Allah help you! It's over, he's gone. How are you?"

"Old," Ibrahim answered. "Everything hurts."

"Want to go for a walk outside? Get some fresh air and calm down."

Daniel helped Ibrahim stand and supported him while he straightened his Golani Brigade baseball cap. He picked up Ibrahim's cane, handed it to him, then guided him out of the room with a hand on his elbow.

Outside, the gardener was disturbing the peaceful surroundings. Daniel stopped Ibrahim in the stone-paved courtyard to wait until the gardener moved away and the cloud of dust settled. Ibtisam walked past them, her eyes smiling at Daniel.

"Let's go to the woods," Daniel suggested.

"It's very hot outside."

"We'll sit in the shade," Daniel tried to convince him. "You love sitting on the bench there."

"Let's go," Ibrahim complied.

"Just a minute," Daniel sat Ibrahim down on a gray plastic chair and ran inside to get a bottle of cold water. Ibrahim stood up by himself, and Daniel hurried to support him. Walking made him short of breath, so they remained silent. Daniel led the elderly man to the same bench they had sat on before, hoping that this time too, he'd bring up memories of his childhood. Ibrahim sat down with a heavy sigh.

"Here," Daniel handed him the water. "Drink."

The old man took the bottle with a shaking hand and brought it to his mouth. Daniel watched the thin, wrinkled skin of his throat move as he sipped.

"They said your mother died. May she rest in peace." Ibrahim gave him the bottle and scratched his white stubble. "I thought you weren't coming back."

"Bless you, Uncle Ibrahim."

"Was she sick?"

"Yes."

"You're lucky, son."

"Lucky?"

"I don't remember my mother or my father. I hardly even remember my brother who brought me here. I don't have anyone in this world."

Daniel felt his heart squeeze. "I must be lucky," he murmured, and his thoughts wandered to his real parents, who he'd left in France. "You know," he went back to his cover story, "my father also died when I was young."

"And you have brothers? Sisters?"

"My mother remarried, and I have siblings from another father, but no one cared about me there. Not even my mother."

"Some orphans have parents that are still alive," Ibrahim sighed and sat silently. His eyes looked around. Suddenly he tried to bend down to the ground.

"This?" Daniel asked, handing him a dry pinecone.

The old man nodded, and just like last time, he picked at the scales until they fell off.

"You like doing that, don't you, Uncle Ibrahim?"

"Yes, I always did." The man looked happy. "Do you have children, Jalal?"

"No. I'm not married."

"You know," Ibrahim sighed, "that's what hurts me most. That I didn't marry and don't have children to love me. This place," he looked from side to side, "is my entire world."

Ibrahim's words hit a nerve. They immediately sent Daniel's thoughts to Yael and the pregnancy he had asked her to terminate. For a split second, he imagined how his life would have been if they had continued their course. He forced himself back to the matter at hand. "Do you remember telling me about the tunnel you found here many years ago?"

"Really?" Ibrahim furrowed his brow. "I told you?"

"Yes! About Zaki, who caught you, and the director..."

"Yes, yes, Zaki." Ibrahim turned his gaze into the woods, a dreamy look on his face.

"Where is it?" Daniel asked casually. "Could you show me?"

Ibrahim laughed. "Who knows, son? Maybe here, maybe there. Everything's changed... new buildings. Maybe they built over it. It was a long, long time ago." Ibrahim swept his hand through the air as he spoke.

Daniel considered his next steps. "Too bad. I'd love for you to see it again."

"I see it," the old man said, his eyelids closing slowly, "in my head."

"Tell me what you see."

"Looong, looong tunnels," Ibrahim dragged out the words, "that you could stand in. Very high!"

"And the walls were stone?"

Ibrahim shook his head and clucked. "Not stone. Smooth, carved from the rock."

Daniel's excitement ramped up. "What else?"

"It was fun inside. Cool. On a hot day like today, we'd want to sit there."

Daniel smiled. "And it was deep down in the ground?"

"Not so deep." The old man opened his eyes. "You'd enter through the opening in the ground, five, maybe ten feet down, and then it continued at the same height and branched off, many times."

"How did you get down there?"

"Stairs."

"Stairs? What stairs?"

"Stairs carved in the rock... you understand, right?"

As Ibrahim spoke, Daniel suddenly remembered a trip he'd taken years ago with his grandfather to the underground tunnels from the Bar-Kokhba period in Herodium. The description sounded similar. "And did you ever get lost?"

"Once," Ibrahim recalled, a look of fear on his face even now. "The flashlight stopped working. I couldn't find the way back. I felt along the walls for hours in the dark until I found my way out. I thought it was the end! Enough!" He threw what was left of the pinecone and rubbed his hands together.

Daniel handed him a new pinecone. "These tunnels, where did they lead to?"

Ibrahim shrugged; his shirt looked like it was hung on a thin wire hanger. "I didn't go into all of them. Some you could reach the end and that was it, nothing there. Sometimes a pile of stones."

"Jalal!" Daniel heard someone calling him and saw Rashid waving his hands and walking toward them. Ibrahim pointed at the bottle of water; Daniel twisted the cap off and handed it to him.

"What is it, Rashid?" he said, greeting the chubby, sweating man.

"It's hot as hell out here!" Rashid replied. "And summer hasn't even started. What made you come sit outside?"

"It's nice in the shade," Daniel said. "And there's a bit of a breeze."

"How are you Ibrahim?" Rashid asked.

"Come sit," he invited Rashid. "Listen to stories about tunnels I found here once," he boasted.

"What tunnels?" Rashid sat, looking pensive. "When did you find them?"

"Tell him, Jalal," Ibrahim said.

"I will," Daniel promised and winked at Rashid. "Come on. Let's get you back to your room. Rashid is right. It's too hot here."

Rashid and Daniel got up and supported Ibrahim as he stood. They led him slowly back to his room and then went back to the main building.

"What's with the tunnels?" Rashid asked again, showing interest.

"It's nothing," Daniel tried to deflect, "just the ramblings of an old man. Every time he goes on about something else. Today it was tunnels, tomorrow it'll be elephants, and the day after, whales."

Rashid looked troubled. "Okay," he said after a moment. The look on his face caught Daniel's attention. I touched on something, he thought.

They entered the staff room. Rashid went to the kitchenette and came back with two cups of fragrant espresso. They sat facing one another at a small table, and Daniel felt it coming – the interrogation by his curious friend. He knew that his first day back at the hospital would be devoted to tying up loose ends and was prepared for any possible question. Outwardly, Daniel remained aloof, detached, to prevent unwelcome interest. But from Rashid, he expected he wouldn't be able to keep his distance – because they were close and also because of Rashid's nature.

"How are you doing, my brother?"

"It's all in Allah's hands!"

"You told me once that you weren't close."

"She was my mother."

"Yes," Rashid sighed and took a sip. Clearly, he was thinking about his own mother. "Was she sick? I mean, were you expecting it?"

"She wasn't well," Daniel recited the changes to his cover story that circumstances had dictated, recalling the fine tuning he had done with Shlomo before his return to Bethlehem. "But I didn't think she'd have a heart attack."

"Allah protect us," Rashid murmured, rubbing his hands together. "How did they notify you? You must have been in shock."

Daniel sipped his espresso. "They came in the middle of the night with my landlord and knocked on my door. I was so stunned that I didn't even ask who they were. They said that they were connected to the French consulate or something. I packed a few things and went with them. They took me to Al-Quds, and I got a taxi to the Israeli airport. I took the first plane to France."

"Lucky there was room." Rashid played with his cup, moving the liquid from side to side.

"Yeah," Daniel replied and pulled out his cellphone before his curious friend asked any more questions. "Look," he held out his phone. There was a picture of Daniel standing beside a freshly dug grave. Rashid nodded and scrolled down. "That's my mother's husband," Daniel pointed to one of the people. "And this is at home, during the mourning period," he pointed at another picture. Rashid had no idea that before returning to Bethlehem, Daniel had gone to France for two days, went to the first Muslim funeral he could find and then visited the family, accompanied by a field agent. The pictures corroborated his cover story, as did the short video chat he'd had with Rashid on WhatsApp while standing in one of the immigrant neighborhoods just before he came back.

"You know," Rashid said, giving Daniel back his phone, "a couple of years ago they brought back a man who had lived in France for many years and buried him here in Bethlehem. They said that most of the Muslims in France prefer to be buried in the homeland."

That was the kind of detail that an undercover field agent had to know, and Daniel was well-versed on the topic. "True," he affirmed, "most families send the bodies to the homeland. You know, the French worship secularism. The authorities don't establish cemeteries for every religion. Everyone is buried in the same cemetery."

"You don't say!" Rashid responded in surprise, stroking his sparse beard. "Muslims next to Christians? Together?"

"More or less. But now there are areas within the cemeteries where the Muslims are buried, so you know..."

"That's awful!" Rashid said, "So how do the Muslims there accept that? What about the burial rites – the position of the body, the headstones... is that even possible?"

"Like I said, it's not the paradise you think it is. It's France, and France belongs to the French people, not the immigrants."

Rashid changed the subject. "Tell me, didn't Israeli intelligence harass you at their airport?"

Daniel tensed. "No. Why should they?"

"Why!?" Rashid laughed. "Because you're Muslim and you were here in Palestine!"

"Let them go to hell!" Daniel waved his hand. "I have French citizenship! They asked questions, I went through the security check, and that was it. Same as for everyone else."

"They only harass Muslims," Rashid insisted.

"Listen, screw them, but I can tell you – it's much worse in France."

"What? The security checks on Muslims?"

"On everyone! They don't care who or what you are, Muslim or not. They don't kid around. They're afraid someone will blow up their planes."

Rashid's phone rang, to Daniel's relief. He took their cups to the kitchenette. From the snatches of conversation he heard in the background, he knew something had happened.

"What happened?" he asked Rashid, who came back looking irritated.

"They arrested my cousin."

"Who? Israel?"

"No. Those sons of whores from the Palestinian Authority! Every few months, they arrest him." Rashid pounded the table, his face twisted in loathing.

"At least it wasn't the Israelis," Daniel said.

Rashid gave a forced laugh and stood up. "You're naïve, Jalal. I wish it were the Israelis. They have laws. Here? They do whatever they want. And he's Hamas, supposedly, so anything goes."

"So now what?"

"Damn them! Like always, some of us from the family will go, threaten them, you know... and bring him home."

"May Allah help you."

"The problem is I'm on shift tonight."

Daniel didn't hesitate to take advantage of the opportunity; he had enough to do there that night. "No problem, go ahead. I'll take your shift."

"Seriously?" Rashid's face softened.

"Sure, no problem. Go take care of things."

2

Daniel was busy with routine tasks for the rest of the day, impatient for night to come. The late afternoon brought a cool breeze with the smell of pine, and the day's heat dissipated. The day shift staff hurried home, and long shadows stretched out until they disappeared with the last of the light. The hospital was shrouded in dark silence, and the outdoor lighting came on. On Daniel's ward, the patients finished their evening meal and were escorted to their rooms.

Daniel visited Ibrahim. The elderly man lay on his back, staring at the ceiling. His yellowed, cracked toes peeked out from under the blanket, which covered half his body.

"Uncle Ibrahim," Daniel said softly, "your blanket." He tucked him in.

Ibrahim smiled. "Thank you, Jalal."

Daniel took a chocolate bar from his coat pocket and handed it to Ibrahim. "Here, I brought it for you from France."

Ibrahim's eyes filled with tears. "May Allah protect you, Jalal. You're a good man."

Daniel sat on the chair next to him, his emotions stirring. The feelings he'd developed for Ibrahim were genuine. His heart sank at the thought of his tragic life, an elderly man essentially with the spirit of a child.

"Can you break off a piece for me?" Ibrahim asked.

Daniel tore open the fancy package and peeled off the foil wrapping. "Here you go." He held out two squares. "It's got cherry cream filling."

The old man took the chocolate and let it melt in his mouth, "Allah!"

"You like it?" Daniel asked eagerly.

"Jalal," Ibrahim's voice trembled, "This is the first time in my life that someone brought me a present... something especially for me."

Daniel patted Ibrahim's hand, choking up. The man's words saddened him. "It's never too late, Uncle Ibrahim. I'll bring you a chocolate bar every day."

Ibrahim coughed and tried to get up. "For now, give me another piece," and he held out his hand.

"It's all yours!"

Daniel helped Ibrahim sit up. Ibrahim broke the rest of the chocolate in two and gave Daniel half.

"Just one square," Daniel said. He watched the old man enjoy the treat.

When he was done, Ibrahim lay back down, and Daniel covered him.

"Good night."

"Wait," Ibrahim said, "sit with me just a little longer."

"Gladly."

Daniel sat back down, and Ibrahim closed his eyes. They were both silent. Daniel took his phone out of his pants pocket and started scrolling.

"You know," Ibrahim said after a few minutes, "the tunnel I told you about..."

Daniel tensed. "Yes?"

"When they came to dig there, the people looking for old things..."

Daniel sat up. "Yes, the archaeologists."

"They took a picture of me for the newspaper, next to the opening in the ground that I found... I just remembered."

Daniel felt overwhelmed. He immediately realized the potential of this discovery. "Did you keep the paper?"

"No. I don't have it. I wish."

Merde, he cursed silently. "And do you remember the name of the newspaper?"

"It was a newspaper, I don't know."

Daniel was disappointed. His brain started running through the options of checking archives from that time. "Go to sleep, Uncle Ibrahim." He got up to go. When he was at the doorway, Ibrahim turned to him.

"The director has that picture."

"What? Which director?"

"Our director, here. He showed it to me some time ago... he has a kind of book in his office with articles about the hospital."

Daniel's hopes rose again. A new mission had been added to the list for tonight. "Okay, Uncle Ibrahim. Good night."

Daniel passed a small storage room on his way out and grabbed a pair of latex gloves from the cabinet. He stuffed them in his pocket. Then he stuck his head around the door of the break room to say that he was going out to get some fresh air and would be right back. His fellow worker nodded. Daniel left, ran down the stone stairs at the entrance and walked down the path to the main building. A single car was parked in the lot. Two workers stood outside, one of them smoking a cigarette.

"Good evening," Daniel said with a nod. He entered the building. Red numerals on the digital clock on the lobby wall showed the time: 20:20. The large ceiling fans whispered in the empty corridors. He slowed down as he passed the reception desk. The shift supervisor was sitting behind the tall plexiglass divider, watching a soccer game on TV. On the desk was a plastic container of cookies. Homemade, Daniel recalled the man saying that morning when he offered some to the rest of the staff.

He immediately decided on his next step. He picked up the pace and entered the staff room. No one was there. He went to his locker, took a flash drive from his bag, and put it in his pocket. Then he turned toward the kitchenette, straight to the espresso machine. The power button flashed, and the machine heated the water while Daniel searched the drawers and cabinets for the supply of coffee. He selected a capsule, and the machine gurgled and filled the room with the aroma of freshly brewed coffee. He took his cup and walked back to reception.

"Good evening," he said to the man behind the desk, lifting his cup to make sure he would see it.

"Good evening," the man replied as Daniel appeared to be leaving the building. "Wait a minute!"

Daniel turned around and saw the man holding the container of cookies. Excellent, he took the bait.

"Please, take one," he offered, tipping the container so Daniel could see its contents.

"I love these!" Daniel replied enthusiastically and entered through the side door. He sat next to his colleague.

"Homemade," the man repeated.

Daniel helped himself and took a bite. "Delicious!" he complimented. "Who made them?"

"My wife," the supervisor said proudly.

"These are excellent!"

"Thank you! You're the volunteer from France, right?"

"Jalal." Daniel shook the man's hand. He usually worked in a different ward, and even though they'd seen each other around, they had never talked. "It's nice to meet you," he added.

The man introduced himself and after they exchanged a few words said, "I haven't seen you for a while. I thought you'd left us."

"I was away for two weeks; I just got back yesterday. My mother passed away. I went back to France for a while."

"May she rest in peace!" the man responded, adding, "My condolences."

Daniel thanked him and maneuvered the conversation to serve his purpose. "Tell me, how many cameras do you have to monitor? There are so many on the screen; how do you do it?"

"You mean that?" the man said dismissively. "There are at least thirty cameras. Who's watching them? There's a game on! The screen shows sixteen cameras at once and switches every few seconds. You can't really monitor them. It's just protocol."

"You know, I used to work security jobs in France." Daniel's cover story had elements of the familiar. "I hated the cameras! To spend hours of your shift staring at a screen with all those windows. I totally understand!"

"And besides," the shift supervisor said, "I'm not worried. If something happens, the people on duty in the ward will call."

"You're right," Daniel led the conversation, "Just watch the other cameras, where there's no one on duty. It's more efficient." He took a sip of coffee and helped himself to another cookie.

"But there are only cameras where there are patients."

"Really? No cameras in this building? Or outside, on the paths and in the courtyard?"

"None. What for? There's a guard at the gate. No one can come in except during visiting hours. And between us, who's going to come to a psychiatric hospital at night?"

Out of the corner of his eye, Daniel followed what was happening on screen. He'd never noticed cameras in the offices, but he knew that didn't mean there weren't any. Now he was almost certain that he didn't see any part of the administration building or its exterior on the screen – only the corridors and public spaces on the wards. Excellent!

Daniel stood, "Hey, it was a pleasure getting to know you and I don't want to be a bother. Tell your wife that the cookies were delicious!" He shook the man's hand, left the building, and sat on a bench near a tractor wheel that had been repurposed into a planter. Across from him, a steel gate blocked cars and people from entering. Cats yowled from the direction of the garbage cans. Daniel looked up at the sky and took deep breaths. He'd had an intensive and exhausting two weeks: the interrogation, the quick trip to France, the return to Bethlehem and the hospital, the stress and anticipation of what was to come.

The silence was broken by loud explosions that made him jump. It was an impressive display of fireworks in the sky not far away. Daniel watched.

"Half-time," he heard the voice of the supervisor, who had come outside and stood next to him. "What's going on? What's all that noise?"

"Must be a wedding," Daniel replied and escaped into the building, taking advantage of the moment while the other man was enjoying the view.

He turned to the offices, putting his phone on silent. The lights in the corridor were on, and some of the doors of the dark, empty offices were open. He stopped at the director's office and put his ear to the door for a few seconds. The fireworks had stopped. When he didn't hear anything, he took the gloves out of his coat pocket, put them on quickly, and gently tried the door. It wasn't locked.

Daniel entered the office and shut the door. There was a key on the inside of the lock. He locked the door, and when his eyes adjusted to the dark, he walked in, taking careful steps. It wasn't completely dark – the glow of an outdoor light came through the only window. The fireworks started up again. The colors illuminated the image of Yasser Arafat on the wall to the right of the window.

Although locating the folder with the articles interested Daniel the most, he first took care of the other tasks that he could only complete covertly. At the center of the room was a large wooden desk, with another table attached at the head to create a T-shape. Writing implements were organized on a glass desk pad next to a sign written in Arabic – Director. Daniel went to the desk, sat in the director's chair and shut off the speakers and screen. He covered the flashing light of the desktop computer with his white work coat, making a tent that covered the flat screen and his head. He made sure that there were no openings on the sides and only then turned the screen back on and moved the mouse. The computer asked for a password. Daniel carefully shifted out from under the improvised tent cover, leaving the coat over the screen, and searched the desk. He tried under the glass, then the drawers. When he opened the first one, he got a strong whiff of paint and lacquer from the new desk. The director was meticulous; the drawers were extremely organized, and Daniel made an effort not to move anything out of place. A small notepad caught his attention. He opened it and smiled. Bingo – a list of passwords. Every page had a heading in precise handwriting, and underneath, the relevant password and password history – the old ones were crossed out. Daniel stuck his head back under the tent and entered the password.

The screen unlocked, showing the desktop. Daniel pulled the USB device out of his pocket, loaded with the malware he'd been directed to download to the director's computer, and plugged it in. The cursor turned into a small shifting hourglass. While the device went to work, Daniel used an app on his cellphone to document all the passwords – for emails, bank accounts, patient files, and more. Every picture he took was sent directly to the Shabak without leaving a trace. When he finished, he got out from under the tent and opened the middle drawer.

The doorknob of the office suddenly rattled. Someone was trying to get in. Daniel froze, glanced at the door, returned the notepad to its place, and closed the drawer. There was a second and third try, but the locked door didn't open. After a few seconds of silence, he heard the wheels squeaking and a woman humming a popular song. The cleaning lady, he realized immediately. *Merde*! He hadn't felt like this in a long time – the exhilaration, heart pounding loudly in fear of getting caught. The feeling was addictive. In such situations, Daniel always kept his cool. He got up and slowly walked to the door and felt to make sure the key hadn't fallen out. He could only hope that she had moved on to another office. He went back to the computer and looked at the device – the indicator light was finally green. "Excellent!" he whispered and removed the flash drive. Underneath his tent, he put the computer back on standby, waited for the screen to turn off, and then removed the coat.

He heard the cleaning lady's humming again and calculated that she was just a few feet away. Her singing got louder as she came closer. The doorknob turned again. Daniel broke out in a cold sweat. The door wouldn't open, and she kept trying her luck. She uttered a curse at the director and moved away. Daniel tried to think of a way out. The window had bars across it, otherwise, he could have dropped down into the yard. He had no choice; she'd just give up after a while. Ninety percent of the time is spent waiting, a phrase he hadn't thought of in a long time. He thought about looking for the article but quickly dismissed it. Better not tempt fate, he decided without hesitation. He hadn't seen anything in the drawers or around him. There were two shelves in the room with knickknacks on them – some patient artwork, and next to them a woven tapestry, like a small rug in some dark color. Maybe red.

Maybe Ibrahim was just imagining things and it would be a shame to take a risk, he thought, and started to put his coat back on. In a careless move as he put his arm through the sleeve, his fist hit a small clay vase on the shelf. The vase rolled across the shelf and fell off. Daniel caught it at the last second. He put it back and felt the blood resume flowing in his veins. Idiot! He was angry at himself and released a weak sigh of relief. He sat on the floor by the door and listened. While he was waiting for the opportune moment to leave, he stared at the light coming in from the gap under the door. His exhilaration dissipated; it never lasted long, reaching a peak and then quickly crashing.

Daniel put his ear to the door; he heard the squeaky wheels and the sound of another door opening, and then what he thought were chairs being dragged in a room nearby. He stood, slowly turned the key, opened the door, and peeked out. The coast was clear. The cleaning cart stood to his left at the entrance to the office next door. He snuck out, closed the door, and quickly removed the gloves. His heart was thudding. He looked to the right down the long hallway and thought that if he went that way, the cleaning lady might see him, and when she realized the room was now open – she'd put two and two together. So, he decided to walk backward, facing the offices.

As he feared, the cart moved, and the cleaning lady appeared. He was already thirty feet from the director's office. In a split-second decision, Daniel switched directions and walked toward her.

"Hello there!" he waved at the elderly woman with a head covering.

She waved back and looked at him as he walked up to her.

"I spilled coffee all over the kitchen," he told her sheepishly, "Can I have a rag to clean it up?"

"It's okay," she replied, "I'll go clean it."

"No!" he insisted and pulled a rag from the cart. "I made the mess, I'll clean it up. You have enough work."

"Bless you, son," she said as he took off. "Just leave it there."

Daniel nodded, then walked away around the corner and out of her sight. The supervisor was still absorbed in the game. Daniel took a circular route and walked up as if he was coming in from outside. He hid the rag when he passed by, but the man was totally immersed. Daniel continued to the staff kitchenette, where he set the scene for the accident, washed the rag, and left it on the counter by the sink.

Filled with a sense of satisfaction, he went back to the ward, relieved his colleague so he could take a break and went on a routine round of the rooms. He returned to the break room, sat on the sofa, and tried to stay alert while watching TV.

3

The next day, after the patients had finished eating breakfast, Daniel walked out of the building. It was a lovely day, and the supervisor had decided to do the shift handover outdoors. He saw Rashid walking up the footpath, breathing heavily.

"That steep path will be the end of me!" Rashid complained when he came up to Daniel.

"The food you eat will be the end of you," Daniel commented, slapping Rashid on the back, "walking up the hill can only be good for you."

"One of those club cars like maintenance uses would be good," Rashid huffed.

"So, how's your cousin? Did you manage to get him released?"

"Motherfucking bastards!" Rashid spat on the ground.

"Shhh..." Daniel hissed.

"They have nerve... But wait and see what happens if they don't release him in a day or two."

"Allah help you," Daniel commiserated.

"Thanks for taking my shift!" Rashid swatted Daniel's arm, "I know I can count on you."

They stopped talking and listened to the supervisor brief them before their shift changed. When he was done, they went their separate ways – Rashid to the ward and Daniel to run some errands before he went back to his apartment to rest. In the parking lot adjacent to the administration building, he saw the hospital director talking to his second in command. Daniel walked past them, giving a slight nod.

"Just a minute, Jalal!" the director called out. "I'd like a few words with you."

"Of course." Daniel's heart skipped a beat. Possible scenarios flashed through his head.

"How are you doing, Jalal?" the director said, straightening his red-striped tie.

"Praise be to Allah, doctor," Daniel responded politely.

"May she rest in peace." The doctor offered his condolences, clasping his hands.

"Thank you, sir."

"We were all worried about you, and I, personally, appreciate that you came back to us so quickly."

"Thank you!" Daniel replied with a short bow, his hand to his chest. "I love this place and the people. Working here is important to me."

"May God give you strength!" the director added. "And you know – my door is always open. I mean it!"

"*Shukran!*" Daniel thanked him with a smile. His nighttime visit to the director's office flashed through his mind. "There is something… Ibrahim Ja'far, he told me you once showed him a newspaper article about him."

"Yes, I did."

"It does him good to talk about those days," Daniel explained, "and I promised him I'd read the article. I don't want to disappoint him."

"Of course, no problem! I'm going up to do ward rounds, but you can ask my secretary for the media folder. She'll give it to you."

"I appreciate it, sir. It will make Ibrahim happy!"

"Yes... such a sad story..." the director said, his expression unreadable. "Goodbye, Jalal."

"Good morning, doctor!" Rashid suddenly appeared.

The director shook Daniel's hand and walked away without acknowledging Rashid.

"Go to hell!" Rashid grumbled. "I can't stand him... those arrogant Christians think they're better than everyone else!"

"That's nothing, you don't know what real arrogance is. Come to France to see how they look at us there."

"What do you mean?"

"They stare at you!" Daniel replied. "Look at you as if you're an animal. Afraid of you."

"I don't believe that. I wish I could leave here," Rashid complained. "In Europe, I'd let everyone walk all over me! No problem!"

Daniel had often heard different versions of that wish during his time at the hospital in Bethlehem. The same with his Israeli friends. People were all the same, he thought, in the end, they'd always think the grass was greener on the other side.

"It only seems that way to you," he told Rashid. "Everything looks rosy from here, but it isn't really. You'd just feel lost, like you were invisible."

"It can't be that bad," said Rashid as he stroked his short beard.

"How would you keep your identity? What language would you speak? What about the weather in Europe, it's so different from here... and that's just for starters."

"And you think it's better for me here?"

"You have a home, a job, close family nearby, your native language. You live where you were born. What are you talking about?"

"All that is true as long as I'm in Bethlehem. But who can leave? We're stuck here, blocked in all directions. And anyway, if that's the case, why did you live there?"

Daniel didn't want to get into a political discussion and have to navigate the potential minefield. "Rashid, my friend, I moved there as a child with my parents. I grew up as a French citizen, and even so I never felt at home there. Can you imagine that? True, it's not ideal here, and all I'm saying is that Europe isn't a paradise either. You'd hang around with different kinds of brothers, each with baggage from where they came from. You might not even be able to communicate with them. Many don't speak Arabic, and the only thing you have in common with them is that you're Muslims. Nothing else matters – being Palestinian, nothing. I think you'd feel suffocated there more than you do here."

Rashid winked at him, "Tell that to Ibtisam, maybe she'll back off with those dreams of hers."

"I don't think it will help," Daniel said, "Bottom line, at least here you're not a foreigner. Watch it," he pushed Rashid aside; a large laundry cart was barreling toward them, the staff member from housekeeping barely able to control it. They moved out of the way under a cypress tree.

"Listen," Rashid started after a short silence, "It wouldn't hurt to change my environment for a year or two, expand my horizons a little."

"That's something else entirely," Daniel agreed. "Find somewhere you can volunteer like I did."

"Okay, man, I've got to go back to my locker, I left my cellphone there. See you later."

Rashid hurried into the building and Daniel followed him. He turned right to the administration offices. The director's door was wide open. His secretary sat behind her desk in the outer office, talking on the phone. Daniel waited for her to finish.

"Hello," he said when she was finished, "I spoke with the doctor, he told me to ask you for the media folder."

"Of course," she got up and turned toward the director's office, "Come in."

Daniel entered the room, trying to guess whether the cleaning lady had finally gotten in. He couldn't decide, and watched the woman, curious to see where the folder was.

She went straight to the red tapestry on the wall and pulled it aside. To Daniel's surprise, it covered a niche in the stone wall. The bottom of the tapestry had woven fringes with little bells hanging from them that tinkled softly. Lucky he hadn't moved the tapestry, he thought.

Inside the niche were glass shelves with some books and a thick album. The secretary pulled out the album and handed it to Daniel. He eagerly opened it, and she watched as he carefully rifled through the newspaper articles, each one protected by a thin plastic sleeve. When he found the page he was looking for, he felt a rush. There was a young Ibrahim, standing tall and proud next to three men in the woods. Behind them, the camera had caught details that he wanted to examine. Despite the many years that had passed, the newspaper clipping was well preserved. Another smaller picture showed the opening in the ground by their feet.

"Can you make me a copy of this?" he asked the woman.

"Certainly." She took the album, and they left the office. "This is Ibrahim, right? We showed this to him not long ago. He remembered seeing this once, ages ago and got very emotional."

"Yes," Daniel affirmed.

She went to the copy machine and centered the page on the glass plate.

"If it's no bother," Daniel stopped her, needing a high-quality image, "it's better to scan it. I want Ibrahim to see the picture in high resolution on my phone."

She made a sour face and took the album to the printer on her desk, "Where should I send it?"

Daniel gave her Jalal's email; a minute later, the photo was safely stored on his phone.

4

That afternoon, Daniel opened his eyes after a few hours' sleep, his body heavy, almost paralyzed. He lay still, eyes half closed as if hypnotized, following floating dust particles in the beam of sunlight coming in through the window. Finally gathering strength, he sat up for a few more minutes, feeling the blood coursing through his body and the puffiness in his face gradually dwindling. He stretched a long arm out to the small nightstand on the right side of the bed to check the time on his wristwatch. Twenty to five. The last few days had been packed and exhausting and, together with an almost sleepless night shift, had done him in.

Daniel got out of bed, opened the window and shutters wide. The afternoon breeze flowed in, refreshing the stale air. He stuck his head out the window, and the last orange rays of sun glinted on his face. The sounds of horns honking rose from the busy street three floors below. His stomach growled, and his hunger intensified with the smell of grilled meat from the shawarma stand downstairs. I need a shower, he thought. Then downstairs for a pita stuffed with spicy meat, back to the apartment for coffee and to organize his thoughts – and at night, communication with the command post.

The high-pressure spray in the shower invigorated him. In the background, his cellphone rang. He stayed in the shower, wondering who it could be. The phone started ringing again. He got out, dried off, and walked naked into the room. Another ring.

"What's up with you?" Rashid barked at him.

"I was in the shower. I went to sleep as soon as I got home after my shift."

"So, you're at home! Great! Get dressed, I'm down here waiting for you."

This wasn't the first time Rashid had invited Daniel out on the town with him, and the excuses were wearing thin. "Join me for shawarma downstairs," Daniel suggested, "I was just about to get something to eat."

"No shawarma," Rashid shouted. "My mother invited you over for dinner. Come on! Get down here!"

No choice, Daniel thought. "How can I say no to your mother?"

Five minutes later they were in Rashid's new car, a dark blue Mitsubishi Lancer that had already gone through several owners but was well-maintained. The sharp smell of artificial cherry irritated Daniel's nostrils. Red plastic prayer beads hung on the rearview mirror, and a clean, green velvet mat lay on the dashboard.

"Congrats on the car!"

"Allah bless you," Rashid thanked him. "Finally, after two months you've found the time!"

"I don't want to be a bother," Daniel said in defense, slamming the car door shut. He reminded himself not to buckle up like he usually did automatically.

"It's no bother. My mother will be thrilled. Believe me, you've never eaten *maqluba* like hers!"

Daniel smiled and thought about his own mother's *couscous*. The local radio station was playing a rhythmic Arabic song, and they both listened without saying much. Rashid navigated the narrow streets carefully, avoiding the potholes.

"Are the streets in Paris bad too?"

"There are roads with potholes everywhere. Not just in Bethlehem."

"Those bastards from the municipality – this city gets tons of money in donations, and where does it all go?"

"Where does it go?" Daniel asked.

"Take a look at where they live, you'll see!"

They heard something hit the back of the car. Rashid hit the brakes and opened the window. "Hey kid, come here!" he yelled at a ten-year-old boy holding a soccer ball. Some other kids stood behind him. "Don't you have eyes?"

"I do! Do you?" the boy jeered, pointing at Rashid's glasses. The punks behind him burst out laughing and ran off to the alleys as Rashid got out of the car to check for damage.

"Bastard," Rashid cursed at the boy. "Did you see that?" he turned toward Daniel, who was cracking up, "I've barely had the car for two days…"

Rashid got back into the driver's seat and a little further down the street, parked his car in front of a four-story building on the corner. Daniel looked up and saw that the windows on the third floor were sealed shut, and the fourth floor was under construction.

Rashid sighed. "That was my brother's apartment, may he rest in peace!" he offered without being asked.

Daniel nodded soberly and didn't say a word. Demolishing terrorists' homes or sealing them was nothing new to him, and when he served in Duvdevan, he'd participated in such missions more than once.

They entered the building and climbed the stairs. Rashid opened a white door on the first floor and announced their arrival – so that the women of the house would know that a stranger had arrived and preserve their modesty. The smell of food filled the air. Rashid's father, an old man with slumped shoulders and a head of thick white hair, came out from one of the rooms.

"*Ahlan wa sahlan!*" he greeted them, "Welcome!"

"Thank you!" Daniel shook the old man's hand.

"Please, come in." Rashid's father gestured with a trembling hand and the two followed him.

Rashid's home was crammed and garish; heavy drapes, hand-carved wooden armchairs upholstered with embroidered velvet, old-fashioned lampshades, pictures, knickknacks, everything in warm colors – even the walls – however, everything was clean and tidy. They entered the *diwan*, a traditional Arabic living room with low sofas and mattresses on overlapping carpets that covered the entire tile floor. One wall showed an enormous picture of the Al-Aqsa Mosque, and the others had pictures of the family patriarchs. One wall was dedicated to portraits of the *shaheed* – the martyr, Rashid's brother. Daniel gave them a quick glance.

"May Allah give you strength!" Rashid's father offered Daniel his condolences over the death of his fictional mother. "May she rest in peace!"

"May Allah grant you long life," Daniel responded, offering his condolences on the death of the shaheed.

While they exchanged courtesies, Rashid's mother and sister entered with a pot of tea and a tray filled to overflowing with refreshments. The stocky mother was old, but younger than her husband. She wore thick glasses, a long robe, and a hijab. Rashid's sister also covered her head with a hijab, but she wore makeup and a long tunic over tight jeans. Daniel greeted the mother and thanked her for inviting him. The women left the room. Rashid poured tea into small glasses and served Daniel and his father.

"So, what's with your cousin?" Daniel asked Rashid. "When will he be released?"

"Idiot!" Rashid's father spat out, waving his hand in dismissal.

Daniel didn't understand. He looked at Rashid.

"Enough, papa!" Rashid raised his hand. "Don't decide what to do for others."

"You're still children! You don't understand anything!" the old man fumed.

"Okay, children..." Rashid nodded and then turned to Daniel and said quietly, "Ever since my brother was killed he's been like this... angry at the 'resistance.'"

"Rashid told me about you, Jalal," the old man said. "I wish our young people would take an example from people like you and help others instead of making trouble."

"Thank you. May Allah give you strength!" Daniel replied. He took a handful of peanuts from the tray. "Your young people are fine. There are all kinds, just like everywhere else."

"Papa!" Rashid winked at Daniel, "What do you think about me moving to France too? Jalal will help me get settled there."

"You want to kill your mother?" his father growled. "Isn't it enough that your brother's gone? You too?"

"He has no sense of humor," Rashid whispered to Daniel. "I love getting him riled up..."

While he was talking, they heard a knock at the door and men's voices. A moment later, they heard women's cries of joy. Rashid raised his eyebrows, got up and went out to the hallway. Daniel and the old man remained in the living room. They heard slaps on the back and greetings. Rashid came back with a few smiling young men. Daniel stood up, and Rashid's father gave them a sullen look. One of the men, who was sporting a beard, came up to him.

"*As-salaam alaikum*, uncle!" he said, and kissed his head.

"*Wa alaikum salaam,*" the old man replied unhappily and added, "you idiot!"

"Why, uncle, why?" the bearded man sat on one of the mattresses and smiled sheepishly. Daniel looked at him. He had a baby face and looked like he was in his twenties.

"Why?" the old man stared at him with tired-looking brown eyes. "Hah!" He nodded his head toward the pictures of his son the shaheed. "You want that my brother cries over you his whole life?"

"Enough, papa! Don't ruin the atmosphere," Rashid begged, sitting between Daniel and his cousin. "Let's be joyful now that he's been released."

Three other men, two of them also bearded, greeted Rashid's father and took their places on the mattresses.

"Nice to meet you," Rashid's cousin shook Daniel's hand, "Toufik."

"Jalal," Daniel replied, on edge. Celebrating the release of a Hamas operative wasn't in his plans for the evening.

The others, sitting further away, introduced themselves and exchanged greetings with Daniel from across the room.

Rashid's mother came in trilling cries of joy. She carried a huge serving dish with the traditional *maqluba* upside-down meat and rice dish, which looked like a sculpted tower. "You came just in time, good that I made a big pot!"

Daniel stared in amazement; a top layer of roasted drumsticks, then thick slices of fried eggplant and potatoes, tomatoes, onions and herbs were piled on top of a hill of yellow rice, fragrant with Middle Eastern spices.

"What are you so happy about?" the old man said irritably, "you should be giving him a good slap on the face!"

"You should be ashamed of yourself," the woman snapped. She put the dish on the low table in the center of the room.

Rashid's sister carried another tray with two pitchers of homemade lemonade, plates, glasses, and cutlery. She giggled at her father's words.

"Bless you," the men praised.

"Did you hear what your son just said?" Rashid's father asked his wife. "He wants to move to France!"

Rashid sighed and shook his head.

"Absolutely not!" his mother scowled, "Unless he wants to kill me! If you go, who will I have left?"

"You have four daughters here!" Rashid replied. He and his cousin pulled the table closer to the guests.

His mother glared at him and left the room with her daughter.

"Really, Rashid?" Toufik asked.

"No! But say it was true. Why not? Why the faces?" Rashid filled a plate for his father, then served himself and sat down.

"Because what exactly do you think you'll find there?" his cousin asked, filling his own plate.

"Tell him, Jalal. What would I find there?"

Daniel hesitated a few seconds before responding, "I don't know, Rashid," he shrugged. "People usually look for what they think they don't have. What don't you have here?"

Everyone in the room turned to Rashid, who had a serious expression on his face. He was silent for a few seconds before he replied. "I don't have freedom. I don't have opportunities in life. Hope..."

Daniel listened as he continued eating. This kind of conversation could quickly go downhill. He wasn't afraid that someone would be suspicious of his real identity, but he wanted to remain in the gray area, not voicing strong opinions – exactly the opposite of his real personality. "And over there, you'll have those things?" he asked finally when he felt their gaze on him, waiting for his response.

"I think so, yes. Will anyone tell me where I can or can't go? Will anyone tell me if I can only move within the city? Will anyone make my life difficult just because I want to marry a girl who lives a few miles away – like in Israel, for example? What I mean is – will anyone determine for me how I can live in my own country?"

Daniel weighed his response. He preferred to talk about France than get into a discussion on the Israeli-Palestinian conflict. "You might not encounter those problems there, but you will definitely have to deal with other issues."

"Like what?" Toufik asked.

"Yesterday, I told Rashid that in France they bury everyone in the same cemetery. They refuse to have separate cemeteries for each religion."

"Seriously?" Toufik spoke with a mouth full of rice, his eyes showing astonishment.

"In some places," Daniel continued, "women are not allowed to cover their heads with a hijab or burka. Boys who want to pray on school grounds – it's forbidden. Even the muezzin is forbidden."

"We've heard about that," one of the bearded men said.

"But how is that possible?" Toufik was clearly getting worked up. "What right do they have? They need to be taught a lesson over in Europe!"

Daniel looked at Rashid's father, who was shifting his legs impatiently and finally said, "I told you that you were an idiot! What do you care about what's happening in France? What does it have to do with you? It's their country so let them do what they want! They don't owe Muslims anything!"

"Uncle," Toufik said, "please stop. It hurts me when my brothers are insulted! Why are you so angry?"

The veins in the old man's forehead stood out. "What brothers are you talking about? The Muslims in Europe are your brothers?"

"Yes!" Toufik raised his voice. "All Muslims are brothers, and we need to help one another!"

"Children!" Rashid's father sighed. "That's what you are – children! You're brainwashed with nonsense and believe it instead of thinking for yourself. Your people in Hamas are hostile toward your PLO 'brothers' in Gaza. What are you doing about that?"

"The PLO is hostile to Hamas here on the West Bank," Toufik replied.

"Wonderful!" the old man laughed. "So now, what can you learn from that? I'll tell you: they're all scum! Whoever wants to lead fills the heads of you young people with garbage, and you believe them and fight one another so that they can steal the money for themselves!"

"Hey!" Rashid raised his voice. "Come on, let's eat in peace."

"Tell me, Jalal," Toufik asked, "How do you feel there, as a Muslim?"

Daniel ate slowly, giving himself time to think of a concise response, "We're not wanted there."

"Why? What do they have against us?" one of the men sitting on the mattress asked.

"I don't think they have a problem with Muslims," Daniel explained, "I mean the French, but I think that also other European countries don't either – after all, they took in our parents and grandparents. Their problem is with the young generation, those that were born there."

"That's interesting," Toufik commented, "specifically those born there?"

"Yes! Take me, for example. My parents moved to France with me when I was a baby," Daniel went back to his cover story. "As far as I'm concerned, I'm one hundred percent French; I went to school there, and French is my native language, not Arabic. I don't know a thing about Morocco... but they, the French, treat me like a foreigner. I'm not a troublemaker, but there are a lot of young men like me who feel discriminated against. They have no hope, so they start making trouble, become religious, and that's when the problems start."

"Being religious is a problem?" Toufik snapped.

"No," Daniel replied calmly, "But some take advantage of the young people to gain power for themselves. They call for Sharia law in Europe and don't hide it from the French, and now that there are also terrorist attacks, the French are afraid and don't differentiate – to them, every Muslim is a suspect. It affects all of us!"

"Exactly what I said!" Rashid's father interrupted. "They brainwash the young people who don't understand anything!"

"But they are being treated with disrespect, uncle!" Toufik argued, "Exactly like us!"

"Toufik," the old man softened his tone, "who treats you with disrespect?"

"The Israelis, of course. Who am I fighting against?"

"Our authorities also, right? An hour ago, you were under arrest!"

Toufik poured a glass of lemonade and didn't reply. Daniel listened to the conversation from the side and was happy not to be taking an active part in it.

"I'm an old man," Rashid's father continued, "and when I was young, I also fought and was arrested and humiliated. But I also lost my first-born son. I told him that he was an idiot, too! And I was right! He became a shaheed, and what then? That was it? The Jews left?"

Rashid elbowed Toufik.

Toufik got the hint. "So, Jalal. What do you suggest our Rashid do? Leave or stay?"

"He should live where his heart is," Daniel replied, and felt how right his answer was for him, too. "There he'll only have religion to hold on to, no national identity. He'll always feel like a foreigner."

"And you?" Toufik asked, "Where is your heart?"

Daniel's lips twitched. This whole scenario and conversation was bizarre – cover story and reality intertwined. "I'm still searching," he replied sincerely. "Once, I thought I found it, but things happened and then I wasn't sure anymore."

"Listen to me, all of you – get married and have children!" the old man said. "That's where you'll find your heart! And stop with all the nonsense!"

"God willing!" Rashid concurred and offered everyone another portion of *maqluba*.

The guests all accepted, and the conversation changed its tone. Rashid's father asked Daniel about his life, about his mother who had passed away, and his reasons for coming to volunteer in Bethlehem, of all places. Daniel gave them his sharply polished cover story, which didn't raise any suspicions. When they finished eating, Rashid's sister brought Turkish coffee and a tray of baklava. They lit a hookah pipe, filling the air with a strong fruity aroma.

The guests thanked their host and his wife and went out into the street. They gathered around Rashid's car and examined it under the weak streetlights. Rashid and Toufik walked off to the side and stood together talking while Daniel and the others stayed by the car.

"We're going to celebrate Toufik's release with some friends," Rashid said when he and his cousin came back to them. "Join us, Jalal?"

"I wish!" Daniel said, "But I'm still tired after the night shift yesterday. I'll pass this time."

Toufik and the others decided where they would meet later. Daniel said his goodbyes and got into the car with Rashid. The streets were empty, there was little traffic, and the ride was shorter.

"Your parents are great," Daniel said when they stopped at the entrance to Abu Elias' building. He thought about his own mother and how long it had been since he'd last seen her or his sister. On his last visit to France, only a week ago, he couldn't contact them.

"Thanks, bro. You can consider them your family too. You know..." Rashid hesitated for a beat, "My cousin Toufik really liked you. He thinks you're a very interesting guy. Maybe we can meet up with him again sometime. What do you think?"

"*Inshallah!*" Daniel gave the Arabic language's most ambiguous response. He got out of the car, waved goodbye to Rashid, and climbed up to his third-floor apartment.

It was almost nine twenty, and he had to prepare for the briefing with command post for the operation, which had the code name "Come to Zion." His ability to switch from Jalal to Daniel and then back to Jalal again within minutes was thanks to mental skills improved with practice and experience. He washed his face with cold water from the bathroom sink and then gazed at his reflection in the mirror. He was satisfied with what he saw; a different look, animated and confident, a face he hadn't seen for a long time. The quest he'd started two months ago to unearth artifacts that were part of the Jewish people's cultural heritage was now official. It had the support he couldn't have dreamed of when he was planning alone in France, and then Yael had come up with the idea to cooperate with the Shabak. "It's win-win," she told him.

"The best deals are those where all sides have something to gain," the Mossad director affirmed, and told him that the Prime Minister himself was the one to demand he continue his activity in Bethlehem.

He had a few minutes before the call. He found the scanned article starring Ibrahim and reread it, word by word, taking a closer look at the pictures, seeking clues to the exact location of the finding. The old photograph was very grainy, and what stood out the most was a pile of dirt and stones – probably from the archaeologists' digging. Daniel focused on the young Ibrahim's face, the tall, gangly young man with a childlike smile that didn't match his age and body. He scrolled to another picture and opened another hidden app. He pressed his finger to the scanner, and a screen appeared with a messaging app similar to WhatsApp. At exactly nine forty-five, he opened the encrypted chat and typed:

-Hello everyone.

-How are you?

-All good. Everything's fine. A soft landing and a very warm welcome.

-We're happy to hear that. Roni says hi.

Daniel's heart skipped a beat. He imagined Yael sitting in the control room and peeking at the text message after the electronic notification sounded on the speakers. Seeing her while he was detained and during the preparations for his return to Bethlehem had ignited strong emotions.

-Say hi back.

-We started working on what you sent yesterday. It looks good—some interesting things.

-What about the article I sent?

Daniel typed rapidly, wanting to confirm that they were fulfilling their part of the deal.

-We're working on that too. Can you come for a meeting on Friday?

-Affirmative.

-Excellent. We saw something in the material you were working on, and we want some clarifications.

-Great. Of course.

They sent another message. Daniel read it and raised his eyebrows. What the hell? With everything else that was going on, why did they focus on that?

-I'll do it.

5

Three days later, Daniel woke up at five thirty in the morning to prepare for his visit to Jerusalem. The stated reason was the same as thousands of others in the West Bank – Friday prayers at the Al-Aqsa Mosque. In reality, he'd be spending the time somewhere else. Since the briefing, Daniel focused on priority intelligence requirements they had asked him to complete before the meeting. He was curious about the Shabak's interest in the same place, but it was all speculation; he didn't have a clue. He knew he'd get an explanation later that day.

After he washed and got dressed, he put the notebook that was supposed to be his manuscript in his bag, turned off the lights in his apartment and took a final look around. He locked the door and went downstairs. He left the building, made his routine stop at the bakery, and took a taxi to the Rachel Border Crossing. Like every Friday, the place was packed with Palestinians who wanted to attend the prayers. Daniel went to the "privileged" lane, breezed through the security check, and within a few minutes was sitting in an East Jerusalem taxi, together with other people going directly to the Damascus Gate.

When they arrived, Daniel crossed the busy street and leaped down the stairs to the stone entryway. Two Border Police officers stood beneath the arch monitoring for anything suspicious – the site had a treacherous history of terrorist stabbing and shooting incidents. Ten feet from them stood a young man wearing faded jeans, a white t-shirt, and a red baseball cap. Daniel glanced at him and made his way through the stone arch. The young man followed him.

Daniel started down the crowded main streets of the Old City, turning into side alleys and back again. He stopped several times at random stalls to buy something. All the while, he noticed the man with the red cap following him. He stopped at the corner of Chain Gate Street, at the end of the Muslim Quarter, just before the Jewish Quarter. The young man walked past him, and Daniel saw that his right fist was clenched – the agreed sign that the coast was clear, and he wasn't being followed. He continued to walk the alleys of the Jewish Quarter. At their meeting point, he identified another man with a yellow baseball cap leaning against the stone wall and talking on his phone. Daniel walked toward him, and their eyes met. The man finished his call and put his phone in his back pocket – another agreed sign. Daniel waited for an elderly woman dragging a wheeled shopping cart to pass him, walked a few feet further and then disappeared behind a blue iron door into a small entryway.

He climbed a short narrow staircase to a small landing and then turned to climb another half flight to a hand-carved wooden door. The smell of fried onions wafted down from the floor above. The door opened. A security guard motioned him to enter and locked the door behind him. At the guard's request, Daniel handed over his cellphone and the guard put it in a sealed metal box.

At first glance, the apartment looked like it was someone's home – far from an impersonal safehouse. The entryway walls were covered with decorative plates and some prints, and there was even a wooden coat rack with two jackets and a hat hanging from it. Daniel heard people talking inside and walked in their direction. The entryway led to a large, brightly lit living room, sunlight streaming through the window. Someone lived here, he thought. The sofas, curtains, soft carpets, ornaments around the room, dining table and chairs, and lighting fixtures were all carefully chosen to harmonize, unlike typical intelligence agency furnishings.

"Eran." Yael came up to him with a big smile and kissed his cheek. She wore her usual form-fitting casual style and signature sweet perfume. Eyeliner accentuated her almond-shaped eyes.

"Hi, Roni," he said, feeling the blood coursing through his veins. The elevated heartbeat from just thinking about her this morning confused and slightly embarrassed him. It didn't matter how old you were, he thought; the butterflies were the same. Just like with Josephine in the first grade, the same with others over the years, and then with Roni – Yael – the minute she'd introduced herself at the end of the exercise in the desert. No one had taken her place since they'd broken up.

She wrapped her arms around him. "Yael," she corrected him. "I'm not in the field anymore... I'll tell you later. They know me here by my real name."

Daniel hugged her back, feeling that her embrace was nothing more than a gesture of affection toward a colleague. It made his heart ache.

"Hey!" Jonathan from the Shabak held his hand out. "How was the trip here?"

"Nothing special," Daniel replied in Hebrew, overwhelmed with a sense of foreignness after a few days of speaking only Arabic.

"Excellent." Jonathan gave him a thumbs up. "So, let's get to work. We don't have a lot of time." He sat down at the large dining table, and Daniel followed him.

Yael remained standing. "Jonathan, you already have your coffee. I was waiting for Eran," she said with a smile and turned to Daniel, "I'm making your favorite."

Daniel nodded. "They have Turkish coffee?"

"You can drink Turkish coffee in Bethlehem," she shot at him and disappeared into the kitchen.

A laptop, folder, and yellow legal pad sat on the polished chocolate-colored lacquered table. Jonathan turned on the computer and Daniel sat next to him. They spent the first few minutes talking about Bethlehem and the Palestinians. Jonathan's part in operation "Come to Zion" was solely related to intelligence – what Hamas was planning at the psychiatric hospital. The Mossad was in charge of the complex field agent–handler relationship, and the complexity was even more exceptional this time; Daniel wasn't an active field agent. No one had sent him there; he was there on his own initiative. If he were caught, no one would claim responsibility. That was the deal he was offered, and he did not hesitate to accept. From his perspective, the situation had only improved. The risk hadn't changed, he knew that even before he took his first step in Bethlehem. Now, with the country's resources at his disposal, his path was even more secure.

Yael came back from the kitchen with two glasses. The hot tea with mint leaves conjured the sweet taste of home. She put the glasses down on the table, and his heart filled to overflowing. "Wait," she said, and went back to the kitchen, returning with a plate of Moroccan anise cookies. One glance was enough to know that they weren't store-bought. He felt a lump in his throat and the emotions triggered by what seemed like such a simple gesture brought tears to his eyes. He was at a loss for words, so just nodded in thanks, picked up the glass, and took a sip. That one sip encompassed everything: the house he grew up in, his childhood, grandmother, grandfather, the home he'd dreamed of, longing, a sense of missed opportunity, new chances, and hope. Everything at once – and too much, all from a glass of tea and a cookie. "Get everything set up," he said to Jonathan. "I'll be right back – gotta pee first." He escaped to the bathroom to calm down. The look Yael gave him showed she completely understood his storm of emotions.

He washed his face, went back, and sat between them. His knee touched hers when he crossed his legs.

"Let's get started," Jonathan announced, looking at the list of questions open on his laptop. "Did you bring the flash drive?"

Daniel fished it out of his pocket and handed it to Jonathan. Then he took one of the cookies, dunked it in his tea and took a bite. "Thank you," he said softly to Yael.

"You did good with the director's computer," Jonathan remarked. "We weren't sure at first, but the virus you downloaded let us penetrate the entire hospital network."

"That's great," Daniel smiled. "I almost got caught, so at least it was worth the effort."

"What do you mean?" Jonathan gaped at him.

Daniel gave the short version of the cleaning lady story. "No big deal," he summarized, "a little bit of excitement, that's all."

Yael shook her head and took a sip of her tea.

"We got tons of information; it'll take a while to review everything and we're working on it. But what immediately caught our attention is the greenhouse. We suspect that Hamas funded it," Jonathan explained.

"So what?" Daniel shrugged, "Hamas funds many civilian projects. It's part of the *dawah*; their charitable and social activities are part of the call to embrace Islam. Why is that an issue?"

"When they fund a project that's supposedly civilian and also make efforts to hide it – that's the issue."

"Okay," Daniel nodded somberly. He dipped the rest of his cookie in the tea, which had become increasingly murky. "The truth is that until you asked, I never had a reason to go there. But I went yesterday as I said I would in response to your message. Nothing looks out of the ordinary; the greenhouse is used for therapy. The patients learn how to grow vegetables. I saw rows of lettuce, radishes, and onions."

"Is there signage?" Jonathan asked, "Anything written?"

"There is something. Only that it was established according to a plan by the World Health Organization, or something like that. Honestly, it's hard for me to believe that the hospital director would cooperate with Hamas. He's Christian, and my gut feeling says he can't stand them."

"I'm not sure he knows that they're behind it," Jonathan explained, "Look, it was funded by a donation from a Ramallah businessman who stays in the gray area and doesn't openly support either side. We knew that he received money from some Hamas *dawah* fund, and now we saw his name in the director's communications from around that time and the amounts are similar."

"Yeah, that's suspicious," Daniel agreed. "Anyway, I get the picture. I'll look into it."

"Good," Jonathan replied. "We also have a list of employees. Let's take a quick look and see what you can tell us about each one. My people are already trying to get more intel."

There were sixty names on the list – medical staff and therapists, also maintenance, kitchen and housekeeping workers. Most of them Daniel knew just by name, nothing more. "You already know about Rashid from me," he said when they reached his name on the list. "I assume you also know about his brother, the shaheed. I thought we'd get to that later – but I guess now is good." He told them about the evening he spent at Rashid's parents' house.

"I don't think Rashid himself is connected with Hamas, and if he is, he does a good job of hiding it. His father wouldn't accept it. I don't know why the Palestinian Authority arrested his cousin, but he's the problematic one there – at least on the face of it. I also think he's sniffing around me, or maybe is thinking about how he can use me because I can travel freely in Israel. Meanwhile, I'm trying to put him off."

Jonathan and Yael exchanged glances.

"What?" he asked.

"I'm not crazy about that," Yael said and turned to Jonathan. "Eran and I will talk about that later. Go on."

Daniel shrugged and continued reviewing the names. When they were done, he had a thoughtful, hesitant look.

"I can hear the wheels turning," Yael said.

"Tell me," Daniel turned to Jonathan, "Did you also go over the list of patients?"

"No." The Shabak agent looked uncertain, his brow furrowed. "Why?"

"Maybe you should check them too. Even superficially. Who knows, maybe someone there is an imposter."

"Imposters..." Jonathan muttered. "You might be on to something. Now that we also have the medical files it will be easier. We'll get on that," he promised.

Yael glanced at her sports watch. "Jonathan, when will the tech operations guy get here? We don't have much time to spare today."

"I know." Jonathan also looked at his watch. "He should be here any minute."

"What about my thing?" Daniel asked, "Did you get anywhere?"

"We're still working on it," Jonathan replied.

Daniel didn't like his response. From the start, he'd assumed that the Shabak would give precedence to Hamas issues before the archaeological search. From the moment he'd left the detention facility he'd thought that maybe they were leading him on, but he didn't have a better option. He doubted the Mossad director's story that the Prime Minister himself pushed for cooperation. That was how they had trained him – always doubt. He recognized that they were treating him as a field agent when it came to his skills, but not his status. Under the circumstances, his current status was that of an informant, but with better abilities. After all, he was well aware that manipulation was their expertise. They fed his dream that the government would recognize the importance of his quest and would invest resources in it.

"Make sure you guys are working on it with the same enthusiasm," he glared at Jonathan.

"Eran, I know how this looks to you. And you don't have to believe me, but I have to say that, to me, what you started in Bethlehem is a thousand times more important than any issue with Hamas! My superiors might see things differently, I don't know. But I do know that whatever is going on with Hamas is what enables the search for the Temple artifacts, and so for me, personally, it's important to show the guys upstairs that they need you."

Even that speech could be part of their manipulation efforts, there was no way to tell. Daniel decided to give them the benefit of the doubt for now. He could always just drop hints and put off tasks they gave him. "I trust you, Jonathan," he said finally, "I hope I won't be disappointed."

They heard the apartment door open, and a red-haired young man who looked more like a boy came into the room. Daniel surveyed him with a critical eye – from sandals to yarmulke.

"Hey," the man called out.

"Move it," Jonathan barked, "Get to work, you're late as it is."

He came over to the dining table and introduced himself. Jonathan and Yael disappeared into the kitchen. The man sat next to Daniel, set his huge backpack on the table and pulled out a small cardboard box.

"New toys?" Daniel was excited. He'd always been fascinated by the tech people's gadgets.

"Totally!" the tech ops guy replied cheerfully, taking a small device out of the box.

The plastic device was similar in size to a cellphone, with a micro-USB connector. "FLIR," Daniel read the white letters on the black device. He was familiar with the name of the company which manufactured night vision devices. "Is that what I think it is?" he asked excitedly.

"I don't know what you think," the young man replied, dropping the backpack onto his lap, "It's a thermal imaging camera. Where's your cellphone?"

Daniel went to the entranceway to retrieve his cellphone from the metal storage box. He switched to airplane mode and handed it over. The tech guy, who had meanwhile taken his laptop out, connected the cellphone and installed a few apps. When he was done, he restarted the phone and connected the device to the phone's charging port, then opened one of the apps. He asked Daniel to put his finger on the sensor on the back of his phone. The screen came to life and showed a scale of colors from cold to hot, representing the temperature of the items around them. The technician explained how to operate the camera and then let him try it.

"I like this toy," Daniel beamed, "What's the most effective distance for identifying a person at night?"

"At three hundred feet, no problem," the tech guy replied, and showed Daniel how to switch the display to black and white.

Daniel was impressed as he examined the room as it appeared on the display. "Simple and easy. But I can't walk around with it openly."

The young man smiled, gestured for him to wait, and took a specially designed messenger bag out of his backpack. "Meet your new bag," he said, showing him the compartment where he could hide the small thermal device.

"Ugly," Daniel remarked, "I'd never buy something like that. Really. But how can I work with this outside at night? I need my hands free, and the biggest problem is that the display will be visible from far away. It's bright."

"Hang on, you'll see the entire picture in a minute." The tech guy had a smug smile on his face. He dug in his backpack again and this time, pulled out matt black VR glasses that looked like a ski mask. Initially, they had been intended to upgrade smartphones for gaming, and now, they had a new purpose.

"Wow!" Daniel exclaimed, "Amazing! I have no problem carrying them in the bag!"

"Yes. We adapted the glasses so that every device will connect to them." The technician completed the set up to connect Daniel's cellphone with the VR glasses.

Daniel took the glasses, put them over his head, and tightened the wide elastic strap. He went over to the window, pulled back the curtain and watched the warm white figures walking on a grayscale background that represented the cold objects. Daniel muttered as he tried it out, "I have to admit the results are similar to that of a military thermal device. Although it doesn't connect to a helmet, the image is identical."

"Will you be done playing soon?" Yael's voice suddenly called out.

Daniel turned around, and she burst out laughing. "Eran, you should see yourself!"

"Five more minutes," the tech guy said.

Yael came over and pointed at her wristwatch. "Finish up and we'll start our part; we don't have much time."

The technician asked Daniel to demonstrate taking apart, connecting and operating the device. Daniel was technically minded and had always excelled in operating these types of equipment. The technician was satisfied, and they said their goodbyes. "Thanks," Daniel shook his hand, then asked Jonathan to give his phone back to the guard at the entrance. He followed Yael and took the plate of cookies with him.

"We're ordering lunch soon," Jonathan called out after them.

"Order for us too. We eat anything!" Yael replied and closed the door behind her.

The room was fairly small and set up like a home office, a desk with a computer, family photos, shelves filled with books, and a sofa bed. Yael pulled back the curtain and opened the window, letting in the unique atmosphere of a Friday in the Jewish Quarter. She sat on the sofa, holding a notebook and pen. Daniel stood at the center of the room, looking out the window. Two young ultra-Orthodox men with towels hung around their necks entered the alley, arguing loudly. He assumed they were returning from the ritual bath. He turned to look at the photos of the anonymous residents of the house.

"Cute, huh?" Yael asked as Daniel focused on the face of a happy-looking baby.

"Very!" he agreed. His gaze wandered to the other pictures. "It's strange," he said.

"What?"

"This isn't a regular safehouse. We're in someone's home, a family's. They live here, maybe they're on vacation and sublet the house, I don't know... but they have no idea that for a few hours their life has entangled with ours. It's just kind of bizarre."

Yael smiled, "You're right, it is."

"Well," Daniel sat on the sofa, keeping some distance between them. "This meeting is also bizarre. You're my handler..."

"Would you prefer someone else?"

"I think you know the answer to that," Daniel replied and added hesitantly, "So that's it? You're not in the field anymore?"

"You could say I haven't been for a while," she replied, doodling in the notebook. For a moment she looked like a shy high-school girl.

"Where are you now? Did you leave the team?"

"I'm not in the division anymore," she explained, a wide smile on her face. "I'm where I wanted to be since I was recruited."

Daniel knew exactly what she was talking about. He was surprised. "Really?"

"Yes! I'm finally using my artistic talents to forge documents!"

"Wow!" Daniel blurted. "I didn't expect that. Why did you give up on operations?"

Yael paused before responding, "We don't have time for that now, we'll talk about it later. So how did the return to Bethlehem go?" She got down to business, "Did you notice anything suspicious, any probing questions, anything unusual?"

211

"I think they all believed my story; it's solid. I didn't feel like anyone doubts me or is suspicious."

"Excellent." She rested an ankle on the opposite knee and balanced the notebook as she wrote. "So, what's the story with the Hamas guy, Toufik? I don't like where that's going."

"It wasn't planned," Daniel explained, glancing at her exposed ankle, "I was in a situation, it was under control. It's possible that there was no ulterior motive, and I'm just thinking the worst."

"Stay away from them!" she warned him. "Don't volunteer where you shouldn't!"

"Maybe it's an opportunity," he persisted, "Hamas?"

"I don't think you need to take unnecessary risks. We also have a clear agreement with the Shabak; all the missions Jonathan assigns to you go through the Office first. I won't approve him sending you on adventures even if you agree."

Daniel was surprised and smiled to himself. Yael seemed very emphatic.

"What?"

"I like your concern."

Yael smiled at him. "Field agent safety comes first!"

"But it's not just that, is it?" He was digging for something more personal. "And I'm not exactly a field agent in this case."

"You're right."

"And what about my concern? The artifacts? Are you making sure that's also being taken care of?"

"As much as I can," she replied. "That's part of the deal. If I suspect that Shabak is putting it off, they'll hear from me. Let's see how they deal with the article you sent – it's a major lead."

"Yaeli, I trust you."

"Did you bring the map and the other material we discussed?"

"Yes." He went to his bag and took out the notebook and his grandfather's sketch.

Yael held out her hand for the notebook and examined his notes. They were written in French, and apart from a few words, she didn't understand anything. "Listen," she said, a smile spreading across her face again, "hiding your notes under the cover of a manuscript is brilliant. But why did you decide to pretend to be an author? Why not something else?"

"Think about it – an author is a great cover for anyone making notes, and I also think that writing a book is no different than developing a cover story – making up a believable character, being in someone else's shoes, making sure there are no loose ends, what-if's, analyzing scenarios. Come on, you know, you've done it before yourself."

"So maybe the Office should start recruiting authors?"

"Maybe," Daniel replied, watching her laugh. He loved her laugh; it had always blown him away, just like now. He handed her the sketch.

Yael's expression turned serious. She pulled the yellowed piece of paper out of the plastic sleeve, spread it between them on the sofa and straightened the folds with her fingers. Daniel watched her hands move and beat down the desire to lace their fingers together. She was wearing her engagement ring, and it kindled a strange, inexplicable feeling, like a single heartbeat that stood out, stronger than the ones before and after.

"I remember this sketch," she said, a slight tremor in her voice. "I don't understand what these shapes mean, the lines between them and the names. But yes, I saw it in the boxes you left. I'm glad I sent them to you."

"So am I," Daniel said. He explained the sketch and his grandfather's findings in depth, using his written notes.

Yael listened closely, taking notes and asking questions for clarification. "You think they're really there?" she asked when he was done.

"The treasures?"

"Yes."

"I really hope so," his eyes gleamed. "I fantasize about it a lot."

"Tell me."

"Sometimes, when I walk along the paths or in the woods with Ibrahim, I imagine that I'm walking right over the room where they have been waiting in the dark for hundreds of years in some old wooden crate or clay jar, or wrapped in cloth..."

Yael smiled at him as he spoke; he looked happy. He was cut off by Jonathan knocking and opening the door.

"We'll be there in a minute," Yael said.

"The food isn't here yet," he replied. "Eran, you've had a few calls from an unknown caller. You want to answer?"

"Uh-huh." Daniel walked out to the living room with Jonathan. The security guard handed him his phone.

Daniel looked at the display, "Four calls?! Interesting. Let's wait until they call again."

A minute later the phone rang. Unknown caller. Daniel motioned to everyone to remain silent.

"Hello? Rashid!" Daniel's face showed surprise. "In Al-Quds. Why aren't you calling from your phone? I would have answered the first time... your battery... I see, no, I don't have a pen, text it to me..."

Yael and Jonathan looked at him with interest. Yael suddenly came up close so she could hear the call, her head against his. A shiver ran down Daniel's spine.

"Right, the battery, okay... I'll get a pen from someone here... call me in a couple of minutes. Bye!"

"What's up?" Yael and Jonathan simultaneously whispered, as if someone was listening in.

"That crazy Rashid," Daniel chuckled, "Someone from East Jerusalem owes him money and he asked me to go get it for him since I'm already here. You get it, right? 'Owes him'..."

"Of course," Jonathan said.

"I don't like it," Yael added.

The phone rang again.

"Get the number from him," Jonathan requested.

"I said I don't like this, Jonathan!" Yael repeated.

"I'm answering," Daniel said, "Just shut up and we'll deal with this in a minute."

"Rashid. I'm writing it down. Zero, five, zero, six... I'll try... you need anything else?" Yael gave him a wide-eyed warning look and Daniel winked at her. "Okay, see you soon." He ended the call and gave the phone back to the guard, who returned it to the box in the lobby.

"If until now I thought Rashid was innocent," Daniel started, "now I'm not so sure. I don't buy that his battery just died. If I had to guess, he's afraid someone was listening, and he made it up. But why would anyone be listening?"

Yael and Jonathan exchanged glances, and Daniel tried to figure out what was going on. It looked like they were hiding something from him.

"I'll check out the number he gave you." Jonathan took the slip of paper on which Daniel had written the digits.

"Let us know when you have something. Let's continue, Eran." Yael lifted her chin toward the room. "We don't have much time."

They went and sat on the sofa, once again facing one another.

"I think he's trying to use me to transfer dirty money," Daniel said.

"As a courier! I think so too," Yael agreed. "And I don't want you to get involved in things like that. That isn't the goal of this arrangement." Her irritation was evident in her hand gestures. "The last thing we need is for you to get in trouble with the Palestinian Intelligence; they'll turn you over to the French, and boom, there goes your cover story."

"Wait for Jonathan to check it out," Daniel suggested. "Let's get back to the archaeology. I want you to have the full picture, so you can explain to them upstairs that everything is backed up. Like I told you when I was detained."

"Daniel," Yael said his real name for the first time that day, "They didn't let you go just like that. You know that the Prime Minister insisted they first validate with people who were close with your grandfather. Respected, trustworthy people. From what I understand, the story excites him much more than what Hamas is hiding there. He's convinced that your grandfather knew something about the Temple and the treasures. Take your notes back with you but leave the sketch here."

Daniel's head wanted to cast doubt, but his heart refused. He trusted Yael, but the tremble in her voice made him slightly suspicious.

"You know, it's hard to believe that's the case," Daniel said honestly, "It's too good to be true."

She nodded, "I agree with you. But it's true!"

"Are you sure about the sketch?" He folded it as he asked. "Why leave it here?"

"Because it's an original document from your real life – Daniel's, not Jalal. You know the rules, even though you didn't follow them: never take anything into the field that can be tied to your real identity. We even change wedding rings! So yes, supposedly, the rules of the game don't apply to you, but there's a reason for them. Official or not, it doesn't matter – you're undercover! And anyway, you don't need the sketch. It shows the general location of the treasures, and your grandfather assumed that they are now under the hospital. It's served its purpose."

Daniel knew she was right and was angry at himself for taking the sketch to Bethlehem. It really did only indicate the area as the Temple treasures' last stop and wasn't needed anymore. "You're right. Take care of it," he asked and gave it to her.

Yael looked pleased. There was a knock on the door before it opened. Daniel and Yael looked up at Jonathan.

"Did you win the lottery?" Yael asked. "You look excited."

"The phone number Rashid gave you was a money changer that we know. We've been trying for a while now to find his contacts."

"That worries me," Yael exclaimed.

"Forget about that," Jonathan said, a huge smile on his face. "I just got the results back on your article."

Yael and Daniel hurried after the Shabak agent and sat around his laptop. The screen showed a full picture of Ibrahim, the hero of the article. Daniel clenched his hands nervously.

"You see that small hill behind the people?" Jonathan pointed. "That's a pile of dirt and stones, probably from a dig."

Yael and Daniel nodded.

"Okay," he continued, "Fortunately, they didn't just cut out the article; they saved the entire page, so we know when it was published. On May twenty..."

"Four, nineteen sixty-seven," Daniel said. "I saw that too."

"Correct," Jonathan confirmed. "We asked the archive for aerial images of Bethlehem around that date – before and after. There were six aerial photography flights."

"Comparative analysis?" Yael asked.

"What's that?" Daniel had mostly been in the field and was less familiar with the behind-the-scenes intelligence work.

Jonathan explained. "We asked an aerial imagery analyst to scan the wooded area at the hospital and look for any sign of changes on the ground that could be related to that pile."

"Great! And what did he find?" Daniel spoke with uncharacteristic impatience.

Jonathan clicked on the mouse and the picture was replaced with a black and white aerial image. "The analyst identified two suspicious areas two days after the article was published. Can you see? Marked by these red circles."

Daniel and Yael leaned toward the screen. Jonathan clicked again, and an enlarged image showed the first area.

"Okay," Jonathan hovered over a light-colored spot at the center of the red circle, "these dark spots are the tops of the trees, and here, the lighter spot – do you see it? Under the shade of the trees – that could be the pile of dirt."

Daniel concentrated on the image, his brow furrowed. Yael looked pensive.

"Sometimes you just need some luck," Jonathan added, "Skill isn't enough. If these trees were denser, we wouldn't have been able to see the pile."

"Are you sure? That's the pile from the image?" Daniel asked enthusiastically.

"Patience," Jonathan said and clicked again. "The second area we found," he pointed to another light-colored spot, "you can see it more clearly. It's at the edge of the forest and not under the shaded area."

Daniel nodded. "Yes. It is clear. But it looks like a flat-topped rock. There are several of these in the woods."

"Nice." Jonathan nodded, "Bingo!"

Daniel gave Yael a satisfied look.

"So, we're left with the first area," Jonathan continued. "The next step is to verify that it is indeed a change in the topography. The analyst checked the aerial reconnaissance flights before the date of publication. The first one he examined was taken eight days before, and this spot doesn't appear in it. He also checked images from two weeks before; there was nothing there either, and it was even taken from a lower altitude and the details are sharper. So, we're pretty sure that whatever that spot is – it's not natural, and from a week before the picture in the article."

Daniel stood up and started pacing. "That must be it! There's no way it could be anything else! What do you think, Yael?"

"I don't know," she sounded thoughtful and was staring at a spot in front of her. "It could be anything."

"Okay, Jonathan, show me the first image again, the one that covers more area. I want to understand exactly where it is in the woods."

"You'll see in a minute. This is the good part!" Jonathan announced, a smug look on his face. "That was just the promo!"

Daniel went back to stand by the computer. "There's more?"

Jonathan clicked and a sharp, aerial image filled the screen. "This is from a few days ago."

Daniel froze, and Yael was startled out of her contemplative mode like she was bitten by a snake. The two exchanged astonished looks. Daniel held both hands to his head in disbelief.

"No way!" Yael blurted.

6

Three hours later, more excited than ever, Daniel was already on his way back to Bethlehem. The events threatened his impressive capacity for self-control, feeding his desire for immediate action. If it were up to him, he wouldn't have even waited for a taxi – he would have run all the way, grabbed a shovel, and started to dig on the hospital grounds.

The taxi stopped at the border crossing. Daniel bypassed the crowd of people with Palestinian passports and went to the "privileged" line. He had mixed feelings about the envelope stuffed with five thousand dollars that the money changer had counted twice before sealing. It was deep inside his bag. If the money was indeed laundered, he hoped that someone at the crossing would find it in a random search and seize it. If not – then let Rashid enjoy it. Yael's objections echoed in his mind. She and Jonathan argued about the risks and chances. And it was Daniel who finally convinced her that it was a calculated risk, that the mission was under control. Although at first he'd thought Yael was being friendly yet keeping her distance, the more time he spent with her, the more he felt that her concern for his safety stemmed from something else, deeper and more emotional. He was almost convinced that she was even trying to stop him from going to Bethlehem and was startled by her reaction to the aerial images that Jonathan had shown them. She seemed fearful for him, as if the Shabak's findings had surprised her.

The envelope wasn't discovered, and Daniel quickly made it to the other side of the concrete wall – controlled by the Palestinian Authority. Rashid was already waiting for him in the parking lot, leaning against the Mitsubishi with a cigarette in his hand, looking agitated.

"Jalal!" he called out, waving to him, his expression changing instantly.

Daniel waved back, walked toward his friend and decided to conduct a little experiment. He slid his hand into his messenger bag, as if he wanted to pull out the envelope. Rashid jumped up, threw his cigarette on the dusty gravel and shook his head, signaling Daniel to be discreet. He rushed over and put his hand on Daniel's arm. "In the car," he whispered.

That was all Daniel needed. He shrugged and sat in the front seat. Rashid took his place in the driver's seat and started the car, refusing an elderly man who wanted a ride into the city, waving him off with some excuse.

"Is that new?" Rashid asked, looking at Daniel's bag.

"Yes," Daniel replied, noting that gossiping went hand in hand with an eye for detail. "Nice, isn't it?"

Rashid rolled his eyes, "Well, as long as you like it!"

Daniel took the envelope out and gave it to Rashid without a word.

"Thanks, bro," Rashid put the envelope on the dashboard in front of him. "You really did me a favor. I don't know when I would have been able to go to Al-Quds."

"My pleasure."

Daniel didn't say anything more, but Rashid, who wasn't known for holding back, didn't stop, "You know, if I'd have asked one of my friends here, they would have stuck their noses in my business and asked questions – and then all of Bethlehem would know about it! Arabs don't know how to keep their mouths shut!"

Daniel bit back laughter at the real-life example sitting next to him.

Rashid continued, clearly riled up, "And an hour after they'd have brought me the money, they'd come back to knock on my door: Rashid, buddy, any chance of a loan?"

"I was just afraid of losing it," Daniel said, in control of his laughter now, "that was some responsibility you laid on me."

"I trust you more than all the thieves here!" Rashid said. Then he changed the subject. "Want to hang out with us tonight at Wisam's coffee shop?"

No way that was happening, Daniel thought. "Some other time. I'm tired and working a double shift tomorrow – morning and night."

"I owe you a night shift," Rashid reminded him.

Excellent, Daniel thought, preparing the groundwork for his next step. "I'll do tomorrow's shift, but if it's no problem for you, can you switch with me next week? I wanted to go to the Dead Sea."

Rashid sighed. "I wish I could go with you... no problem. Have fun for me too."

He stopped the car at the entrance to Abu Elias' apartment building. "So, you won't come out with us tonight?"

"Next time, *inshallah*. I'm exhausted." Daniel shook Rashid's hand, got out, and disappeared into the building.

Abu Elias was sitting in his modest office. "Hey Frenchman!" he called out to Daniel, who already had one foot on the first step. "Jalal?"

He walked back. "Good evening, Abu Elias. How are you?"

"Praise be to God!" the landlord replied. "And you? I wanted to ask – until when are you staying with us? I mean, when are you going back to France? Don't get me wrong, it's just that people are interested in the apartment, and I need to know..."

Who knows when I'll be done here, Daniel thought. "At least until the end of next month," he replied. "Then we'll see."

"Okay, son." The elderly man stood, shut off the light and walked into the lobby with Daniel. "Let me know as soon as you can. It's almost Easter and there are lots of tourists in town."

"Of course," Daniel confirmed and hurried away to avoid any more questions.

He turned toward the stairs. Two tenants on their way down nodded hello. He climbed to the last floor, strode to his apartment at the end of the hallway and locked the door behind him. The small apartment felt like home, as absurd as it was. He was happy to return there at the end of the day, and it had become a safe haven for him. He could peel back the protective layers and breathe easily before pulling them back on. He took off his clothes and lay back on the bed. He folded the pillow in half to raise his head a bit higher and inhaled the fresh scent of the local laundry. He grabbed his cellphone and sent the prearranged signal to command post that he'd arrived safely. He pulled up the scanned article with Ibrahim's picture. This time he focused on the pile of dirt and thought about the surprising discovery. There was now a greenhouse on the spot they had identified as suspicious. Some of the trees that had grown there were cut down shortly before it was built.

One of the most challenging things for Daniel was the dead time, especially before storming into an operation. It was too early to go to sleep, but there were mostly Arabic channels on television, and the Israeli channels were restricted. Wandering the streets of Bethlehem might draw needless trouble, and he had already memorized the article on Ibrahim. Ninety percent of the time is spent waiting, his instructor Arik's words surfaced every time he found himself with dead time. When he first heard it, he couldn't have imagined how accurate the statement was. He was fortunate to have the necessary control. Maybe he'd been recruited to the Mossad after he'd shown that same ability in the entrance exams – for example, surveillance on a building in Tel Aviv until a man whose face he'd been given just a few minutes to memorize showed up. Finally, after a hot shower, a light supper and some random television, he fell asleep.

The next day Daniel felt completely different. He woke up refreshed and energized and arrived at the hospital just in time for the shift handover. He had two main missions for the day, operational and personal. First, to find a way to get into the greenhouse and wander around freely. Second, to walk through the woods and try to verify indisputably that the location of the greenhouse was identical to that of the historic dig.

When the briefing was over, he went to the shift supervisor, a senior nurse at the hospital and Christian like the director, judging by the gold cross necklace he wore.

"No problem," the supervisor said when Daniel asked to participate in the occupational therapy program in the greenhouse. "Talk to Ibtisam, she's the coordinator."

Daniel was surprised. She wasn't the coordinator of the entire occupational therapy program, and he hadn't known that she was involved. Ironic, he thought.

Until then, he'd classified Ibtisam as a risk, and now he had to find a way to turn her into an opportunity.

He spent the morning hours helping the medical staff. Today it was a routine doctor visit going from room to room, asking the patients how they were, examining any problems and checking their blood pressure, accompanied by two nurses. When they were done, just before lunch, Daniel went to Ibrahim's room. He found him dozing on a white plastic chair by the window.

"Uncle Ibrahim?"

The old man opened his eyes, glanced at Daniel, smiled, and shut them again.

"Go to sleep after lunch," Daniel said, laying his hand on Ibrahim's bony shoulder. "Now look at this," he showed Ibrahim his cellphone with the scanned article. Ibrahim half-opened his eyes again and immediately shut them.

"What about lunch? You want me to take you?"

His response was a dismissive wave. "Take a nap," Daniel said, and left the room. He helped his colleagues get the rest of the patients organized in the cafeteria for lunch, and then left while they were eating. His target was Ibtisam in one of the women's wards. With every step in the direction of the main building, his excitement grew, the rush of the operation diluted with inherent reticence. What he would say and how he would present his request was easy enough but knowing that Ibtisam was interested in him and didn't bother hiding it made him uncomfortable. Cover story or not, you couldn't hide sexual tension, just suppress it. Maybe.

He entered the women's ward building and stopped in the public area at the entrance. One of the workers greeted him and asked if she could help. He asked her to call Ibtisam. Three minutes later, Ibtisam appeared at the end of the long corridor. She walked toward him quickly, looking both happy and surprised.

"Hi, Jalal." She spoke in her usual soft voice.

"Hi, Ibtisam." This time, Daniel deliberately left out the title of sister that he usually made a point to include in every greeting.

"What can I do for you?" She smiled at him, a shy look in her eyes.

"I'm thinking of joining the greenhouse activities," he said, getting straight to the point. "A little change in routine. I was happy to hear you're in charge."

Ibtisam's face glowed under her head covering. "Of course! No problem. I'll put you on the schedule! Do you have any background in agriculture?" she asked enthusiastically.

"I had plants on the balcony in Paris, does that count?"

Ibtisam giggled, covering her mouth with her hand. "What kind of plants? Did you grow vegetables?"

"Roses," Daniel replied coolly.

"Oh!" she blushed, "Of course, it counts."

"Wonderful! When can I start?"

She glanced at her watch and hesitated, "Ahh, well, I'd better give you a short tour, so you see what we do there, and on Sunday, I mean tomorrow, you can join the group. You can accompany one of the aides, and next time you can work with a patient. Are you free now? I have fifteen minutes."

"If you have the time now, let's go!"

Ibtisam went to one of her colleagues to let her know and joined Daniel, who waited outside the ward. They walked side by side, at an appropriate distance, until Daniel broke the silence.

"So how long has this program been running? I understand it's fairly new."

"Around six months," she replied. "And it's been very successful. The patients love it."

"That's why I wanted to join. It's different from everything else we do here. I was surprised to hear that you're coordinating it. I didn't know. Do *you* have a background in agriculture?" he joked.

Something flashed across Ibtisam's face for a split second. "No," she admitted, forcing a smile, "but it interests me. So, I asked, and they let me be the coordinator."

Daniel let it go. "Established according to the guidelines of the World Health Organization," he read off the sign by the entrance to the greenhouse.

"Yes," Ibtisam said, adding, "Someone from Ramallah, a businessman, started the project. He even brought the workers, he paid for everything!"

"Good for him. It's great that successful people donate to causes like this."

"You're also like that, Jalal," she complimented him, "Even more... really, I'm not just saying that. I think it's wonderful that you're volunteering here!"

Daniel listened, a sheepish look on his face, as would be expected, but not because he was being humble; he felt ashamed. He didn't think the real Daniel would volunteer at any mental health facility for altruistic reasons, not even in Israel. Acknowledging that fact disappointed him a little.

"And at a place you have no connection with!" she continued. "You should be proud of yourself!"

That last sentence only proved just how complicated his life was.

"You're exaggerating," he blurted and followed her into the greenhouse.

It was warm and humid inside. The place reminded him of a nursery; it was tall and wide, and the bare metal frame was covered with rigid, partly transparent plastic panels, not with the usual plastic sheeting. He saw rows and rows of new seedlings sprouting from the ground. Ibtisam wandered among the rows, telling Daniel about the different varieties: lettuce, onions, radishes, eggplant, tomatoes. Then she explained the patients' work groups, the tasks, the treatment method, and more. Daniel's senses were divided: his ears listened to every word she said, and his eyes tried to take in his surroundings. The upper layer of dirt was a mix of compost and tree shavings. On one side of the greenhouse was a wide wooden platform, and on it was a large blue plastic crate usually used for gathering crops from the fields. He could see the handles of gardening tools peeking out from the top. Next to the crate was a water valve for the drip irrigation system, a few plastic chairs, and a table. Daniel noted two circulation fans on the ceiling. Ibtisam finished the tour and the two walked out.

"I have to get back," she said. "I'll schedule you for Sunday, okay?"

"Perfect. I have to get back too."

"So, I'll see you later," she gazed at him with bright eyes filled with hope and went on her way.

"Thanks," Daniel called out after her, thinking so far, so good.

Once she was further away, he did a quick survey outside the greenhouse. Abutting the wooden platform from the outside was a rectangular metal structure, around six feet tall and three feet wide. Daniel walked up closer and saw a door with a padlock. He stood in the space between the metal structure and the plastic sheet of the greenhouse wall, and under the guise of urinating, he noted other details: the back of the metal structure had horizontal air vents tilted downward. He didn't hear motors, the buzz of electronics, or any other sound. Possibly a storage closet, something to do with the greenhouse.

He took a different path back to the ward than the one he'd taken with Ibtisam. He wanted to get a complete picture and plan his return there in a few hours, after dark, and maybe find some clue that this was the same place as in the newspaper article. Unfortunately, he didn't see anything unusual under the pine trees, the cypress trees, and hidden in the piles of dry needles on the ground.

At around eight, after the patients had finished eating dinner and were back in their rooms getting ready to sleep, Daniel went to the supervisor on duty. "I'm just going over to the main building to get a book I brought with me," he notified him, and left the building. The outdoor lighting was on, illuminating the paths between the buildings, but the other areas were in the dark. The woods were a black shadow, and on his way to the administration building, Daniel noted the best spot to disappear between the trees – the longest dark area between two lamp posts. Inside the building, he went to his locker in the staff room, slung his new messenger bag over his right shoulder and headed to the washroom. He set his phone to silent mode, attached the thermal camera, opened the special app, scanned his fingerprint, and checked the screen. It was unlocked and ready. He connected everything to the VR glasses and put the device at the bottom of the bag. He knew that if someone went through his things, he wouldn't have any plausible explanation, and yet, the two minutes it would take him to disappear between the trees were certainly an acceptable risk.

Daniel left the building and took the path along the woods, on high alert. He approached the spot he'd located earlier. The path ahead was clear, and a quick glance behind showed he was alone. Out of range of the lights and under the cover of the dark, he quickly pulled out the device, placed it over his head and walked off the path, around fifty feet into the woods. Heart racing, he stood by a tree, stripped off his white coat and stuffed it into his bag. He looked deep into the woods to make sure he was alone, and waited another minute, in case someone was hiding behind a tree. The coast was clear up ahead, but he heard footsteps coming from the path. He slowly knelt on the ground and waited. He wasn't worried. As a professional, he knew very well that no one would be able to hear him at that distance. When the threat passed, Daniel stood up and focused on the woods.

The pine needles crunching under his feet grated on his nerves, but he knew the chorus of crickets drowned it out. The greenhouse was clearly visible in the dark with thermal imagery. The sensors picked up the heat absorbed by the metal frame during the day. Daniel stuck his head in the entrance to make sure it was clear and walked in. He didn't know what he was looking for. The goal was to examine the place undisturbed. He walked among the rows of plants systematically, then went to the low wooden platform against the wall. Nothing seemed unusual except for the large crate used as storage for garden tools. It looked like it had been moved a few feet away from where it had been just a few hours ago. He didn't think it was important.

Daniel went back outside and circled the greenhouse. When he got to the locked metal structure, the thermal cameras showed that the air vents were hotter than the outer walls, as was the air coming out. He put his hand on the metal wall and it was relatively cold. The vent openings were narrow, and the angle didn't allow him to see inside. He thought for a moment, detached the phone with the thermal camera from the goggles and inserted it part way between the slats. When he was done, he pulled it back, reattached the device, made his way back to the path, disassembled it and put it in his bag. Before he reached the path, he put his white coat back on. He looked right and left, making sure the coast was clear, and under the cover of darkness, continued as if nothing had happened.

It had taken less than thirty minutes from the moment he left the ward until he returned, but it felt like half the night had passed. Before joining his fellow shift worker, he went to the washroom, took out his cellphone and played the video from inside the vents. He was stunned at what he saw. There was no doubt he'd found the smoking gun.

7

Four days had passed since Daniel had sent in the findings from his nighttime reconnaissance. After many weeks of not driving, he rented a car. It was exhilarating. He found a radio station that played classical music and felt himself relax. He would have preferred listening to music in Hebrew, but there was no way to know if the rental car was bugged.

The desert landscape on his way east stirred a longing for Yael and an eagerness to see her again. That combination of desert and Yael was the core of his identity as a Sabra. There was nothing about the yellow scenery that reminded him of France. It was all about his army service, navigation training, trips he'd taken and of course the unforgettable exercise that had sparked their relationship. Lately, when his thoughts wandered, he realized that his resolve to stay away from Israel and Yael was not as strong as it used to be, even feeling a spark of hope that he could be reinstated into the Office.

The northern end of the Dead Sea appeared on the horizon in a flash of blue, and a big green sign marked the end of the *Megilot* Dead Sea Regional Council jurisdiction, the region where the Dead Sea Scrolls were found. Just after the gas station and the adjacent inn, the road took a sharp right south, continuing parallel to the Dead Sea from a distance. Right after the turn, Daniel noticed a police patrol vehicle blocking part of the road, stopping cars for a routine check. When it was his turn, he stopped and showed his passport to a man he assumed was in the Shabak. The man let him pass, and in the rearview mirror Daniel saw him halting the other cars so they wouldn't trail behind him. Daniel drove a few miles and turned east onto the road that led to the shores of the Dead Sea.

He parked alongside other cars, turned off his cellphone and joined the security officer, who was waiting to take him to the nearby Kalia Kibbutz Guest House. Just before the entrance to the kibbutz there was a sign directing toward the Qumran National Park. He'd visited there with his grandfather when he was younger. He only now realized the similarity between the chance discovery of the Dead Sea Scrolls by a Bedouin looking for a lost goat, and Ibrahim's discovery of the tunnels. He hoped for a similar outcome. It was certainly possible.

Yael, Jonathan and a few other intelligence officers he hadn't met yet were waiting for him in the sparsely furnished room. The next few hours were intense, and he quickly realized that there was no hope of stealing a few private moments with Yael. The conversation with the Shabak agents centered around the intel from the greenhouse and the surrounding area, but also coordination and preparation for the next stages. The ventilation shaft he'd discovered four nights ago in the metal structure next to the greenhouse left no room for doubt; there was an underground space beneath the greenhouse that had been deliberately hidden. The entrance, the size of the underground space and its purpose – all of that was still a mystery.

Their plan of action was complex. This time he wouldn't be operating alone; the technology, skills, equipment and scope of the operation were beyond the capabilities of a single field agent. The surprising news triggered conflicting emotions and uncertainty in Daniel. The operation was moving forward; they were getting closer to the answers – but his hopes were shattered. It could mean the end of his quest just as he was on the verge of significant findings.

The meeting ended in the early afternoon and Daniel went back to the Dead Sea. He decided to stay away from the area frequented by Palestinians to avoid unnecessary contact with them. At the advice of Yael and the Shabak agents, he chose a beach more popular with tourists. He had to spend the next few hours there to rest up and establish a credible story should anyone in Bethlehem ask him about his day. The beach looked like a resort village, with swimming pools, shaded grassy areas, a bar and restaurant, even a venue for events and small cabins that didn't look very inviting. Except for a group of Asian tourists, only a few other couples had found the time for a mid-week respite.

Daniel changed and went down to the beach, which had seen better days. He dragged a plastic chair behind him, slathered on a layer of black mud and sat on the waterline. Nature cooperated and arranged cloud cover to hide the sun, so sitting outside was bearable. Ripples washed over his feet, and Daniel stared at the horizon, where the sea met the crimson-colored Moab Mountains. His mind wandered aimlessly to Yael and their engagement ring on her finger that morning. He wondered why she wore it, and the most logical reason was that she still held hope for them. On the one hand, her behavior showed otherwise. Today, she was being friendly, nothing more. And since he'd left for France, she hadn't done a thing to try and get back together. She even sent him all his belongings. On the other hand, she told him that she wasn't in a relationship. Maybe she was waiting to see the outcome of this adventure she'd been drawn into because of him. He buried the thought that the ring was cheap manipulation to get him to trust her. He knew that Yael wasn't like that. And what would she get out of it? But he couldn't stop thinking about it, letting himself hope she was hinting that the door was still open.

After a while, the dried mud started to annoy him. Daniel went into the water and tried to float. After a few tries, he gave up. He rinsed off most of the dry mud with a hose on the beach, then went to the public showers. After a late lunch at the beach restaurant, he found a quiet, shaded area on the grass where he could rest and set the alarm on his phone. Staring at the canopy above him, he fell into a deep sleep.

Hours later, at seven twenty in the evening, Daniel entered the apartment building in Bethlehem, his bag slung over his shoulder. He turned straight to the stairs, but heard Abu Elias calling him from his office, "Jalal?"

Exactly as planned, Daniel thought, and turned around. He entered the cubbyhole office. "Good evening," he said from the doorway.

"Good evening! Just in time – God must have sent you!" Abu Elias replied, turning to a couple sitting across from him with a sheepish smile on his face.

"Jalal, my friend," he explained, "these two arrived a couple of hours ago, and may God help them, they don't speak a word of English. She speaks French and he speaks Spanish. I could barely explain to them about the rent. What do they want from me?"

"Good evening," Daniel spoke to Yael in French and nodded at the man with her, Mariano – a Shabak agent recruited for this operation. They had met that morning at the kibbutz.

"Julie," Yael introduced herself with a smile, speaking in French with a slightly odd accent but not so much that Abu Elias would pick up on the nuances. She and Daniel spoke briefly and then shook hands.

"So?" Abu Elias asked, "What's the story?"

"They want to take a walk around town and asked where they should go and if I could recommend a restaurant," Daniel replied.

"Good," the old man turned toward the door, hinting that they should follow him, "you know Bethlehem better than I do by now. Will you help them?"

"Don't worry," Daniel assured him.

"Wonderful," Abu Elias clapped his hands together, "You can catch up on news from France."

"She's not French," Daniel explained, "She's from French Guiana. That's in South America."

"Never heard of it," Abu Elias muttered as he walked out.

The first stage was successful, Daniel thought. They assumed that the old man informed Palestinian Intelligence about any foreign guests, so there was no one better to be a key player in a scenario of which he was completely unaware.

Daniel promised to come back in ten minutes and accompany them for a tour around town and dinner. He led them to wait in the courtyard between the apartment building and Abu Elias' private residence amid the fragrant smell of herbs and a small fountain typical of traditional Arab-style inner courtyards.

He returned dressed like them, in dark clothing. They left the building together and Yael suggested, as planned, that if the center of town was far, they could take their rental car. Daniel agreed, and the three went to the car parked at the entrance to the building. The license plates were Israeli – not a rare sight in Bethlehem, considering people from East Jerusalem, Israeli Arabs, and tourists came there every day. Yael drove, her partner sat next to her, and Daniel in the back seat as their tour guide. The streets of Bethlehem were illuminated with yellow streetlights, and there was little traffic. Safe in their car, they had a different kind of conversation.

"Did everything go okay until I arrived?" Daniel asked Yael in Hebrew.

"Smoothly," Yael answered. "We found the place pretty quickly and the room is fine."

"Great," he said, and for a split second he felt a spark of jealousy. Yael was going to spend the night with another man, presumably her partner. He knew that some of Abu Elias' apartments were furnished only with double beds. He wasn't used to feeling jealous. It wasn't the first time she'd shared a room with another man during an operation, but when they were a couple, he'd never been jealous – he knew for sure that she was his.

"Are the beds comfortable?" he asked hesitantly.

Yael glanced at him through the rearview mirror, a smile in her eyes. "We haven't checked yet," she said deliberately, "but I'm sure Mariano will let me choose. We got a room with two twin beds."

Daniel nodded. Mariano made a face and said, "Of course you can choose."

"Where's your apartment?"

"Next to yours," Yael answered.

Daniel nodded again. From his detailed descriptions, Yael knew exactly where he lived. Their apartment was usually given to random guests, mostly tourists, but also Israeli Arab couples who wanted to have a good time far from watchful eyes upholding the codes of family honor. The shared wall between the two apartments wasn't well insulated.

"We have around two and a half hours," Daniel said, "Let's take a short tour in the town center and then eat. At ten, we get to work, as planned."

Mariano and Yael nodded. As they got closer to the center of town they saw more cafes, restaurants, colorful string lights and young people enjoying themselves. They parked in a well-lit area across from the restaurant where they planned to eat and were happy to note two Palestinian police officers patrolling the area, ensuring their car was safe. They focused their short walking tour on the old city's main draw – The Church of the Nativity. The illuminated crosses on the bell towers, the bells ringing in the hour and the old limestone walls suggested a vacation abroad rather than an undercover operation.

Two hours later, on the outskirts of one of Bethlehem's suburbs, they got authorization from the command post; the team operating the drone circling high above them confirmed that the area was clear. Yael stopped the car in a dark area. It took Daniel exactly three seconds to get out of the car with two black backpacks that were hidden in the car ahead of time in Israel, and another five seconds to disappear into the dark valley across the street. Yael and Mariano drove a bit further and parked in a big gravel parking lot next to other cars.

Daniel got organized, frequently glancing at the parking lot to note the movements of his partners. He removed the military night vision goggles from one of the packs, and quickly scanned the valley. The area looked clear. Next, he put on the black multi-pocketed tactical vest with adjustable straps, pulled out a gun secured in a holster, checked that it was loaded with the safety on and the silencer attached properly, and put it back. Then came the headset, a wide, flexible headband with a microphone and earpiece connected to a small tactical communication device from another pocket. He attached the night vision device above the headset.

Yael and Mariano slowly walked toward him and also disappeared into the darkness to join him. Daniel handed each one the same equipment, gave Mariano one backpack, and shouldered the other. When they were ready, they conducted an internal communications check, contacted the command post, and set off.

They had a short route ahead of them, around a mile along the ravine that led from the outskirts of a sparsely populated neighborhood to one of the outer walls of the psychiatric hospital complex in Bethlehem. Yael was first. Daniel followed her, and Mariano brought up the rear. There was very little illumination from the night sky. In the distance, they heard dogs barking and a donkey braying, but close around them only the chirping of crickets and the soft shuffle of their footsteps. With each step Daniel's mood lightened. He hadn't felt this happy in a long time. Every breath he took filled his lungs with the unique blend of scents that was Israel. Like the flavors of fine wine, he recalled the fragrant aroma of hyssop, fig and pomegranate, mint and sage, although none were growing on their route. He watched Yael walking ahead of him in the dark. Her confident, purposeful, almost casual stride, and the disparity between her young, innocent look and the experienced field agent that she was ignited an intense desire in him to stop and embrace her with the love that had never died.

Yael passed by a large shrub and suddenly jumped back. Daniel's heart skipped a beat. The silence was suddenly broken by the loud flapping of wings from some warblers whose sleep was disturbed. Mariano chuckled from behind them, and Yael cursed under her breath. Walking through the valley amplified every sound; every step, pebble or crunch of dry vegetation underfoot – at least that's how it sounded to them. From experience they knew that as long as no one was within sixty feet of them, there was no danger. The amplifying effect also worked in the other direction. They heard distant sounds clearly, the laughter of women perhaps sitting in a backyard, loud music from a passing car, the buzz of a generator and high voltage lines.

They made their way down old stone terraces and crossed through an olive grove where the ravine intersected the main channel, and then up the other side. Although a short climb, it was a steep slope with high stone steps. Three hundred feet before they reached their destination, they saw the outer wall of the hospital like a black streak. Sweaty from the exertion, they reached an eight-feet high stone wall. On the other side were the woods. Yael wiped the sweat from her forehead. Mariano, who was taller and broader than Daniel, rested the palms of his hands on the rough stones. Daniel climbed on his back, stood on his shoulders, and quickly pulled himself up onto the wall. He lay on his stomach, held his hand out to Yael, and helped her climb up. Her hand was soft and firm. Daniel helped Mariano next then they both jumped down to the other side and joined Yael, who scanned the area to make sure no one was there.

Daniel led them in the direction of the greenhouse. Dry needles and twigs crunched underfoot and settled softly, as if they were walking on a foam mattress. They moved forward slowly and cautiously. Around sixty feet before the greenhouse, they stopped for a quick briefing. Daniel gave a rundown on their surroundings and Mariano reviewed their tasks and priorities – what they needed to get done that night and report so that the intelligence officers at headquarters could process and plan their mission for the following night. Daniel and Mariano entered the greenhouse and Yael stood watch outside and to guard their heavy packs.

It was warm and humid inside. Beads of sweat ran down their faces, their bodies heated from the exertion of the climb and from carrying their equipment. They walked between the rows and planned the next stage of the operation before unloading the devices they had brought with them. On the wooden platform Daniel noticed the large plastic crate with the gardening tools had again been moved a few feet to the right of its regular spot. Mariano went out into the woods, notifying Yael that they were starting to do their ground scan, and returned to the greenhouse with his backpack.

Following the preliminary plan for their main mission, they took out a ground penetrating radar that had been specially adapted for their operation. The main component was a receiver and transmitter in the shape of a flat, rectangular plastic box. Two long straps were attached to each side. A thick communication cable connected it to the control panel, a flat screen with a few push buttons. Mariano and Daniel took off the night vision devices and let their eyes adjust to the dark. Mariano switched on the radar and wrapped a strap around his neck to support the control panel slightly below his chest. Daniel held one of the radar straps and Mariano held the other, and together they lifted it a few inches above the ground. They started their scan at the point closest to the wooden platform, in a straight line relative to the ventilation shaft in the metal structure outside the greenhouse.

The indication on the control panel left no room for doubt from the first minute; there was an open space below. Mariano noted the location they saw on screen a few feet away from where they started, and they continued to systematically scan along the rows of the entire greenhouse, inch by inch. No other anomaly was detected. They returned to the location where they had seen the anomaly and repeated the scan. It appeared there was an underground space from that point toward the ventilation shaft and under the wooden platform. They decided to continue their scan outside in the vicinity of the metal structure and reported to command post. Yael confirmed that the coast was clear, and they could leave the greenhouse. Mariano covered the control panel screen to hide the illumination.

They walked back and forth among the trees, trying to cover as much ground as possible, because without the control panel they couldn't know what they were revealing. Daniel's hands were tired from holding the radar and he figured Mariano must feel the same. Neither one of them dared complain.

After forty-five minutes that felt like an eternity they joined Yael, sweaty and thirsty. They each downed a bottle of water and then packed up the radar. They switched roles for the last mission of the night. Mariano stayed to guard, Yael shouldered Daniel's backpack, and together they went to the metal structure that hid the mysterious ventilation shaft. Daniel got to work with a lock-picking tool he pulled out from his vest. A few seconds later they opened the creaking door, entered the narrow structure, and closed it behind them. Yael took an endoscope camera out of the backpack, holding the handle with a small screen, and Daniel inserted a long optic cable through the wire mesh covering the air vent. A weak flow of air came through, and they heard a dull knocking sound – maybe a fan, Daniel thought. The display showed the metal interior of the air duct, lit by the glow of the optic fiber's end, but the further down it went, the greater their disappointment. They saw nothing but the inside of the duct.

"I hope the cable is long enough," Yael furrowed her brow.

"Man in the woods!" Mariano whispered into the radio.

Daniel stopped immediately and looked at Yael.

"Roger that. Man in the woods," Yael replied coolly and whispered to Daniel, "How much more cable do we have?"

"Not more than five-six feet."

"Keep going!"

"Advancing in the direction of the greenhouse," Mariano reported.

"Advancing in the direction of the greenhouse," Yael confirmed. "Hurry!" she urged Daniel.

"Stopped. Thirty feet away from you," Mariano reported, and Yael repeated his words again.

"That's all," Daniel whispered, "I'm at the end."

Yael shook her head. "Not good. Pack it up!"

Daniel pulled the cable out of the air duct.

"Moving toward you," Mariano said, following the person's steps.

"Moving toward us," Yael confirmed and tapped Daniel's shoulder twice, signaling him to hurry.

"Stop! He's on you!" Mariano said, not expecting a confirmation from them.

Daniel and Yael, who hadn't finished packing up the equipment, froze in place. They heard footsteps crushing dried twigs. The man leaned against the outer wall. Daniel's heart pounded, prepared for the worst-case scenario. They smelled cigarette smoke. He and Yael stood close together in the dark. Their night vision devices hung down on their chests. Daniel assumed the man wasn't there because of them and tried to guess what he was doing there. He knew that Yael was having the same thoughts.

"There's someone else!" Mariano reported. Now he sounded worried.

Daniel raised his eyebrows in surprise. He couldn't see the expression on Yael's face, even though she was just a few inches away. He could only hear her breathing and smell her sweat.

"It's a woman," Mariano said, "and she's coming toward you too."

Daniel was dripping with sweat. It was stifling inside the structure, which was like a big metal closet. He could feel Yael's quiet, steady breathing. The man outside mumbled to himself. Mariano was reporting the incident in real time. They heard the man's footsteps and estimated that he'd walked three to six feet away.

"Sweetheart! Over here!" The man called out quietly.

"I can't see a thing," the woman replied. "Where are you?"

"Right in front of you! Come here."

Daniel and Yael could hear both of them. Yael took advantage of the fact that the threat had moved away a bit, put her hand at the nape of Daniel's neck, and whispered in his ear, "You know what's going on here, right?"

He enjoyed the feel of her whisper. "We'll soon see," he replied.

"They're coming back in your direction," Mariano reported.

"Ok, stay alert." The commander's tone in response matched the drama unfolding under the fluorescent lights in Tel Aviv. Mariano was too far away to hear the conversation between the two intruders; anyway, he didn't know Arabic.

Daniel and Yael heard the rustle of the couple's clothing just outside. Now they could hear them more clearly and Daniel tried to figure out who they were, but the voices weren't familiar. Yael was listening, too.

"I missed you," the man whispered.

"Liar," the woman giggled.

"I swear! I'm going crazy! Counting the days until the night shift!"

"I'm sick of this," the woman complained, "Meeting like thieves!"

"What can we do?"

The sudden silence indicated a kiss.

"I don't know... I don't care... I'll tell him and say that I want a divorce!"

"Don't start with that again," the man's voice was louder this time, and then he whispered, "They'll kill us both!"

The woman sighed. "If it weren't for the children I wouldn't care. May Allah take him and my parents for forcing me to marry him!"

"Shhh," the man said gently, "everything will be okay... trust Allah!"

The sounds left no doubt as to what was about to happen; kissing, soft moans, giggles and whispering between lovers. Mariano updated the command post, and Daniel and Yael heard the commander wish him pleasant viewing.

The banging against the metal wall of the structure and the sounds of pleasure increased in intensity, and with them, the efforts of the lovers to be quiet. With only a thin sheet of metal separating the couples, the two inside took the opportunity to move around and get the blood flowing. So that they wouldn't bump into the wall, they stood even closer together. Inadvertently, the intimacy outside forced an intimacy of their own.

Daniel mulled over the conversation they'd just heard and wondered if Yael was, too. What absurd lengths he had to go to, to realize what he'd given up on. His hands and feet kept bumping into Yael's, the tension in the air escalating. Hesitantly, but without thinking too much, Daniel lifted his hands to Yael's short hair and brought his lips to hers. He felt her hesitate a bit, perhaps in surprise, but certainly in consent. There was nothing of the passion or arousal of the couple outside; it was a kiss of mutual longing.

Daniel and Yael separated, and under the circumstances, stayed still and didn't say a word. The sounds of activity outside diminished. They heard the click of a lighter and the woman asking him to light a cigarette for her too. The man was sweet-talking the woman; excessively, Daniel thought. Being very familiar with the Muslim mentality, he wondered how the adulterer would have behaved if his wife had been caught with another man in a dark wood – even if she was only smoking.

They heard the two start to walk away. When the lovers were out of hearing range Daniel and Yael went back to packing up the equipment. They double-checked to make sure they hadn't forgotten anything, strapped the night vision goggles on their heads, and waited. Mariano finally gave the all-clear, and they walked out into the woods. The smell of pine wafted on the light breeze. Yael joined Mariano while Daniel stayed to lock up and erase any tracks. When he finished, he joined them.

"Did you recognize them?" Mariano asked, curious.

"Their voices didn't sound familiar."

"The woman had a head covering," Mariano noted.

"Most women here wear a head covering," Daniel chuckled silently. "But that also teaches you something about religious people."

"Save these conversations for later," Yael interrupted. "Mariano. Are we done here for the night?"

"Yes," he replied. "Unfortunately, we have no need for the endoscope anymore. It's too short. We'll send the ground mapping to the command post and wait for tomorrow night."

Mariano reported that they were wrapping up and got the okay. They confirmed that they had everything and started to walk toward the wall. It was almost midnight.

"Have you started to move out?" They suddenly heard the commander on the radio network.

"Affirmative," Yael, who was in the lead, responded.

"We see movement in the greenhouse." The commander described the real-time thermal images coming from the drone, transmitting them directly to the command post.

The three came to an abrupt halt.

"Are you sure?" Mariano asked.

"Absolutely. Someone is wandering around in there."

"Mariano?" Yael whispered. "Are you sure those two left?"

"Of course," Mariano huffed.

"So how did someone enter the sterile area?" she demanded.

"No idea," Mariano answered, "Maybe from the back?"

"Even so," Daniel interjected, "the greenhouse has one entrance. We would have seen him."

"He's coming up to the entrance," command post reported.

The three of them lay flat on the ground and turned their heads toward the greenhouse entrance. A man walked out. They followed him until he left the woods, reached the path, and disappeared. Daniel thought he recognized his profile and stooped gait, but he wasn't sure.

"The night is getting more and more interesting," Yael noted. "Where the hell did he come from?"

"I'm telling you he didn't go in from the main entrance. I wouldn't have missed it!" Mariano said. "I suggest we go back and take another look inside. Maybe we'll see something."

"I think so too," Daniel agreed.

They notified the commander and got approval within a minute. Yael stood watch while Mariano and Daniel cautiously entered.

"All clear," Mariano reported. He and Daniel scanned between the rows, their eyes on the ground searching for any clue. "The crate," Daniel whispered excitedly into the microphone. "It was moved aside before, and now it's back in its usual place."

They went over to the crate with gardening tools. Mariano also recalled that earlier it had been a few feet to the right. They stood on the wooden platform, examined it on all sides and finally moved it to where it had been before. Even though it was filled with tools, it wasn't very difficult. Nothing seemed out of the ordinary. Daniel went to the far end of the platform where the crate had been originally, knelt and slid his fingers along the wood panel. He felt something protruding slightly. He tried to pull the panel up, but nothing happened.

"It's not budging," he told Mariano, who stood above him.

"Move to the side and try to pull it," Mariano suggested. "Maybe it's because you're standing over the panel."

Daniel took Mariano's advice and tried again. A section of connected wood panels around thirty inches wide, lifted easily.

"What?" Mariano blurted, astonished. They had not expected this. Daniel stood and pushed open the hidden door. He kneeled at the opening and peered inside. The night vision goggles revealed a greenish, grainy image of a couple of stairs leading into the darkness.

"Going down?" Mariano asked.

The question surprised Daniel. He felt a sudden weakness in his body. "Let's consult with the commander," he said to gain time, fending off a wave of disturbing thoughts. He hoped that these stairs would lead to the ancient tunnels that Ibrahim had discovered, but what if his grandfather was right and the Temple treasures had indeed been buried there, and Hamas had found them first? If that was the case, they were doomed just like the other findings far less important that had been found at the Temple Mount over the years. How could he know? Maybe they didn't even know what they had and sold them at the market? He recalled how the Dead Sea Scrolls were discovered. He waited impatiently for the command post to respond and almost prayed to hear the command to abort. The commander wanted to hear Yael's opinion. No one had asked for his.

"Let's go in and be done with it already!" Yael answered.

Daniel was furious. What did she mean by that? Done with what? It sounded as if she was asking them to rid her of the burden called Daniel Ben Atar. He didn't want to go down there. Let them tell us to abort. We'll go back in a couple of weeks, he thought, it's much safer and more logical. We'll gather more intel, prepare...

Confirmation from the commander cut off his thoughts. They were going down. He felt like he had heavy weights chained to his legs. That's it, he told himself, the journey is about to be cut short, for better or worse. Snapshots of his miserable life in France flashed before his eyes, as if ridiculing him. He recognized his real fears immediately – how could he stop living a life that held meaning? What would he do? Where would he go? What could compare? And even if he found the lost treasures, then what? What would he do next?

With his gun cocked and loaded Daniel went down first. Mariano followed. The air was cool and pleasant.

"We're in," Mariano reported as he went down. Yael didn't respond.

"Yael, do you hear me?"

They both stopped.

"No signal," Daniel said. They went back to the stairs, and Mariano climbed up to the wooden platform.

"Yael, do you hear me?"

"I hear you," she answered.

"There's no reception down there," Mariano reported. "I'll wait at the entrance."

Daniel confirmed and continued. The night vision goggles alone weren't very helpful underground. Daniel lit the way with an infrared flashlight. The low ceiling forced him to stoop. The tunnel was narrow, not much more than shoulder-width. His arms, which were in front of him holding the gun and flashlight, grazed the mold that covered the stone walls. On the wall to his right were wired lighting fixtures every few feet. They weren't lit, which he assumed meant no one else was there. There was no trace of the air duct. Daniel walked for around sixty feet. He was on high alert, anticipating what might lie ahead. The beam of the flashlight danced across the damp walls;

the silence was deafening. The tunnel branched off, and Daniel cautiously peered right and left, lighting up the dark corners. Excellent, he thought, encouraged. We'll have to come back and check out every turn. The operation wouldn't end so quickly. He turned in the direction of the light fixtures, reported to Mariano and moved ahead twenty more feet.

Another branch-off. This time the lighting infrastructure turned right. Daniel continued walking through the winding shaft, following the unlit light fixtures, until he saw a metal door up ahead. He moved closer and put his ear to the door. Silence. He turned the handle. The door didn't budge. He took a deep breath, relieved.

"I've reached a locked metal door," he reported.

"You have the lock-pick kit?"

"Yes, but there's a keypad."

"Can you insert an endoscope?"

Daniel holstered his gun, bent down and stuck his fingers under the door.

"It's possible," he replied and brushed soft chalk from his fingers. "Yael has the kit. I'm coming back up to get it. I need some air."

"Copy that!" Mariano replied.

Daniel heard him update Yael but didn't hear her reply.

He pulled out his gun again and went back the same way, walking more quickly. He was angry at his earlier thoughts. This moment would have arrived sooner or later anyway. I can't change reality, just expose it – whatever it is. With every turn on his way back he felt more encouraged. We have nights of work ahead of us no matter what we discover behind that door. He reached the stairs and climbed up.

"Well?" Mariano asked.

"We'll know in a few minutes," he whispered and adjusted the night vision goggles on his head. "I'm coming out," he said to Yael.

Daniel exited the greenhouse. The heady fragrance of pine was even stronger now. He hurried to Yael.

"What's happening down there?"

"A few branch-offs in different directions, but I followed the lights. There's a lot to check out down there," he said, lifting the backpack onto his shoulder.

"Twenty minutes tops we're out of here," Yael said tersely. "No adventures! Straight to that door!"

"You want to be done with this already, don't you?" he retorted, and hurried back to the greenhouse. He went to the opening, down the wooden stairs, and ran to the metal door. He took the endoscope and began to connect the cable to the control panel and screen.

"Man in the woods!" he suddenly heard Mariano repeat Yael's report.

"Man in the woods," he repeated, and continued what he was doing.

"Stop!" Mariano cried out. "Abort!"

Daniel assumed that the man was about to reach the greenhouse. "Copy that! Aborting!" he confirmed.

He quickly stuffed the parts into his backpack and hurried to the stairs.

"You won't make it!" Mariano exclaimed. "I'm closing the entrance!"

Daniel realized that the threat was very close, and his partner had no choice. He was a few feet away from the stairs but above him he heard the crate being dragged, and backtracked quickly to the first branch-off, looking right, then left. He hoped that if the man entered the tunnel, he would continue toward the door. He decided to turn right. It was even narrower than the main tunnel. Daniel walked another few feet and reached a stone wall. *Merde*! He cursed. He lowered his backpack to turn around, pulled out his gun and ran forward – maybe he should have turned left. What was happening up there? He strained his ears, thoughts racing.

After a few long seconds, he heard noises. The door in the wooden platform was opening! He stood still and alert, waiting for a signal from Mariano. The radio was silent. He heard a dull slam. The door closed; he assumed the man was on his way down. He turned back. The lights in the tunnel went on, and he heard someone humming the latest popular Arabic song, the sound echoing. Daniel went further in, stood in a dark niche with his back against the stone wall and pointed his gun. The branch of the tunnel was long and dark; the man who was walking down the tunnel would never have imagined that his life depended on Daniel remaining hidden. "It's four fifteen and you haven't called..." The singing was getting closer. Like a flash flood through a dry gorge, Daniel felt a rush of adrenaline. He stretched his arms in front of him and looked through the gun sight at the lit section of the main tunnel. "Four fifteen and you haven't..." The singing stopped. The man was between the sights. If before he had only suspected who it was, now he knew.

A minute later he heard the click of the electronic lock, the door opened and then slammed shut. Daniel hurried to the entrance and quickly climbed out.

8

When they got back to Abu Elias' apartment building it was three am. Despite his busy day – from the Dead Sea to the tunnel – it took a while for Daniel to fall asleep. He discovered, perhaps for the first time in his life, what it was like to feel intense jealousy. It drove him crazy to think that his Yael was lying in bed in another room next to another man, with a shared wall between them through which he could hear every word. What he wouldn't give to get into bed with her after a hot shower together, snuggle and fall into a deep sleep. In all the weeks in Bethlehem, in this room, undercover, by himself – he'd never felt as alone as he did just then. Even though he assumed nothing would happen there, on the other side of two sheets of drywall that separated them by three inches, he still felt a pang of doubt. That Shabak agent, Mariano, was a good-looking guy; broad shoulders to lie against, the accent of a Latin lover and a face that could be considered handsome. After all, they were undercover as a couple – they couldn't act like complete strangers. Big Brother might be watching, and they had to play the part. Someone might also be watching him too, and that made it even more difficult. He couldn't pace the room or put his ear against the wall to listen in next door.

He sat by the wall and imagined Yael getting into the shower. Did she undress in front of him? Maybe just stepped out wrapped in a towel? Maybe just wearing panties? She wasn't shy. But even if she had no intentions, maybe the guy would think she was flirting with him and try to start something? How tempting was it to relieve the accumulated stress from the night? A one-night stand – who would know? Who would even ask? And even if she acted like Mother Theresa, maybe that Don Juan would decide to strut around naked?

Daniel's thoughts hit him like the break shot in billiards, the balls scattering across the table. When he heard her giggling, he was ready to burst into their room. Finally, he pulled himself together, showered, and lay in bed. The jealous thoughts tormented him until he fell into a restless sleep for three hours.

The next morning at seven he could barely open his eyes. There was silence from the room next door. They didn't have to wake up as early as he did. He got ready quickly, random thoughts about what did or didn't happen on the other side of the wall last night flitting through his head. He stopped at the bakery as usual and took a taxi to the hospital, still half asleep. He arrived just in time for the morning shift handover. Rashid silently nodded good morning while the supervisor was talking. Daniel responded with a nod.

"What's up, bro?" Rashid came up to him after. "How was the Dead Sea? Are you feeling okay?"

"Yes, why do you ask?"

"You look like you didn't get any sleep last night."

And you? You dirty terrorist! Daniel wanted to say when he thought of the split second that Rashid was in his gunsight. If he only knew how close he was to dying last night. "Yeah, I went out with a couple of tourists that are staying at Abu Elias'."

Rashid patted him on the shoulder, "You won't join me, but you'll go out with tourists. Noted!" he said, as if insulted.

Daniel didn't reply and just forced a smile. The two parted – Rashid had a day off after the night shift, and Daniel went to see the patients. He had mixed feelings. Although he had been somewhat suspicious of Rashid since the money incident, he hadn't known for sure that he was a member of Hamas and involved in terror. He'd continued to act as his friend; their connection had seemed genuine and honest. And now, it seemed that Rashid was hurt – he always asked Daniel to join him when he went out and Daniel always had to find an excuse.

"Jalal! Jalal!" He heard Ibrahim call him from the end of the hallway, waving at him to come with trembling hands. Daniel's pensive expression turned into a smile. He was happy to see the old man.

"Uncle Ibrahim!" he called out, hurrying over to him, "How are you today?"

"Praise be to Allah," the old man replied, coughing.

"Why are you dressed like that, only in your undershirt?" Daniel asked, his eyes on the man's thin shoulders.

"I like it," Ibrahim said dismissively. His legs almost gave out.

"Let's go," Daniel said, linking arms to support him. "Do you want me to take you to your room?"

"No!" the old man said adamantly, "Maybe some sun. Will you go outside with me?"

"Of course!" Daniel said.

They walked slowly to the stone courtyard outside the ward. Daniel dragged a plastic chair from the entrance and sat Ibrahim down by the wall – mostly in the sun. Ibrahim adjusted his Golani Brigade cap. Daniel sat silently next to him on a stone bench, almost dozing off.

"What's bothering you, son?" Ibrahim asked after a few moments of silence.

Too many things, Daniel thought glancing at Ibrahim, who had one eye open, the other squinting in the sun. "You know me well, I guess," he said.

"Jalal, I spent my entire life here observing people."

Daniel thought about the moment he'd seen Rashid in the tunnel last night. "You know, sometimes people can surprise you. You think you know them, and then learn that you don't know them at all."

"We all have our secrets," Ibrahim said, "You don't?"

"I do."

"So, what's the problem? Everyone leads a double life." Ibrahim's choice of words surprised Daniel. "Look around you!" he added with a hoarse laugh.

"True," Daniel said, laughing with him, thinking about the lovers in the woods.

"Let me tell you something," Ibrahim sobered. "You and I, and everyone – we all need it."

"Need what?"

"Secrets! Another life that we live only in our imaginations. A fantasy! Otherwise, how would we make it through the day?"

Daniel paid close attention to Ibrahim's words.

"Look, I'm past seventy years old, and every day I imagine that today my mother and father will come to take me home. You understand?"

"Hope..." Daniel whispered and nodded. He thought about his fantasy suddenly becoming a reality and now seemed to be coming to an end. "I understand, Uncle Ibrahim. I understand."

They sat silently after that exchange, each in their own thoughts. Daniel felt the exhaustion taking over his entire body, cell by cell. He dozed off, leaning against the wall, and every time he jerked awake, he glanced at Ibrahim, who also seemed to be napping. At least an hour passed.

Suddenly he heard a familiar cry. "Jalal! Jalal! *Bonsoir*, Jalal!"

"*Bonjour*," Daniel muttered, yawning. "What did I teach you? *Bonsoir* means good evening, right?"

"They beat me and tortured me with electric shocks too!" the young man wailed as he always did and lifted his shirt, "See?"

"You're crazy!" Ibrahim called out angrily. "If they had given you electric shocks, maybe you'd be normal. Who beat you today?"

"Hamas!" the young man shouted, "Hamas, may Allah take them!"

"May Allah take you!" Ibrahim waved at him. "Let's go, Jalal; take me to my room."

Daniel pointed at the bicycle abandoned in the center of the courtyard and sent the young man, as he always did, to ride around. Then he helped Ibrahim back to his room, arm in arm, and was almost tempted to bring up the tunnel again.

Ibrahim asked to rest a bit before lunch, and Daniel helped him into his chair by the window while he continued with his tasks for the day.

At four pm, he went to the greenhouse, like a criminal returning to the scene of the crime. From a distance he saw the group of patients and their aides standing near the metal structure by the greenhouse. Ibtisam was with them. Since he'd joined this activity, she'd made it a point to be there, even though she didn't have an active role. She waved to him, and he forced a smile, wondering if she was aware of what was going on beneath their feet.

"Hi, Jalal," she greeted him with a shy smile when he reached the group.

"How are you?" he asked. He kept a friendly tone; he may yet need her at some point.

"Praise Allah!" she said, her eyes shining. "How is it going with the group?"

"Great!" You won't believe who I saw here last night, he thought to himself. "It's refreshing. I'm enjoying it, and I have to admit, I'm learning new things."

"Wonderful! So, when you go back to France, you can grow tomatoes too, not just roses."

"I'll certainly try."

"You'll be leaving soon, no?" she asked hesitantly.

The question surprised him. Even people 'in the field' felt he was close to ending this chapter of his life. "The truth is that I'm in no hurry to go anywhere. I like it here."

"Good!" she said, but her tone changed. "I'm sure everyone will be happy for you to stay on."

Daniel thanked her, but the disappointment in her voice that she couldn't hide bothered him.

The group of ten patients and five aides entered the greenhouse. They were relatively high-functioning people who came to the hospital for the day and went home to their families in the evening. The greenhouse program helped them to gain confidence, good work habits, and independence. While the instructor explained what they would do for the next hour, Daniel's gaze wandered over to the wooden platform. The crate was in its place. He replayed the events of last night. Ibtisam stood next to him and listened to the instructor. Daniel felt her body touch his lightly once or twice. She was probably very hot under the hijab and the long dress that covered every inch of her body, Daniel thought. The instructor finished and everyone got to work. Daniel accompanied two of his patients to the large crate, where they grabbed garden forks and went over to turn and aerate the soil around the seedlings.

Daniel liked working in the greenhouse. He didn't grow up in the country and had never gardened, except for the roses on his friend's balcony in Paris, and even then he'd only watered them once a week. The instructor's impassioned speech about the rewards of gardening and what it does for the soul spoke to him. He didn't plan to become a farmer but added nurturing a garden to his bucket list.

When the activity in the greenhouse was over, so was his shift. He threw his white coat onto the hanger in his locker and hurried out to get a taxi.

When he reached the apartment building, he went straight upstairs. Eagerly, he knocked on the neighbor's door. He decided to ignore the jealousy. He heard the sound of a television program.

Yael opened the door. "Jalal!" She kissed him on both cheeks and started to chatter loudly in French.

Daniel smiled. Yael's talent to switch identities had always impressed him. How far the real Yael was from the peppy and talkative girl in the doorway. For the benefit of anyone who understood French and might be listening in the hallway, she told him they were planning to leave that night and invited him to join them for dinner. Daniel said he'd be happy to, and they planned to meet at eight thirty. Mariano waved at him from inside the room and Daniel went to his apartment.

He was exhausted and planned to sleep for two and a half hours until they went out. He undressed, dropped onto the bed, and was asleep in seconds, until the alarm went off at eight. He went straight to the shower, woke up under the strong spray, dressed and went out to meet his neighbors.

Like the night before, they sat at a local restaurant and then went straight to their destination, taking a more roundabout route this time. In the hospital grounds, they set up across from the greenhouse, scanned the area, and Daniel and Mariano went in when they were sure the area was clear. The crate was in its usual place, suggesting no one was below. They lifted the large crate together and set it aside. Daniel lifted the hidden hatch and hurried down the stairs. He moved slowly, holding out his gun and infrared flashlight, did a radio check and went straight to the steel door. He tried his luck and turned the handle. The door didn't budge.

Daniel kneeled, shrugged the backpack off his shoulders and removed the endoscope camera kit. After putting it together and turning on the control panel, he inserted the thin flexible cable under the door. The space behind the door was dark, and Daniel continued to feed the cable deeper inside, but couldn't identify anything except for the legs of tables and chairs. He tried again and again but the picture didn't improve. Disappointed, he carefully pulled out the camera cable, rolled it up and returned it to his backpack. He reported to Mariano and started to go back. When he reached the stairs, he saw Mariano peeking in from above. He started climbing, but suddenly froze, and then ran back inside.

"What happened?" Mariano called after him on the radio. "Did you forget something?"

"No, on the contrary," Daniel panted into the radio, "I remembered something."

He reached the door and pressed the numbers one, six, one, five on the keypad. He heard a short mechanical click. "It's four fifteen and you haven't called!" he sang as he pushed the heavy door open.

"I'm in!" he reported and examined his surroundings with a regular flashlight this time. It was a large room carved into the stone, furnished like an office. He walked in further, scanning back and forth along the walls, and a reflection from the flashlight caught his eye. He pointed it in the same direction again and walked up to a glass partition that overlooked an inner space. He held up the flashlight and peered inside. He couldn't believe what he saw.

PART THREE

Cultural Heritage

1

It was quiet in the darkened conference room. Jonathan, the Shabak officer, sat next to the oval table and gave a short intelligence brief. The listeners paid close attention to his explanation, their serious expressions concentrated on the presentation scrolling down the screen. At the head of the table, Amos, the director of Shabak leaned back in a padded faux leather executive chair, hands clasped behind his head. To his left and right sat the senior officers of the security agency and the heads of the Jerusalem and the Judea and Samaria field offices. Daniel and Yael sat next to Jonathan, and across from them sat the Commander of Sayeret Matkal. The rest of the seats were taken by representatives of different units in the Military Intelligence Directorate and Shabak, a total of twenty people.

It was the closing meeting of an intense day; a marathon effort whose outputs would be presented by the director of Shabak to the Prime Minister with suggestions on how to handle the laboratory that Daniel had exposed the week before. The discovery was immediately defined as the most urgent issue to handle and had stunned everyone in the inner circle. A project of that magnitude operated by Hamas under almost complete secrecy in the West Bank and not in the blockaded Gaza was surprising, although certainly not new. To some of the experts it seemed pretty logical, in hindsight. The big surprise for Shabak, even though they knew that Hamas was stirring things up over there, was the fact that none of the operators who were categorized as requiring close monitoring were directly involved in this activity. If they were – there were no leaks.

But the biggest surprise was Rashid. For Daniel, it was learning of his fellow worker's duplicity. Not only was he a member of Hamas, but he had also been an informer for Shabak for several years and had even reported to them about Jalal the volunteer. On his involvement in the greenhouse, he didn't bother to inform the Israelis. Daniel didn't hold a grudge against Yael who knew about Rashid playing both sides and didn't brief him about it; he knew that was the only way he could have effectively played his part.

There was only one explanation for what Daniel saw and documented from behind the glass partition underground: a laboratory for biological weapons. It didn't look amateur; it had cutting-edge equipment and technologies. To the experts it was clear that this wasn't about a few bags of blood contaminated with HIV that someone wanted to explode at the scene of a terror attack and not anthrax powder sent in anonymous envelopes. Daniel had spent an hour taking pictures of dozens of documents and reports at the laboratory – what they were about, he had no idea. Now he was hearing the analysis; Hamas had gotten hold of a deadly virus that until today was thought only superpowers had. They didn't know how and where they'd got it; all they had were guesses. What they planned to do with it – how and when they planned to spread it – these were also unknowns, and under the circumstances, the solution was to take immediate action to stop it. The sooner the better. One possibility was to blow the place up, certainly not to leave it to the Palestinian Authority, despite their cooperation with Israel on security issues.

Jonathan reported on the findings. Amos poured cold water into a disposable plastic cup and drank. The head of the Operations Division said a few words, then gave the floor to the Commander of Sayeret Matkal. In a quiet and confident tone, he outlined the main points of the raid he would order his officers to plan. The Commander spoke of the importance of the element of surprise and his hopes for a completely covert operation – at least until the stage of arrests in Bethlehem conducted by Shabak agents with IDF soldiers.

Daniel listened closely. Most of the participants didn't know who he was, but the Commander of Sayeret Matkal did. Daniel had spent most of the day with him and his Intelligence Officer, providing in-depth details of the hospital complex, the structure of the lab, the woods and the greenhouse, in efforts to exhaust all avenues of information. After all, he'd be going back to Bethlehem and wasn't sure he'd be able to leave again before the raid. His personal interest in the underground space under the hospital wasn't mentioned at all throughout the day, not even during the time he spent with the Commander. That bothered him. As far as he was concerned, the raid would be an excellent opportunity to examine the remaining tunnels, to break down blocked walls and try to find some clue to find the lost Temple treasures. He took a small slip of blue paper from the pile at the center of the table, scrawled a few words with an exclamation point at the end, and passed it to Yael. *I don't know, let's wait until the end of the meeting and we'll see*, she wrote back. He folded the note, now even more worried, and folded his arms across his chest.

Amos straightened in his chair. "This isn't the first time we've had more luck than sense. I have to be honest," he glanced at the relevant field officer. "Hamas was cooking this up right under our noses, and even though we knew something smelled bad, we didn't know just how bad and why... but we'll leave that for the investigations, so we can learn something from all this," he said with a sigh. "And now to the issue at hand. We have two options – one, to use every means we have at our disposal and investigate, write reports, argue at meetings on situation analysis, interpretation, and whatever. That can keep us happily occupied for months. The other option is to end this immediately before it's too late, and that will be my recommendation to the Prime Minister. We'll handle it as the Commander of Sayeret Matkal said – a covert raid. No one wants to fight battles at a psychiatric hospital at the heart of the Palestinian Authority while neutralizing a bioweapons lab. The last thing we need is some test tube to get hit by a bullet and for bacteria to fly through the air." People around the table chuckled. "You get the picture, I see. Excellent. Let's get to work!"

The conference room started to empty. Daniel, visibly agitated, turned to Yael and announced, "I'm going to talk with him!"

"It doesn't interest him right now. There are more important issues," she said and added hesitantly, "Maybe let it go?"

He didn't answer her. Yael looked at him and sighed, a worried look on her face, but he turned to catch up to the director of Shabak before he disappeared.

"I'd like a few words with you," Daniel said.

"Come!" he said, looking at Daniel with tired eyes.

They took over the empty office, sitting across from one another at a round table in the corner of the room. Amos asked the aide to bring them Turkish coffee.

"The luck I mentioned earlier was your search for antiquities in Bethlehem," the director of Shabak said.

"I got that," Daniel replied. "And those antiquities are yours just as much as they are mine. This raid is an opportunity to search."

"This raid is not the time for that," Amos said bluntly. "We have to focus on the lab and not on archaeology."

"How can you say that? It's our cultural heritage!"

"Daniel, you're a smart man, and you already know what I think about those relics – it's better for all of us if they stay buried. They can only cause trouble!"

"What? You mean the Palestinians?"

Contrary to the impatience Amos had demonstrated at their last meeting, now he took the time to answer. "That's the least of it. It's not just another clay vessel or shard of pottery... finding artifacts from the Temple would be catastrophic! I mean the crazies who want to build the Third Temple."

"I'm not sure they're crazy and that's also nothing new. There are all sorts of organizations like that, and they make their own vessels," Daniel retorted. "And you think that's what they're missing? Only a trumpet or candlesticks?"

The aide knocked on the door and entered carrying a tray with two cups of coffee. She placed them on the table and left.

"Daniel, listen," Amos said, "You don't have the complete picture. The issue is extremely complex, and there's nothing more dangerous than religious fanatics."

Daniel took a sip of his coffee and put the cup on the table. "I think you're exaggerating. If there's an opportunity to search for relics like these, the government has to take it! They are incredibly important!"

"To whom? Take the Temple Mount, for example. I don't see masses of Israelis going to visit it. It interests a small and particular group, which is growing... still, it's only a handful, and the common denominator is very clear."

"That's exactly what I'm talking about!" Daniel's face lit up as if they had agreed. "And that has to change! No one will build a Third Temple if we find something; that's just alarmist talk. The treasures would be displayed in the Israel Museum... there won't be a single Israeli who won't come to see them – it's even more significant than the Wailing Wall!"

"Like I just said – it's extremely complicated."

"The Palestinians pass decisions at the UN that state we have no connection to Jerusalem and the Temple Mount. And others support them."

The director laughed, "Who cares! I don't give a rat's ass about legitimization by Arabs or any other antisemites in the world. I don't need their recognition. Let them live in denial. We've had a country for decades already."

"I was under the impression that the Prime Minister thinks differently," Daniel said, wondering whether the expression on

Amos's face was actually an effort to hide his opinion of the Prime Minister, or maybe he wanted him to know.

"So you thought," the director replied.

"Think of the headlines the Palestinians make every time they petition in the UN," Daniel said hotly, "and the energy Israel invests in it: putting pressure around the world, asking the United States to veto, to condemn, to get involved... Think what would happen if we found the menorah, for example – end of story! Who could deny our connection to this land? There was once a Temple here! It's ours – from all sides of the political divide."

"Daniel, you know what your problem is?"

"I have many."

"You're still stuck in the past, thinking like a minority in France."

"You're right! And I want that to change! I came to Israel so that I would have a common identity with my people, my brothers, but you Israelis don't have to think about it. You were born here and to you, it's clear that this is our homeland. You don't understand that it's not something that can be taken for granted."

"And another trumpet or golden urn will change that? The people you're talking about want to raise families in Israel and live quietly like anyone else in the world. It's that simple!" Amos glanced at his watch. "Listen, Daniel, your values and ideology are commendable, really, but let them go. Don't waste your life on things like that. You might be disappointed. Go raise a family! The Zionist stories you heard in France – they aren't the reality, my friend. It was good for dreams. And let me tell you something about dreams," he added with a sigh, "they never come true the way you think."

Daniel thought how true that was for him – his dream had gone off course a long time ago. They both sat silently, drinking their coffee.

"You know," Amos said softly, changing his tone, "if your grandfather had been alive today, he would tell you how he and his friends were almost slaughtered at that dig under the Temple Mount. Thugs from the Muslim Quarter came with bats and planks of wood, and it was a miracle that it didn't cost anyone's life. And that was back when they were really afraid of us..." he added glumly.

Daniel also glanced at his watch. It was getting late, and he had to get back to Bethlehem. He slammed down his cup. "I'm not convinced. You still have to fulfill your part of the agreement!"

"Daniel," the director held out his hand, "you are exceptional, and I'm proud that we have men like you. I hope you don't have any stupid ideas. Take care of yourself in Bethlehem."

Daniel shook his hand grudgingly and left. Yael was waiting in the hallway.

"Well?" she asked, looking distraught. "Did you come to an agreement?"

Daniel was lost in thought and didn't respond immediately. "Let's go out to the parking lot. I doubt they'll do their part."

"Don't say they haven't done anything. They tried to find the dirt from the picture in the newspaper. What can we do when it's exactly where the greenhouse is? What did he say to you?"

"To go raise a family and stop dreaming."

Yael was silent.

"You know," Daniel continued, "I'm not hurt, but I don't understand why he's so dismissive, as if I'm searching for some elusive pirate's treasure. I hope that when the time comes the Prime Minister will give the order."

Yael's expression was tight, and she was clenching her teeth. They went out to the parking lot surrounded by a tall concrete wall, and Daniel stopped. The last rays of the setting sun lit the sky. They could hear Hasidic music playing in the distance – a sign that Sabbath eve was fast approaching.

"I understand you," Yael said, biting her nail, "but I can also understand his attitude. Just think what he has to deal with right now – this biological weapon has the potential to kill thousands of people. Why should he do anything about the past when he has the future to deal with?"

"That's got nothing to do with it. I'm not saying that we don't have to destroy that lab, just let us search at the same time. It's not that complicated – they can bring two more soldiers, we'll do a quick scan of the tunnel walls, we'll go in where we see an opening and see what we find. Either we see something, or we don't. We won't get another opportunity like this."

They stood alone at the center of the parking lot, which was already empty except for the car that waited to take him to the outskirts of Bethlehem. Yael grabbed his hand and said, "Maybe it's enough already? Maybe you should just let things be? The universe is balanced – remember? It takes one thing from you and gives you something else... let it offer something else."

"Yes... balance..." Daniel's heart was racing. He felt the ring on her finger and looked into her eyes, shimmering with unshed tears. Her gaze was different now from what he'd gotten used to over the past few weeks. "I can't, Yael... not now," he said, and let go of her hand.

"Don't do anything stupid!" she called after him, and muttered, "I'm afraid that something will happen to you in the end..."

Daniel turned to her and just nodded. He was too emotional to speak.

2

The drive to the border crossing didn't take long on a Friday evening. Wearing a baseball cap and slouching down in the back seat, Daniel looked out at the quiet streets of Jerusalem. The Sabbath atmosphere filled him with longing for his parents, his sister, his grandparents, Yael's family, and the traditional blessings that her father, who was completely secular, recited every Friday evening. The memory was physical. Daniel could smell the sweet challah bread and feel its smooth texture. And then, just as tangible, he smelled the gunpowder and the sound of the two bullets in Sweden. And the silence that came after that, until it was broken by Yael's voice on the radio.

"Jalal!" the driver called out to him, "we're almost there."

Daniel nodded, and a few minutes later he got out of the car. He heard the pickup driving away, adjusted the strap of his bag over his shoulder and forced himself to separate from his thoughts as Daniel. "Jalal," he muttered in Arabic, "I volunteer at the psychiatric hospital. I'm a Muslim from France and live in Abu Elias' apartment building. I left for prayers at Al-Aqsa this morning and had some errands in Jerusalem..."

Daniel quickly went through the border crossing into the Palestinian Authority and as usual, took a taxi to his empty apartment. It felt different now. He didn't have the same sense of coming home. Daniel opened the window and sat in an armchair. The only illumination came from outside and the light near the front door. He sat quietly in the dark contemplating his next steps before notifying the command post that he'd arrived. He set his cellphone on the low coffee table in front of him and stared out the window. It felt like the end. How and when – he didn't know, but it was imminent. A matter of days. He had to find a way to say goodbye to Ibrahim. Loud music floated up from a passing car. Ninety percent of the time is spent waiting, the mantra from the training course played in his head. He wondered about his instructor, Arik. He probably knew what was going on. How would he grade his performance on so many days undercover? He had broken records; it wasn't the way things were done anymore! He felt professional pride. Who else knew about it? One thought led to another. And Yael? He felt that she was being honest with him but that it was over too soon – building something but not getting to where he wanted them to be. He couldn't define it exactly; it was just a feeling. If she had wanted to get back together she would have said something. He already knew that he wanted her back. True, he came here for the treasures and would do what he could to find them, but he also understood a different truth, and it had nothing to do with the outcome.

Bells pealed in the distance, echoing through the streets of the city. He didn't need a watch to know that it was eight pm, and his thoughts seemed to freeze until the ringing stopped. Now the smell of roasted meat wafted in from the shawarma stand just under his window. It didn't tempt him; he didn't have an appetite. He got his notebook, turned on the light in the room and flipped through it, amusing himself with the thought that he might actually write a novel. His phone suddenly vibrated and rang, startling him.

"Rashid," he answered the phone, forcing a friendly tone.

"Jalal, you're back from Al-Quds? You'll end up growing a beard like all the religious men."

"I'm back home."

"Great, I'm coming to pick you up. You can't get out of it this time!"

"Where are we going?"

"Wisam's coffee shop. I'll be there in twenty minutes. Be ready!"

"Okay, I'll be waiting." Daniel hung up. He went to the bathroom and splashed cold water on his face. He went to his bag, opened the hidden compartment, and took out a device that looked like a plastic coin in children's games, a little bigger and thicker than a real coin. He pressed the center of the coin until it emitted a short, sharp beep. He put it in his pants pocket, changed his shirt, and waited for Rashid. In no time, he heard him honking under his window.

It was a short drive to the center of town. The radio played popular Arabic music, and Rashid, as always, chattered nonstop, reporting the latest gossip from the hospital. Daniel didn't say much, just a word here and there to show interest in a way he knew Rashid would expect.

"Hey," Rashid said, turning up the volume, "I love this song!"

"Me too!" Daniel said, enjoying the moment, and joined Rashid singing the chorus in a hoarse voice, "It's four fifteen and you haven't called... four fifteen and you're late!"

They sang along until the end, and Daniel's gloomy mood turned around. It was a rare moment, heightened feelings that no one else would understand – supreme satisfaction rarely experienced during that ten percent of time that isn't spent waiting.

They reached the town center and Rashid parked across the street from the lively coffee shop. A large hookah pipe made of twisting neon lights hung above the entrance. They crossed the street, and just before they entered, Daniel turned to Rashid.

"I left my cellphone in the car," he said, checking his pockets, "give me the key for a second."

Rashid threw him the key, "I'm going in, we'll sit outside?"

"Sure," Daniel agreed, and crossed the street. He rounded the car to the door by the sidewalk, took out the toy coin, opened the car door, bent over and pushed the coin deep into the gap between the armrest and the back of the passenger seat. He grabbed his cellphone, which he'd left on the seat, and locked the car. Now anywhere Rashid drove to would show up as a waypoint on the Shabak tracking system. The battery would last for two weeks, but Rashid's time as a free man was less than that. If he did happen to find the plastic coin, he'd assume it was left there by the former owner's children.

"Catch." Daniel threw the keys.

Rashid sat in the corner of the open outdoor area under soft lights, on a mattress covered in floral fabric. The fruity aroma of tobacco filled the air, and Arabic music played in the background. "Your hookah is ready," he said to Daniel, slowly blowing out a puff of smoke.

"What flavor?" Daniel asked as he took his shoes off and leaned back.

Rashid coughed. "Tastes like heaven! What does it matter?"

Daniel picked up the flexible hose and inhaled. The water bubbled in the glass bowl, and as he exhaled, he remarked, "Apple."

"I told you, like heaven," Rashid laughed, "How was it at Al-Quds today?"

"The usual. You know. Crowded."

"You should visit Tel Aviv," Rashid said, surprising Daniel. "Now that's heaven! The Israeli women – oh my god!" he chuckled. "Here, there's nothing to see. Covered from head to toe."

"Rashid, my friend," Daniel laughed at him, "Did you forget where I come from? Forget Tel Aviv, it can't compare to Paris!" He waved his hand in the air and wondered if the secularism Rashid was displaying was for real or just a cover for his connection to the terrorist organization of religious fanatics.

"Oh man, Paris!" Rashid sighed, his eyes dreamy, and then teased him, "You dog you, Jalal!"

"And anyway," Daniel said after another few puffs, "how would you know? When were you in Tel Aviv?"

Rashid sobered. "I used to have a work permit, but they canceled it after my brother became a shaheed."

Daniel nodded and puffed on the hookah mouthpiece. Canceled so that no one would suspect that you were an informant, he thought to himself. "Really? You worked in Tel Aviv? Doing what?"

"About a year," Rashid said, "Cleaning, dishwashing at restaurants, hotels... when my brother became a shaheed, Allah have mercy on him, I went to study, and since then I've been working with the crazies."

"Isn't that better?" Daniel asked. "It's good work. Close to home."

"I guess," Rashid shrugged. "What about you, Jalal? You know when you're going back to France?"

Daniel sighed. "No, not yet. The truth is, I like it here. Maybe I'll go for a visit and come back, I don't know..."

"You like us, the Palestinians?"

"Muslims are brothers, right?"

"Only when they interview them on television..." Rashid pushed up to sit and grumbled, "Brothers help one another!"

Daniel breathed in the apple-scented tobacco vapor, his senses alert. It seemed that the conversation was taking an interesting turn. "Absolutely!"

"You could help us." Rashid raised his hand to signal someone. "Come here," he mouthed silently.

"Us?" Daniel ventured.

Rashid smiled as if he were about to tell a secret and exhaled smoke. "There's just one problem," he said, his expression suddenly serious. "I think you're Shabak!" he threw at him.

Daniel felt the blood drain from his face and prayed the dim light hid his response. He forced an amused expression onto his face. "*Shubak*? A window? What are you smoking Rashid?"

Rashid gave him a piercing look for a few seconds, and then burst out laughing. "Never mind... it was a joke." He got up to greet the friend who stood next to them.

Daniel shrugged and took another pull from the hookah. Rashid and the other man embraced and exchanged the traditional cheek kisses, blessings, and small talk. He introduced him to Daniel and lowered back down to recline on the mattress.

"So, how can I help the Palestinians?" Daniel asked.

"We'll find a way," Rashid replied vaguely. "I'm hungry. Do you want to order?"

"Yes," Daniel replied. They both ordered hearty sandwiches. While they ate, Daniel wondered what Rashid had meant.

3

The next morning, a Saturday, Daniel woke up later than usual, which only added to the sense of urgency, as if a timer had started a countdown. The future was unclear. When the raid would take place and what his part was, he didn't know yet, nor did he know when or how he would leave Bethlehem. The Shabak had promised they'd send further instructions; meanwhile, he had other missions – none of them underground. He had completed the first one successfully yesterday when he hid the tracking device in Rashid's car.

On the way to the hospital, he planned what he would do today and what could wait until tomorrow. What he could do during the day, and what needed the cover of night.

The minute he crossed under the stone arch, he felt a flurry of activity. An ambulance with the symbol of the red crescent parked at the main building, and groups of patients and aides crowded around. He noticed a large group of people coming down the path from his ward.

"What happened?" he asked one of his colleagues.

"Old Ibrahim... may he rest in peace..."

Daniel's heart stuttered. "What?!"

"He went to sleep and never woke up."

Daniel felt as if his heart was being squeezed. Ibrahim was dear to him, and his sudden passing hit him like a punch to the gut. He didn't see him as an enemy, the same as with almost everyone else in

Bethlehem. It was a professional choice, not personal – you can't live among people for such a long time and look at them through a sniper's sight. On the contrary, the friendlier and more personal the contact, the safer you'll be. And Ibrahim, as fate would have it, was the anchor Daniel could tie to all his missions.

The group of people came closer, and now Daniel saw that they were carrying a body on a stretcher. When they walked past him, he saw Ibrahim's toes peeking out from under the sheet that covered him. People around him clucked and muttered about fate and the will of Allah.

"May he rest in peace," Ibtisam said, coming to stand next to him.

"Yes..." Daniel's eyes followed the stretcher.

"At least he died in his sleep," she repeated the cliché. "They say the funeral procession will leave from here after his body is purified."

Daniel glanced at Ibtisam. Her expression projected unease. "You look worried," he told her.

She sighed, but didn't meet his eyes, just stared at the group carrying the stretcher away. "*Inshallah*, everything will be okay, Jalal."

"What? Ibrahim?"

Ibtisam forced a laugh. "No... other things... I'll be fine."

Daniel thought for a few seconds and decided it wouldn't hurt to offer his help. Maybe she had a part in what was happening under the greenhouse, and something was bothering her. "If I can help with something – please don't hesitate."

She turned to him and for a moment, looked heartened. "Thank you, Jalal. I'm happy that I don't make you uncomfortable anymore."

Daniel felt his cheeks flush. "I think I'll be going back home to France soon. So maybe that's why."

Her expression sobered again. "You're going? When?"

"I haven't decided yet," he said with a smile, "you know, just a feeling. Listen, I have to go. We'll talk later." He walked away before she could respond.

The ward felt different. Although most of the patients were busy with their usual routines, some looked agitated. They rocked back and forth restlessly, fidgeting. Daniel approached the patient who always claimed he was beaten. He was crying hysterically, and two aides were trying to calm him down.

"Jalal... Jalal..." he cried, "They'll kill me like they killed Ibrahim..."

"Who would do a thing like that?" Daniel rested a comforting hand on his shoulder. The young man curled into him.

"The Israeli army," he answered, "They gave him electric shocks. They hit him in the head and he died..."

"Shhh," Daniel soothed him, "everything will be fine. Ibrahim was an old man. Nobody killed him. Don't be afraid."

"Of course they did!" he said and tried to shrug off Daniel's hand. "They did! Look," he lifted his shirt like he did during every outburst and exposed his torso, "Look what they did to me..."

Daniel pulled him close. "Don't worry. I'm watching over you. Let's go take a walk outside. You want to ride your bike?"

The young man pulled away from Daniel and turned to go outside. He stopped crying and started repeatedly muttering, "*Bonsoir* you say in the evening... *bonsoir* you say in the evening..."

Daniel joined the shift handover that had started late and heard what happened during the night and early morning. The funeral procession would leave as soon as the body was purified, and patients were invited to join if they wanted – but they shouldn't be encouraged. When it was over, Daniel went back to his daily routine on the ward.

When he got to Ibrahim's empty room, he peeked inside. They had already stripped the bed. His ratty slippers were underneath, and the closet door was half open, showing faded sweatpants and folded shirts. His Golani Brigade baseball cap was nowhere to be seen. Daniel stood there for a moment and then continued making the rounds.

Half an hour later, whispers that the funeral procession was starting passed down the corridors. Daniel hurried to the main building and joined the group waiting by the coffin – mostly employees and a few patients. Ibrahim lay in an open wood coffin, his body wrapped in a white sheet, his face peaceful as if sleeping. The procession set out from the hospital, which had been his home and family for almost seventy years, the coffin on the shoulders of six men, through the stone arch of the main gate to its first stop – the neighborhood mosque. The hospital director, staff, and patients who were allowed to leave the complex walked silently ahead of the coffin. The women were not allowed to participate in funerals, Daniel knew. The noticeably small group made their way along the narrow alleyways. As in a military procession, the people carrying the coffin switched along the route. It was customary for passersby to join in funeral processions that went through Arab streets. That wasn't the case this time. People who didn't realize it at first drifted off once they learned the identity of the deceased. Only a few unprejudiced people or those who didn't fear being "infected" with mental illness continued with the group of "lepers." Daniel took his place helping to support the coffin several times. Images of his mother's imaginary funeral in France just a few weeks ago came to mind, as well as the distant memories of the funerals of *shaheeds* that he had participated in undercover with his comrades in the Duvdevan Unit, to catch wanted terrorists.

At the mosque the coffin was lowered and placed before the Imam. The small group stood behind the religious leader as he started the funeral ceremony. Daniel repeated the phrases together with the others and thought about how similar they were to their Hebrew equivalents: mercy, praise to God and the return to dust. When the ceremony was over, Ibrahim's face was covered and the procession continued to the cemetery, a ten-minute walk. They reached the plot, and the coffin was placed beside the grave that cemetery workers had dug earlier. Ibrahim's body was removed from the coffin and lowered into the ground, lying on the right side, his face in the direction of Holy Mecca. One of the attendants spread branches of sage over the body, and the grave was filled until there was a small mound of dirt and two stones at the head.

With no family to offer condolences to, the group dispersed and piled into two large vans sent by the hospital administration. Daniel sat in one of them in the back row, by the window, his sense of loneliness intensifying. He thought about Ibrahim's life, surrounded by changing strangers, waiting every day for almost seventy years for his beloved parents to come and take him home. Every day he was disappointed anew, but he never gave up. Daniel felt deep sorrow; the old man had left this world without knowing what an important role he had played in it.

They arrived at the hospital and went back to work. Another patient was already in Ibrahim's room, and the world was back in its routine. Daniel decided to postpone his intelligence-gathering mission to the next day.

4

Daniel returned to his apartment that evening, exhausted and depressed. He turned on the TV, lay on the sofa, and fell asleep with the remote in his hand. He woke up at nine forty, his stomach growling. There was nothing edible in the small refrigerator except for a few wrinkled apples. He went to the grocery store down the street and bought some fresh fruit, eggs, rye bread, and a container of labneh, the Middle Eastern-style thick, creamy yogurt cheese. On the way to the cashier, he hesitated at the shelf of beers, stocked for the city's Christian residents, but decided against it. When he got out into the street, he felt he was being watched. He stopped for a moment, pretending to rearrange the grocery bags, and when he didn't notice anything unusual, he made his way back to the apartment and prepared a light supper.

After he ate, he took a shower, standing under the spray of hot water for a while. His thoughts went back to Ibrahim. The funeral with so few participants saddened him. A man lives for almost eighty years and leaves the world as if he had never been. He recalled the Arab belief that a man lives on through his children. Ibrahim had never loved or been loved and had no one who survived him. While he was soaping his body he shut the water off, a habit from his years in Israel, and heard knocking on the door. "Just a minute," he shouted, hoping whoever it was, heard him, and quickly rinsed himself off. He dragged a towel over his body, wrapped it around his hips, and went to open the door a crack to see who was there.

"Ibtisam?!" he exclaimed, stunned to see her at the door. "What... what are you doing here?"

"Jalal," she looked at him, embarrassed, her eyes filled with tears, "can I come in?"

Daniel was astonished at her request, a young, unmarried religious woman coming to his house alone at night. He knew that something terrible had happened. "Ibtisam, *ukhti*, are you sure you want to come in? You are a respectable Arab woman. What will people say?"

"You offered," she reminded him and burst into tears. "I don't want to beg."

"Come in," Daniel opened the door. She was very agitated.

Daniel quickly glanced down the hall, making sure no one was watching her, and shut the door.

"Are you alright?" he asked. "It's ten thirty at night, and..."

"I... I..." she stuttered, "I don't know what to do." She glanced at his half-naked body.

He brought her a glass of water from the kitchen. "Here, calm down. Excuse me; I'll just get dressed... this isn't decent." He gathered some clothes and went into the bathroom to get dressed. I'll find out what's going on, he thought. It has nothing to do with the greenhouse; I'll calm her down and send her home. He walked into the living room wearing jeans and a white t-shirt.

"Ibtis..." he froze. He had not seen this coming. She stood in the center of the room, naked. For a moment, he didn't recognize her, as if someone else had taken her place. She looked so different without the traditional clothing that always covered her – clothing that right now was on the sofa together with her head covering. Daniel stood there in shock and felt himself waking up. He looked away. "What are you doing?" he asked.

"Look at me," she cried, "Don't humiliate me... I'm already dying of embarrassment."

"This isn't right," he replied. "You're a good woman, respectable, why are you doing this?"

"I'm not a girl! Look at me!" She sounded almost pleading.

Daniel knew he had to shut this down quickly and send her on her way. He looked at her, only now noticing that she had turned off the ceiling lights and turned on the lamp by his bed, bathing her body in warm yellow light. Slightly embarrassed, Daniel avoided eye contact. How brave she was, he thought. She took a few steps toward him, and he looked down to keep himself from meeting her eyes. Now she was standing very close to him, and he lifted his head to scan her body, from bare feet to chin. She was very thin. Her skin, which had never seen sunlight, was pale, her breasts firm and high. Her pubic hair had never seen a razor. She reached her hand out to his chin and lifted his head to look at her. Her eye makeup had smudged a bit from her tears, and lush black curls he'd never seen before flowed over her shoulders.

"Do you want me?" she whispered.

Daniel remained silent. If she looked down, she'd see his response. His body wanted, very much even, but his brain shouted that it would be a mistake. "It wouldn't be fair to you..."

"Be quiet!" She pressed her lips to his and waited. He immediately realized that she hadn't planned this evening and hadn't prepared for it. Her scent was delicate and pleasant but also carried undertones of her workday. He also knew that she had no idea what to do and that this was her first time doing anything that night might bring. A million thoughts ran through his head, but their physical closeness overcame everything. Months had passed since the last time he'd been with a woman, and the memory of that time, the bitter disappointment at the lowest point of his life, was still fresh. Then, he was Daniel, now, he was Jalal, and the bulge in his briefs was the evidence. The loneliness, the stress, the fears, the past and the future – they all swirled around him like a tornado and pulled him in. He held Ibtisam's face in both hands and guided her in her first kiss. What started as a hesitant lip touch quickly turned into raging desire on her part, as if all the societal dams that had held her back for twenty years had suddenly burst. The sound of brakes squealing came from outside. Daniel released her lips and lay her on the sofa. Her black curls with their faint scent of conditioner hid part of her face. He took off his white t-shirt and leaned over her. He had no doubt that she was a virgin and knew the consequences she faced for what they were doing. And Yael? His conscience nagged him – but there was no reply. He slowly moved down from her neck, breathing in the scent of her warm body. His lips glided over smooth skin, and she shivered at the contact. Her nipples were hard; every touch brought soft sighs of pleasure. He pressed his cheek to one breast, scraping her skin with his stubble. When he reached her waist, she jerked as if electrocuted. Daniel enjoyed every minute. He was fully aroused but kept caressing her, keeping his clothes on. He held himself over her, shoved his face in her neck, and put his hands between her legs. She trembled. He asked her if it was okay, and she said yes.

"Open the door, you daughter of a whore!" They heard shouts from outside the apartment and the loud banging of fists on the wooden door. "I know you're in there! Open the door!"

Daniel jumped up and looked at the naked Ibtisam. She looked even paler than usual.

The door shook. "Open the door, I said! You whore!"

"What's this?" Daniel asked.

Ibtisam stood and froze in place. The shouting got louder. "This is why I came... they'll kill me..." She burst into tears.

Daniel acted quickly. The picture still wasn't entirely clear to him, but the immediate threat was indisputable. "Come on," he pulled her into the bathroom. "Get dressed quickly but don't come out." He handed her her clothes, turned off the light and closed the door.

"I'll kill you! Open up!" The door threatened to break open.

Daniel put on his shirt and shoes quickly, went over to a kitchen drawer, and with the skill of an expert, chose a sharp knife with a smooth stainless-steel blade that ran through the wooden handle – so it wouldn't break at the critical moment. He hid it under his shirt just in case and went to open the door.

Before he could get a word out of his mouth a furious young man burst in. He shoved Daniel aside and with violence in his eyes he searched for Ibtisam. "Where are you, you daughter of a whore!"

"Calm down, man!" Daniel yelled, "What's the matter with you?"

"Jalal! What's going on?" Abu Elias appeared at the door, dressed in traditional sleepwear.

Daniel realized that the entire building was already involved. "Everything is fine, Abu Elias. Don't worry!" he answered and closed the door.

"Get out here, you bitch!" The man was like a raging bull, almost tearing the closet door off its hinges.

"What's wrong with you! Calm down! There's no one here! Get out of here!" Daniel came closer to him.

"We'll see about that!" the intruder yelled, eyeing the bathroom door.

Daniel tried to stop him but failed. The man entered the dark bathroom and found Ibtisam.

She started screaming and wailing. "Go away! You won't force me to get married!"

Daniel heard and immediately understood everything – why she came to him that night and why she had clung to him from the moment he'd arrived at the hospital. He went into the bathroom and tried to free Ibtisam from the man who was going wild and beating her mercilessly. He turned to Daniel and shoved him, then dragged Ibtisam out by the hair and flung her against the wall. Her face was dripping with blood. She was still naked and tried to protect her head while holding her dress against her body. The image was brutal.

"Jalal! Jalal!" shouted Abu Elias as he knocked on the door.

Ibtisam was lying on the floor, and the man spat on her and kicked her hard. Everything happened fast. A minute, maybe a few seconds longer, had passed since he'd burst into the apartment. Thoughts rushed through Daniel's head at the speed of light. It all came up again: the spit rolling down his mother's face, his father not doing a thing, the helplessness, the fear. He analyzed the situation in a split second; it was all over. He wouldn't be able to stay there anymore. It was too dangerous. He pulled out the knife, came up behind the man, kicked the back of his knee and bent him over. He held him in a chokehold, raised the knife to his neck and ordered him to shut up. The man coughed and tried to shake him off, but Daniel tightened his hold and barely restrained himself from slitting his throat.

"I will slaughter you like a lamb if you don't calm down," he threatened.

Ibtisam crawled to the corner of the room, sobbing.

The man was breathing heavily and stopped fighting. Daniel dragged him to the bathroom. "Come here," he ordered Ibtisam. She obeyed immediately. "Take off my belt," he said. Weeping and frightened, she pulled the belt from his pants. "Hold your hands behind you, you dog!" he said to the man. "Tie them!" With shaking hands, Ibtisam bound the man's hands with the belt and stepped back.

"There's another belt in the closet. Bring it to me!" he said, holding the man tightly. She returned with the belt and Daniel instructed her how to tie his legs. He lay the man down on his stomach. All the while, the man continued to threaten Daniel, cursing and promising Ibtisam that it wasn't over. Daniel shoved a washcloth in his mouth. He went to the living room and came back with a rug, rolled the man in it and shut him in the bathroom. The apartment was quiet now; all he could hear was Abu Elias knocking and calling Jalal's name.

"Hide in the closet," Daniel ordered Ibtisam. Then he went to open the door.

"Everything is fine," he said, opening the door a crack. Abu Elias stood there with some tenants who had come out into the hallway. "I'm sorry," he said to the landlord, "It's someone who works with me at the hospital, he drank a little, you know... he'll sober up and then I'll take him home. His parents are very religious, and I don't want them to see him like this."

Abu Elias gave him a sharp look, then sighed and turned to go. "I hope he didn't break anything," he said as he walked away.

"Don't worry," Daniel called out after him and shrugged at the curious onlookers from his floor, who went back into their apartments.

He went back and found Ibtisam hiding in the closet like an obedient soldier. "You can come out," he said, looking at her still-naked body. Her forehead was bleeding, and blood flowed down her neck and along the side of her breast. Daniel took a towel, wiped her beaten body and ordered her to hold the towel to her forehead to stop the bleeding. "Where are your clothes?"

She tipped her head toward the floor. Daniel gave her the pile of clothes. She let go of the towel and put on the traditional dress. She held her head covering while her eyes seemed to be searching for something.

"It's still bleeding," he told her, and she put the towel back on her forehead. "Looking for your shoes?"

"My underwear," she replied, hanging her head in shame.

299

Daniel looked around him, and when he couldn't find them, he said quietly, "Never mind. Put your shoes on and fix your head covering. We need to get out of here quickly."

Ibtisam nodded and did as he said. "I'm so sorry," she said as she tied her shoelaces.

"It doesn't matter now, explain later."

"Where are we going?" she asked, adjusting her head covering over her curls and the cut on her forehead.

We? The plural surprised him. "Is there somewhere you can be safe?"

"I can't stay in the West Bank, they'll kill me... I don't even know how my brother knew I was here. Maybe he followed me, or someone saw and told him," she said, her eyes pleading.

He thought for a few seconds. "We'll go to Al-Quds," he whispered. He started to stuff things he didn't want to leave behind in a backpack. "You'll be safe there."

Ibtisam nodded. He went to the door and opened it slowly. The hallway was empty. She went out first and he followed with a final glance at what had been his home over the past few weeks. He locked the door and put the key in his jeans pocket. "Let's go," he said, walking to the staircase. She walked behind him, looking from side to side fearfully. It was eleven fifteen – only ten minutes had passed since they had been interrupted. Daniel entered the lobby first to make sure the coast was clear. He gestured to Ibtisam, they hurried to the front door of the building and out onto the street. Three men stood near a parked car to their right. They turned left down the street that led to a main road, where Daniel planned to hail a taxi.

"Thank you, Jalal," she said. "I don't know what to say... I never imagined something like this could happen."

Daniel looked at Ibtisam and felt distant. He had been with women in the past that he'd known for only five minutes, but this intimacy he'd suddenly found himself in felt completely different – strange and foreign. "That was your brother?" he asked, looking behind him as he heard feet pounding on the sidewalk.

"Yes, they arranged a marriage to..."

"Ibtisam!" yelled a man running after them. "Stop, you whore!"

She turned around, horrified. Daniel saw the other two who had stood near the car hurrying after their friend. "Run!" Daniel grabbed her hand and dragged her with him. Ibtisam ran as fast as she could. The shouts behind them didn't stop, and the cool night air carried their profanities. Taking advantage of a turn in the road once they were out of sight, Daniel pulled Ibtisam into a narrow alley. He hoped to lose their pursuers, but it was futile; in the dark alley, which acted as an amplifier, the menacing threats sounded closer than they actually were. Ibtisam started to slow down, but Daniel pulled her after him. He also wasn't in peak physical condition and felt his lungs starting to burn. "Turn right," he hissed just before the alley ended. "This way," he said, entering the staircase of an apartment building, and shut the blue metal door behind them. "Go up to the top floor and wait until I call you," Daniel ordered.

"I'm scared," she replied, panting.

"Me too," he replied, and watched her go up the stairs. He pulled his cellphone out of his pocket, opened the app he used to contact command post, placed his finger on the sensor on the back and sent a distress signal. Then he sent a text message, "On the way to Jerusalem. I'm not alone." He knew the message would get to the right person, and now his phone would broadcast his location to every screen at command post. He put the phone back in his pocket, opened the creaking door and went out into the street. A quick scan showed no sign of their pursuers. He waved at a passing taxi. "Wait here a minute," he told the driver, "I'll call my sister."

Daniel went back in and called Ibtisam. He heard her coming down the stairs in the dark. "I got a taxi. Come on, hurry. We'll go to the border crossing."

She stood facing him. "Jalal, I'm not sure it's possible to cross at this hour, and I don't have a permit to enter Israel. They won't let me pass."

"That's a problem," Daniel said.

"But I know where we can cross," she continued. "Everyone who doesn't have a permit sneaks in through there, but we might get caught. I've got you into enough trouble already..."

Daniel saw this as an opportunity. If they were arrested, it would be easier for him to detach from her. "Let's go. Tell the driver where to take us."

They got into the taxi and Ibtisam explained to the driver, an elderly man with a friendly face, that they had to get to Jerusalem. He understood immediately and even knew where to take them. They sat silently as he drove, each in their own world. The prayer beads on the driver's rearview mirror swung back and forth, the beads clicking. The radio played a dramatic song by the famous Egyptian singer Umm Kulthum accompanied by a string orchestra, a scratchy recording from an old concert. Daniel, gradually processing the implications of the past hour, stared out the window at the crowded streets of Bethlehem. This was the last time he'd be able to get around openly. When he came back, probably within a few days, it would be with a special ops force – they'd probably want him to join. His next thought was the missions he hadn't had time to accomplish. It angered him, and he tried to console himself with the fact that intelligence was never complete. He stole a glance at Ibtisam. She was staring silently out the window, frozen and beaten down. Daniel felt sorry for her. That evening, he knew from experience, would always haunt her. He thought her brother deserved to die, but he also didn't regret that he had been satisfied with simply tying him up – there was no room for more death in his dreams.

The driver slowed down and turned into a dirt road. The taxi rocked back and forth. The prayer beads clinked rapidly, sounding like a clock ticking. Umm Kulthum's powerful voice was still singing. After a few minutes of bumpy driving, the taxi stopped in a dark area. Daniel paid the driver, and they got out. The taxi's headlights lit the suspended dust particles, two parallel beams disappearing into the distance.

Ibtisam led. Apparently, this wasn't her first time. Daniel mused at the surprising role switch, and the two advanced into the dark landscape, paved with steep terraces of olive trees.

"Those buildings up there," Ibtisam said loudly, panting, "that's Israel."

"Not far," Daniel whispered and thought how indiscreet she was.

"Why are you whispering?" she asked, again loudly.

His lips turned up in a small smile, "I don't know." He raised his voice and felt like he was shouting in the middle of a library, "maybe because we're doing something illegal?"

Ibtisam didn't respond and continued climbing. After a few minutes, she told him, "I thought you were much gentler, Jalal. Before, you looked like it wasn't your first time holding a knife."

"I worked as a bouncer in Paris, I've been in fights before," Daniel replied, and felt the same distance. "But I prefer to live quietly."

The last few feet were especially steep. Daniel took the lead silently. Every time he gave her a hand up, he felt her embarrassment, even though she had exposed her naked body to him. Strange, he thought, how holding hands can be more intimate than making love. They reached the top and found themselves on an asphalt road illuminated with orange streetlights. It was the far end of an Israeli neighborhood. Cars were parked alongside houses, the night quiet. Ibtisam stopped, looked back at the valley they had come from, and stared for a moment at the twinkling lights of the life she had left behind. She removed her head covering and threw it into the dark valley. Daniel watched her and wondered how far they would get before the Shabak people following the signal from his cellphone found them. It didn't take long; at the end of the road there was a police vehicle, flashing its blue and red lights.

Ibtisam sighed. "They'll take us to the station and tomorrow morning return us to the border crossing. I'm sorry, Jalal, I hope you won't get into trouble," she said, as if she knew their paths were destined to separate.

"Tell them everything," he told her. "Maybe they can help you."

"If they take me back, I'll escape again," she said with determination. "Even if they put me in jail... there's no way I'll stay alive in Bethlehem."

Daniel looked at her and his heart sank. He didn't have a chance to respond as the police car stopped next to them. Two officers who were sent to arrest them sat in the front seats. Daniel didn't recognize their faces and had no idea who they were. The instructions they had received from the Shabak, who had been following the events not far from there, were certainly focused – arrest the two and bring them to the police station.

"Where are you from?" the driver asked in Arabic with a terrible accent.

"Jabel Mukaber." Ibtisam gave the name of a neighborhood in East Jerusalem.

"So, what are you doing here?" the officer continued in Hebrew. "Aren't you a little far from home?"

Ibtisam shrugged. "Just here walking," she tried to say in her limited Hebrew.

"Identity cards," he demanded.

Daniel handed him his French passport and Ibtisam her Palestinian identity card.

"You came with her from Bethlehem?" the police officer asked Daniel in Hebrew.

"*Français?* English? Arabic?" he replied.

The police officers got out of the car, handcuffed the two of them and put them in the back seat. During the drive, Ibtisam and Daniel exchanged occasional glances. She tried to say something, and the officers told her to be quiet. When they were led into the police station the large clock on the wall showed it was one forty-five. It seemed like even at that late hour there was activity at the station – they weren't the only ones being detained. The officers separated them and sent Ibtisam to a female officer with dyed hair and tired eyes.

"Allah be with you, Jalal, you're a good man," she said, as she disappeared with the officer at the end of the long corridor.

"This way." The officer from the police car led Daniel to one of the interrogation rooms and left him handcuffed.

Three minutes later the door opened, and Yael entered with the officer. "Take the handcuffs off," she ordered. "It's okay."

The officer removed the handcuffs and left. Daniel stood there. Yael came over and gave him a long hug. He wrapped his arms around her.

"You're dirty and you stink." She shoved him playfully.

"I showered not long ago." He bent his head to sniff himself.

The only scent in his nostrils was that of Ibtisam. He hoped it was only in his memory.

"What happened, Daniel?" she asked, a grave expression on her face. "I sped here all the way from Haifa, I didn't know what to expect, I was so worried."

Daniel's face relaxed. "Thank you," he said, "and I'm sorry, but I'm here now and it's all good."

"Who's the woman you brought with you?"

"Ibtisam," he replied, "from the hospital. There's a chance she knows something about the project. I don't feel comfortable suggesting this, but she was in a delicate situation..." He hesitated for a few seconds. "She'll do anything not to go back to the West Bank. You know what I mean."

"I'm sure Jonathan and his friends will know what to do with her."

Daniel sat down and told her the events of the past few hours. He decided to leave out what happened from the moment Ibtisam knocked on his door until her brother arrived. It was not relevant to the operation, and he didn't want to hurt Yael. She sat next to him at the table, facing him with her chin resting in her palm, and listened. When he was done, she stared at him and sighed. "I'm proud of you," she told him, "But do you know why?"

"Maybe," he smiled at her.

"That you didn't kill her brother."

"Yes... but I'd be lying to you if I said the thought hadn't crossed my mind."

"So, that's it?" she asked him softly. "Over and done with?"

"Almost." Daniel stretched out his palms and then stretched in his chair. "After the raid."

"That's someone else's job."

"No," Daniel said bluntly, "there's no chance I'm not joining them – exactly as planned. What difference does it make if I join them there or come from here?"

Yael's face reddened. She stood up. "I don't believe this," she muttered and walked around the room.

Daniel followed her with his eyes, trying to understand her reaction. "What?" he exclaimed.

"Just stop it already!" she cried, her voice raised.

Daniel was surprised at her sharp reaction. "Yael, what is it? Why shouldn't I join them? I'm the only one who's been there. Doesn't that seem important enough to you?"

"Why do you keep giving me this crap?" She raised her voice even more. "They'll do just fine without you. You just can't let go of those Temple treasures, can you!"

Daniel was astonished by her emotional response. "Yes, the treasures too. You're right. Why should I let it go?"

"Because it's dangerous, Daniel! Dangerous!" She was almost screaming now. "You did your part, you did more than enough. It's a raid! It could turn into a battlefield in seconds! It's enough if this Rashid or one of your colleagues turns up. What do you think will happen? You almost blew his brains out too!"

"Of course, it's dangerous," he replied, "All the past few months have been dangerous. But I have to finish what I started."

Yael sat down, distraught, and held her head in both hands, shaking it from side to side. Daniel went to her, hesitated for a minute, and then stroked her hair. She lifted her face to him, tears in her eyes.

"Give up on it already," she said in a choked voice, and hit his chest with her fists, "give it up... for me... okay?"

Daniel took a deep breath. He was confused and didn't understand why she was so upset.

"Yaeli, I can't... not now... I'll never be able to rest if I give up. It's too serious, too important."

Yael got up and looked deep into his eyes.

"You won't find anything there, Daniel, nothing that you're looking for."

"Come on," he laughed.

She hugged him tightly. "I'm sorry, so sorry... I never expected that this would happen."

Daniel wrinkled his forehead at her words.

"Don't be angry," she whispered, crying, "I didn't think you would go this far."

Her words made him shudder. He pushed her away gently and looked at her face. "What are you talking about? Yael, I don't understand."

"And also, this coincidence," she continued as if she hadn't heard him, "that of all places, that damn laboratory was there... you have to forgive me."

Daniel let go of her and took a step back. "Enough, Yael! Explain! Because it's clear something is going on here!"

She wiped the tears from her almond-shaped eyes, red from crying, blew her nose with a tissue she took from her purse, and took a deep breath.

"I made everything up. Everything! And it was too successful!"

"Made it up? What did you make up?"

"The sketch that led you to the hospital isn't your grandfather's. I drew it and added it to the boxes I sent you from our apartment."

Daniel burst out laughing. "Yael. Don't you have a better story than that to convince me?"

"I know it sounds crazy, but it's the truth. This isn't what I expected or wanted to happen, but like always, reality follows its own rules."

Daniel didn't believe her. "Forget it, let's talk about this tomorrow. I'm tired. Drop me off at a hotel and come pick me up tomorrow – there's a lot of work to do."

Yael gave him a piercing look. "Daniel, I'm not kidding. I was afraid you wouldn't believe me if I told you... I wanted to tell you back then, when the Shabak arrested you by accident. But with all their suspicion, when they thought you'd gone over to the other side, that you were spying for someone else, I couldn't... I should have gotten you out earlier. It's all my fault this happened."

"What are you talking about, Yael?" Daniel still refused to believe her. He sat down. "What are you going on about?"

Yael sat down. "You thought I gave up on you when you left. But no. I didn't. I just left you alone for a while. I thought you'd calm down and come back. I was in touch with your mother the whole time."

Daniel's eyes widened in shock. "My mother?"

Yael nodded. "Yes. All the time. And she told me what was going on with you. I even came to France once to speak with her, to try and get you back. But seeing you, I realized –"

"Seeing me?" Daniel yelled and looked at her in disbelief. "What do you mean?"

"Yes. I was very close, and you weren't very sharp. I realized that if I tried to talk with you in the state you were in, you would just be embarrassed and distance yourself even more."

Daniel started to process what he'd just learned. He stared at the stained floor and muttered to himself in French.

"I came back to Israel because I had to. But I knew it wasn't the end of us, that I had to do something. I kept thinking about it, and I remembered all those boxes from your grandfather that you'd left... I started reading everything I could find, to understand. I knew how important he was to you, how significant he was in your life, and I came to a decision. To give you a little push to continue on his path." She stopped talking when Daniel got up and started pacing around the room. His body language signaled irritation and anger.

"Yael," he said impassively, "if what you say is true, I never want to see you again. You played me."

"Don't you dare judge me!" she admonished. "When you left just before we were supposed to get married and you told me to get an abortion, I didn't judge you for that. I understood what you were going through. You'd killed two people, that isn't easy to cope with. But I loved you and wanted to raise a family with you and I didn't lose hope. You did!"

They stood silently staring at each other.

"Why did you choose the West Bank?" he asked finally, as if he still didn't entirely believe her.

"I didn't. Your grandfather was convinced that the treasures, after they had gone around half the world, had come back to Jerusalem to some church or monastery, and after a while, when they weren't safe there, they were taken to Bethlehem. He didn't have time for more."

"And the hospital?" Daniel continued, sounding suspicious.

Yael smiled. "I looked for a place that was built over ruins."

"There are many others in Bethlehem, why there?"

"Yes, there are others, but all the other sites are active monasteries, churches, or privately owned. I wanted a place that you could get access to. I did some research and saw that the hospital was looking for volunteers. I knew that if the map pointed you there, you'd find out all you could about the place. And when you discovered that you could volunteer there, you might consider it. I didn't think you'd go that far and turn it into a whole operation. All the rest is coincidence. I had no idea the Shabak was monitoring what was going on there and I didn't know that it used to be the site of a dig. I just wanted you to come to Israel to check it out, and then maybe you would get in touch with me."

Daniel nodded and sighed. He was confused and wasn't completely convinced; he didn't know what to believe anymore. It was the busiest day of his life; Ibrahim, Ibtisam, escaping, and now this. "I'm tired, Yael," he said. "I want to sleep. Call the officer to handcuff me and take me to the police car, to keep up the story for whoever sees me outside, and then take me to a hotel. Tomorrow or the next day I'll take the first flight to France, and we'll forget this whole thing."

Yael looked at him, and he looked at her to see her reaction. She looked hesitant and uncertain. Then she came up to him. "Not yet," she said softly. "You have to meet someone first."

"Meet someone?" Daniel glowered. "Who?"

"This is the last thing I'll ask of you. Then you can go back to France, if that's what you decide to do."

Daniel stared at her silently.

"I get what you're feeling right now. But think for a minute. Your life was at an extreme low. I had to do something extreme to get you back to yourself, to this country, to your home! And look at you now," she said sounding proud, her eyes glistening. "Look at what you've done. I just gave the first push – the rest is all you."

Daniel listened to Yael and his expression softened. She was right. What she did had rebuilt him, brick by brick. It was much more than restoring his self-confidence. Suddenly he realized that she had done it all to bring him back to her.

"Who are we going to meet?"

"We're going to Haifa," she replied.

Probably to meet her parents, Daniel thought, I owe her at least that.

5

It was almost five am, the radio was playing soft music, and the sky was getting brighter. The further north they drove, the more cars were making their way in the opposite direction, to start a new work week. Yael drove and Daniel sprawled in the front seat, his head slumped against the window. He was exhausted, emotionally and physically, and was half asleep for most of the drive. From time to time, his eyes fluttered open just enough to get a glimpse, then closed again. They didn't exchange a word.

When they arrived, Yael touched his shoulder to wake him. He opened his eyes, stretched his arms as he yawned, and looked outside to see where they were. Yael was already standing out in the street, and he joined her in the chilly morning air with the smell of pine trees typical of the Carmel Mountains. It was a residential neighborhood, not the one that her parents lived in or one that he was familiar with. He stole a glance at Yael and saw she looked anxious. "Come on," she said and crossed the quiet street. He followed her silently along the narrow sidewalk that led to the well-kept yard of an old apartment building. Now he was really curious. At the entrance to the building, they passed an elderly woman coming down the stairs with a small dog. She said good morning and gave Yael a disapproving look. Daniel wondered why. They returned her greeting politely and climbed up to the second floor. Yael went to a white door with no name on it, rummaged through her purse and took out a keychain. She opened the door slowly, as if trying to keep quiet. Daniel followed her in and immediately knew that this was her apartment. There was no doubt – the familiar scent gave it away. Yael hung her purse on a hook by the door, took off her fleece jacket and turned to Daniel. "This is mine," she said, her voice trembling. "Make yourself at home," she added, pointing at the sofa in the living room. "I'm making tea – do you want some?"

Daniel nodded and Yael disappeared into the kitchen. He looked around curiously and went over to sit on the sofa that used to be his favorite. It felt good. Although he'd never been in this apartment, everything was familiar. It was all from their old apartment, when they'd lived together, only now it was in Haifa and not Tel Aviv, and his personal things weren't there. He looked around at Yael's oil painting landscapes on the wall, and remembered how he would watch her paint, amazed by her talent. He smiled. Forgotten memories emerged, and he closed his eyes to try and recreate them.

"Hi." He was surprised to hear an unfamiliar voice behind him, "Good morning." He turned around and saw a young woman looking at him awkwardly.

"Good morning," he replied, wondering who she was. It was clear that she had spent the night there.

"Where's Yael?" she asked.

"In the kitchen."

She replied with a giggle and went to the kitchen. She looked around twenty, maybe just after her army service. Maybe she was a roommate, he thought. A minute or two later they both came out of the kitchen. Yael carried two glasses and offered one to Daniel.

315

"Thanks, sweetie." Yael kissed the woman on the cheek who picked up a tote bag from the floor by the front door and hurried out. "I'll call you," Yael called out after her. She sat on the sofa facing Daniel and warmed her hands on the glass.

"Your roommate?" Daniel asked, sipping his tea. She still looked on edge.

Yael laughed, shook her head, and took a sip. Her face relaxed a bit. "No, not exactly. I'm not really into living with roommates anymore," she said after a pause, checking the time on her watch.

Daniel shrugged. "So, why am I here?" he asked, looking at the coffee table and wondering why it was so far from the sofas. He looked for a place to set down his glass, and finally just held it. The table was right up against the television, leaving an open space with a carpet between him and the other sofa.

Yael had a serious look on her face. She glanced at her watch again and stood. She took a deep breath. "I'll be right back," she said, sounding anxious.

Daniel felt his heart start to speed up and followed her with his eyes as she disappeared into the hallway. Something was happening, he thought. He finished his tea, got up, took a few steps, and set the empty glass on the coffee table. Then he stood looking at a painting he wasn't familiar with.

"Daniel?" He suddenly heard Yael behind him.

He turned around and his heart dropped. He broke out in a cold sweat and his legs felt weak. Yael stood there nervously, holding a little boy wearing a blue onesie decorated with yellow teddy bears.

He had messy light brown hair and was sucking hard on a pacifier. His big innocent eyes examined Daniel with curiosity.

"Say hello," Yael said to the boy.

Daniel was trembling. He looked into the boy's eyes and felt like he was looking into his own. "Hello," he said in a shaky voice. He touched him gently.

The boy stuck his head in Yael's neck and peeked at Daniel from the corner of his eye.

"What's your name?" Daniel asked, his eyes moist.

"Don't be embarrassed, sweetheart," Yael said, gently pulling the pacifier out of his mouth. "Tell him."

"Fael," the little boy said so quietly he almost couldn't hear him.

"Rafael?" Daniel's eyes widened, filling with tears. It was his grandfather's name.

"Yes." She also couldn't hold back her emotions. "I always knew I'd bring you back to us."

Daniel came closer and kissed her forehead. "I don't know what to say..."

"Tell him who you are," she suggested, wiping away her tears.

Daniel held his hands out to Rafael, "Come here."

Rafael kept peeking at Daniel from his mother's neck, and after a few seconds, held his arms out.

Daniel held the boy and kissed his cheek. "Rafael, my sweet boy, I'm your daddy!"

"Mommy, mommy!" Rafael cried, holding his arms out to Yael.

She held him in her arms and kissed him. "I have to get him ready and take him to preschool."

"Preschool? Why can't he stay home today?"

"If you want, you can have all the time in the world with him. He loves school and I don't want to disrupt his routine. Will you come with me?"

Yael sat Rafael in his highchair, and Daniel looked at him, hypnotized while he ate banana yogurt. When he finished eating and making a mess around him, the three of them went to his room. Yael changed Rafael's clothes and organized his small toddler's backpack. Daniel watched her in awe. She moved quickly and confidently, exactly as she had with a paintbrush or a gun.

Daniel lifted Rafael, who didn't object this time, and they went to his preschool together, a short walk from the apartment. They said goodbye and he went straight to play with the toys.

"Daniel," Yael said as they walked out, "take your time and –"

"I don't need time, Yaeli," he cut her off. "I've wasted enough. I realized that a few weeks ago, at a time and place that surprised me. I knew it then and I'm sure of it today."

"When was that?"

"At the Dome of the Rock," he replied, and saw the smile in her eyes. "I went in there and that was it. Of all places, surrounded by thousands of Muslims, I understood. I don't want to live anywhere else in the world."

"I'm glad," she said. "I'm happy you understood that even before you knew about Rafael."

"What now?" he asked her.

"Let's go to the grocery store and get some bread. Then we'll make breakfast. I'm starving."

"Great, me too."

They crossed the street, now loud with morning traffic, and went into the store. When they walked back out, he turned to her, "Tell me, I didn't get the chance to ask you yesterday – did you tell the Shabak what I told you about Ibtisam?"

"Yes," Yael replied, "but they decided to send her back to Bethlehem without questioning her. She probably crossed back this morning with the other illegals."

Daniel was surprised, "Really? Why?"

"Because the decision to raid the lab was already made. If they arrest her and she really knows something, Hamas might get worried and take preventive measures, and that might screw everything up."

He nodded, "That makes sense. And Rashid? What's the plan? Arrest him?"

"From what I understand, Rashid... will probably drown," Yael replied dryly.

"Drown?" Daniel was dumbfounded. "What do you mean, 'drown'? Where? In the sea that Bethlehem doesn't have?"

"It's just a term... Jonathan explained that Hamas can be trusted on this. After the raid, the Shabak will make sure to spread the word that Rashid is the one who sold them out. They'll settle things with him their own way. They'll probably tell his family that he went swimming and drowned or something like that... you know, so that they won't be shamed. After all, his brother is a shaheed and a hero."

The image of Rashid's elderly father flashed in Daniel's mind, and he felt for him. "And the raid?"

"I think it's a matter of days," Yael said, "I'm sure they'll call you to fill in some of the details they're missing."

"And we have to wrap things up in Bethlehem."

"They're taking care of that too. Don't be worried. Your escape with that girl set things up for an excellent excuse to deport you from Israel back to France."

He nodded, "That's what I thought."

They entered the apartment, made breakfast, and sat down to eat. Yael told him everything about Rafael, and Daniel hung onto every word. When they were done, they turned the TV to a morning show while they did the dishes.

"I'm going to take a shower and then take a nap," Yael said, "After the night we had, we should get some sleep."

"You think I can fall asleep now? I just found out I have a son!"

"In a few hours you'll discover that a little boy is much more tiring than an all-night operation."

A breaking news announcement caught their attention. "A suspected terrorist attack at the Rachel Border Crossing," the news anchor reported. "A young Palestinian woman attacked IDF soldiers standing at the barrier and tried to stab one of them. The soldiers responded quickly; she was shot and killed."

Daniel's heart skipped a beat. He hoped that Ibtisam hadn't been that desperate.

"Daniel? Are you alright?"

He took her hand and played with their engagement ring. "Yaeli, you've done so much, but you haven't really told me... do you want me back?"

"You know the answer to that." Yael put her arms around his neck and kissed him.

Epilogue

Two years later

She climbed the stairs from the Metro up to the bustling street level, squinting in the sunlight. It was early afternoon; the sky was blue, and the street was full of people casually strolling along the street of designer stores. The noisy traffic didn't bother them much. She looked at the beautiful buildings, the facades blending into one another. Too often, when she walked past Muslim women with head coverings, she felt as if they were giving her accusing looks that said, you won't get away with this. We know who you are! It was frustrating. Who could have imagined feeling threatened in far-off Paris. Muslim immigrants stood out everywhere, and although it had been almost two years, the fear that they would find her never went away. It was a daily struggle to combat the fear and not give into it, and whenever she got out of work early, she took long walks along the streets of Paris. She dressed differently now, hair dyed and styled, and she thought that was enough, that the demons were just demons and weren't real.

Wearing fashionable large brown sunglasses she wandered past the boutiques, window shopping. When she walked by a bookstore, she glanced at the display in the large window. One of the books caught her eye. Copies were arranged in rows showing the same program in every window. The cover was turquoise and the title, *Insane?*, was printed in large letters in Arabic and French, in black and white. It piqued her interest, and she entered the store.

The bookstore was huge. Customers stood around or sat at small tables, browsing through books that interested them. There were endless rows of books on different topics, in different colors. Her heels tapped as she walked on the light wood flooring until she found the right shelf. There was a pile in each language. She picked up the book in Arabic and read the blurb on the back cover:

Young Ibrahim arrived at the orphanage when he was four years old, during the Algerian War. When the French army withdrew, the orphanage was turned into a psychiatric hospital. Alone in the world and frightened, he decided to pretend he was mentally ill, so he could stay in the only home he knew.

This novel tells the story of a brave man who spent his entire life in the same compound behind a fortified wall and finds creative ways to stay sane in an insane reality.

With every word she read, Ibtisam felt her heart pounding louder. She was trembling as she read the last line:

About the author: Daniel Ben Atar is a former intelligence officer, born in France, who currently lives in Israel. He is married and has a son and a daughter. This is his first novel.

Tell Your Friends!

Did you enjoy this book? Please scan the QR code below to share it with your friends.

Acknowledgments

First and foremost, I would like to dedicate this book to the brave secret heroes of Israel. These are the men and women who serve beyond the lines, often lonely and unknown, but always humble and, most importantly, brave. They are armed only with civilian clothes, sharp senses, wise words, and rare courage. This book is for you.

I would like to express my deep appreciation to my editor, Amnon Jackont, who once again, with rare modesty, guided me through the writing process without deviating from my path. I am also grateful to Bella and Avery A, Zion N, Daniel S, and Jonathan D for their insightful comments and feedback during the writing process. I must also thank Amichai A, who always goes out of his way to help me when I ask. I owe a great debt of gratitude to two dear friends: Moshiko, for the persistent debates, long conversations, scientific arguments, and relentlessness that helped shape this book, and to Udi, for the trust and willingness to share with me the most personal experiences, heart to heart talks, comments, and unique angles that make all the difference. I would like to thank Avishy N, who told me about the "Warren's Gate" events that inspired a crucial part of the story, and to Shaked, who threw a sentence into the air that unexpectedly resolved a significant issue. I also want to acknowledge Dov Eichenwald and the professionals at Yediot Books who helped bring this book to life in Hebrew, including Navit Bar-El and, of course, Hila Shafir. If I have forgotten anyone, I apologize.

The soul of this book is Israeli, and it was initially written in Hebrew, a language with thousands of years of history, heritage, and memory. This language has a distinctive tone and sounds that are as much a part of the landscape of the Holy Land as its physical features. Translating into English without losing the uniqueness of the original language was a complex and challenging task. I am incredibly grateful to the translator, Dalit Shmueli, who created a version that remained faithful to the original with great sensitivity and professionalism, and to Ally Mitchell, who edited the translation in such a meticulous manner. Thanks to Yaniv O and Gadi N, who read the manuscript translation and shared their insights.

Finally, I want to express my heartfelt appreciation to my wife and children for their patience, love, and support throughout this journey. I am grateful for the many hours they allowed me to work on this novel, and I apologize for any time I took away from them.

About The Author

 Yariv Inbar is the pseudonym of an Israeli novelist whose real identity has been banned from publication by the Israeli authorities. With a wealth of experience serving in sensitive positions within the Israeli intelligence community for many years, Yariv brings a unique authenticity to his writing. He is a devoted family man, married with three children, and still serves as a lieutenant colonel Reserve. In 2016, Yariv burst onto the spy fiction scene with the publication of his novels in Hebrew, which quickly earned bestseller status in Israel and received high praise from critics and readers.

Author's Note

Operation Bethlehem is a work of fiction. The names, characters, and incidents portrayed in the story are the product of the author's imagination or have been used fictitiously. Any resemblance to actual people, living or dead, businesses, companies, events, or locales is entirely coincidental, yet the core of the story is rooted in reality.

In 2007, while serving as an intelligence officer, I watched a documentary called "God's Gold." The documentary followed British archaeologist Dr. Sean Kingsley as he searched the world for lost temple treasures. Kingsley claimed that Mar Theodosius, a Greek Orthodox monastery located east of Bethlehem, is the last known hiding place of one of the greatest treasures of antiquity: the gold and silver vessels of the Temple in Jerusalem. Unfortunately, the Palestinian police and the monastery nuns refused to let the documentary team in, which sparked my imagination. I wondered how it could be possible to covertly investigate the location. Over the years, many others shared similar thoughts, inspiring the novel I have written.

All the places mentioned in the book are real and accurately described. I replaced the original monastery with an existing psychiatric hospital located in the heart of Bethlehem. The "Warren's Gate" events mentioned in the story really happened, and it is perhaps important to expand on them.

On July 22, 1981, as part of the archaeological excavations in the Western Wall Tunnels, an arch blocked with stones was discovered at the northern part of the Wall, an ancient gate from the Second Temple period. It is called Warren's Gate after the British archaeologist who worked in Israel in the latter part of the nineteenth century. Charles Warren identified its location at Cistern 30 in a survey he conducted around the Temple Mount.

During the excavations, workers broke through the wall that blocked the gate, which is believed to be the closest to the historic location of the Holy of Holies. Behind it they discovered an enormous space. Peeling back the plaster, they discovered hewn stone similar to the stones of the Western Wall – attesting to its history.

Government authorities and other official entities were informed on the finding by Rabbi Meir Yehuda Getz, the Rabbi of the Western Wall and the holy places, and the driving force behind the Western Wall Tunnel excavations. Rabbi Getz believed that finding the lost Temple treasures was of national importance and got permission to continue secretly digging to expose the rest of the tunnel that led from Warren's Gate east to the space under the Dome of the Rock.

The work to clear out the mud and water was conducted secretly for a month, until it was leaked to the media and broadcast on August 27 that year, sending shock waves around the world. The Arab world was quick to accuse Israel of an attempt to weaken the foundations of the mosques at the Temple Mount to build the Third Temple. The political storm brought about a temporary blockade of wooden boards over the opening.

In the early morning of September 1, 1981, on the order of the Waqf, a group of young Muslims used ropes to descend into the tunnel from the Temple Mount carrying tools. They started building a wall with bricks and mortar to seal the gate. Israeli police officers who were at the site saw them but didn't stop them. Only the next morning did officials from the Ministry of Religion, led by Rabbi Getz, discover what had happened. They went to the police who allowed the Muslims to complete their work.

The afternoon of that same day, a violent clash broke out between a group of young Jewish men and the Muslims who were building the wall. It quickly escalated into an underground riot and drove hundreds of Muslim believers to the Temple Mount, where they clashed with the Jewish men inside and outside the tunnel. Border Police who were stationed at the Temple plateau took control of the event and arrested a few of the Jews, and the Muslims were allowed to continue.

Rabbi Getz wrote in his diary:

I saw the government in all its weakness and disgrace, total capitulation and I pin no hopes on them. My entire support is our Father in heaven. Even the British put on a proper face, but our government has always caved in throughout, to our shame and humiliation.

Today, a synagogue named after Rabbi Getz is located at the site inside the Western Wall Tunnels and is open to visitors. What remains hidden behind the blocked gate, or on the grounds of the Temple Mount? For now, that is left up to the imagination.

Made in United States
North Haven, CT
20 July 2024

55226869R00183